# UNTHINKABLE

# UNTHINKABLE:

The Triumph and Endurance of
Forgotten American Hero T. J. Bowen

BY JIM HARDWICKE

XULON PRESS

Xulon Press
2301 Lucien Way #415
Maitland, FL 32751
407.339.4217
www.xulonpress.com

Unless otherwise indicated, Scripture quotations taken from the New American Standard Bible (NASB). Copyright © 1960, 1962, 1963, 1968, 1971, 1972, 1973, 1975, 1977, 1995 by The Lockman Foundation. Used by permission. All rights reserved.

Front cover photo is courtesy of IMB.

Printed in the United States of America

Paperback ISBN-13: 978-1-6628-0957-6
Ebook ISBN-13: 978-1-6628-0958-3

# Encouragement to Read *Unthinkable*

"I have read many missionary biographies and researched mission history but have never encountered such a gripping story as that of T. J. Bowen as written by Jim Hardwicke. Bowen intrigued Baptist churches and all America by his exploits as the first missionary to Central Africa in the mid-19th century. In a time when early missionaries to the dark continent packed their belongings in caskets because they never expected to come home alive, Bowen penetrated a primitive culture in what was to become Nigeria in the face of formidable challenges, tropical disease, tribal warfare, and uncivilized people with an obsession to plant the gospel. His survival was miraculous due to life-long suffering with a disease-ravaged body and eventual mental illness, but his legacy is remarkable. Missionaries today go to unreached peoples and suffer from deprivation and risks but know nothing of the sacrifice and cost entailed by this pioneer missionary. Every missionary candidate and, indeed, every Christian would better understand the call to share the sufferings of Christ by reading this well-researched book."

—Jerry Rankin, President Emeritus, International Mission Board, SBC

"In this volume, Jim Hardwicke has brought to light one of the most important, yet largely unknown missionary stories: the life of Thomas Jefferson Bowen. Bowen was a pioneer American missionary in 1850 to what is today known as Nigeria (the Yoruba people). Bowen's contributions (in a short period) as a missionary, explorer, ethnographer, linguist, and writer are simply astounding. Hardwicke relates Bowen's life and times with the factual rigor of a skilled researcher, the spell-binding ability of a great story teller, and the compassionate love a sympathizing Christian friend. Bowen's life was filled with pain and hardship and Hardwicke unflinchingly paints every stroke. We need to hear this story. If you read it, you will clearly see the suffering it costs to get the Gospel to the peoples of the earth. You will also realize that no other message, purpose, or person can bring more meaning and joy to your life than Jesus Christ and His Great Commission. Hardwicke has given us a gift. Take and read. You will never be the same."

—Dr. David J. Brady, Pastor of Christ Community Church of Mount Airy; author *One Sacred Effort: Southern Baptists Proclaiming Christ Around the World; Not Forgotten: Inspiring Missionary Pioneers*

"How is it possible that we've not heard the story of Thomas Jefferson Bowen? Here is a gripping account of one man fighting wars, climbing mountains, trekking jungles, opposing slavery, and building missions, all for the cause of Christ. The lessons from his life will inspire you and re-ignite your own fire for giving your life to the glory of God."

—Jim Walters, Executive Director, Servants of Christ International

"Jim Hardwicke writes with the precision of a scholar, the heart of a pastor, and the skills of a gifted storyteller. Bowen was a soldier, pioneer missionary, explorer, linguist, anthropologist, public speaker—and to use Hardwicke's term, a hero. The reader experiences the faithfulness and the victories of T. J. Bowen. Yet, like all of us—Bowen was a sinner with faults and shortcomings that Hardwicke never hides from the reader. Hardwicke painfully but faithfully traces Bowen's life from the pedestal of honored missionary to Bowen's death as a broken, neglected, and poverty-stricken outcast. Not knowing how to handle the paradoxes of Bowen's life—Bowen has been forgotten. Hardwicke calls us back to remembering T. J. Bowen. It is a worthy call that the reader will find to be rewarding and challenging. May we not forget today's less than perfect heroes."

—Al James, Professor of Missions / Associate Dean for Ministry Studies / EQUIP Coordinator, Southeastern Baptist Theological Seminary

"*Unthinkable* is a timely and challenging book for Christians interested in missions, and especially for those persons who are current or future missionaries. In it, Jim Hardwicke details the life and missionary career of forgotten American hero T. J. Bowen, perhaps the most significant American missionary whose life story has never been told. Bowen's life was full of tragedy and pain, including crippling mental illness, and yet God used him in powerful ways. Highly recommended.

—Bruce Ashford, Fellow in Public Theology at the Kirby Laing Centre for Ethics; author of nine books including *The Doctrine of Creation*

"Chances are you have never heard of T. J. Bowen, a mostly forgotten nineteenth-century missionary. For a time, he was arguably one of the most famous American missionaries. Bowen helped pioneer mission work in two different continents and, while in Central Africa, became the first Southern Baptist missionary to engage with a predominately Muslim people group. But Bowen was also captive to the prejudices of his era, struggled with alcohol abuse, and battled significant mental illness. He was not an abstract missionary hero without faults. Rather, Bowen was a real person who loved Jesus and wanted others to know Him, despite Bowen's own shortcomings, struggles, and sins. Though Bowen died in obscurity, the legacy of his mission work—especially in what is now Nigeria—is still evident to the present day. God is faithful! I'm so thankful that my friend Jim Hardwicke has written this biography of Bowen. I trust it will be a realistic-but-hopeful encouragement to many readers, as it has been to me."

—Nathan A. Finn, Provost / Dean of the University
Faculty, North Greenville University

# Contents

Foreword by Jeff Iorg . . . . . . . . . . . . . . . . . . . . . . . . . .xi
Preface. . . . . . . . . . . . . . . . . . . . . . . . . . . . . . . . . . . xiii
Chapter 1—Charging Forward . . . . . . . . . . . . . . . . . . . 1
Chapter 2—Surrendering Everything . . . . . . . . . . . . . 8
Chapter 3—Risking It All . . . . . . . . . . . . . . . . . . . . . 17
Chapter 4—Enjoying Adventure . . . . . . . . . . . . . . . . 30
Chapter 5—Enduring Hardship . . . . . . . . . . . . . . . . . 42
Chapter 6—Inspiring Others . . . . . . . . . . . . . . . . . . . 51
Chapter 7—Overcoming Tragedy . . . . . . . . . . . . . . . . 62
Chapter 8—Dreaming Big. . . . . . . . . . . . . . . . . . . . . 75
Chapter 9—Capturing the Imagination of a Nation. . 97
Chapter 10—Mixing Politics with Ministry. . . . . . . .111
Chapter 11—Struggling with Racial Bias . . . . . . . . . 128
Chapter 12—Accepting Change . . . . . . . . . . . . . . . . 138
Chapter 13—Fighting Physical and Mental Illness. . 156
Chapter 14—Facing Rejection . . . . . . . . . . . . . . . . . 174
Chapter 15—Leaving a Legacy . . . . . . . . . . . . . . . . . 201
Chronology of T. J. Bowen's Life . . . . . . . . . . . . . . . 210
Author's Note . . . . . . . . . . . . . . . . . . . . . . . . . . . . . 217
Notes . . . . . . . . . . . . . . . . . . . . . . . . . . . . . . . . . . . . 218
Acknowledgements . . . . . . . . . . . . . . . . . . . . . . . . . 281

# Foreword

S tumbling across the life of Thomas Jefferson Bowen proved to be an embarrassing admission of my ignorance of the history of missions – particularly the mission history of my denomination, the Southern Baptist Convention. Bowen's life story impacted me profoundly and I started talking and writing about what I was learning. My good friend, Jim Hardwicke, heard me mention Bowen and reminded me his doctoral dissertation was on this forgotten hero. What a serendipitous, providential moment that conversation turned out to be! I immediately read the dissertation and strongly encouraged Dr. Hardwicke to morph that academic treatment into a book for everyday readers. The result is this outstanding volume.

T. J. Bowen's life is an inspiring story of a visionary leader who impacted three continents with the gospel. It is also the tragic story of a broken man whose illnesses were misdiagnosed in his era. Had Bowen lived today, he would have received far better medical treatment and would have largely avoided the stigma attached to his ailments. When viewed through the better lens our perspective on history provides, Bowen emerges as a remarkable man who struggled with ailments over which he had no control and for which he should not be held responsible.

Rather than a troublesome ending, his life is better viewed as heroic quest with a tragic outcome.

In a time of unprecedented need to get the gospel to billions who have not yet even heard the name of Jesus, Bowen's story can inspire a new generation of missionaries. My hope is this book will catalyze many who – like T. J. Bowen – are saddened by the lostness of humankind and captivated by the power of the gospel to produce new life in Jesus Christ. May God use this book to help fulfill the ancient and yet timeless prayer for more workers to join the harvest!

Dr. Jeff Iorg
President, Gateway Seminary

# Preface

Standing on the city wall, squinting in the hot African sun, he watched the enormous enemy army approaching, led by six thousand fierce female soldiers. It was Monday, March 3, 1851. Georgia-born T. J. Bowen had been enduring seven lonely months of language study there in the city of Abeokuta, waiting for doors to open for his missionary work. Abeokuta means "under the rocks." Under its large granite outcroppings forty years earlier the first inhabitants of the city had found protection. They had been driven from numerous cities in the north by Muslim jihads and from over 300 area towns raided by tribes who wanted to sell them into slavery. Abeokuta was a city of about 60,000 war-torn refugees, and now they were under siege by the most frightening army in the region.

Marching against Abeokuta was Ghezo, King of Dahomey, West Africa's most vicious slave trader. For 25 years his soldiers had successfully devastated numerous cities, never suffering a significant defeat. They had recently decimated the town of Oke Odden, killing and capturing 20,000 people, selling many of them to a Brazilian slaver. Through the influence of missionaries, Abeokuta had become the rallying point of opposition to the slave trade, and Ghezo, determined to destroy it and expel any missionaries there, brought his largest army ever.

Leading the attack were Ghezo's most ferocious fighters—the women. These "Amazons" experienced dehumanizing training. To steel them to pain, they were forced to scale walls of acacia bushes with two-inch thorns. To desensitize them to death, often their initiation involved killing someone without flinching. French naval officer Jean Bayol watched as a teenage recruit "who had not yet killed anyone" was tested. He writes that when given a prisoner bound in a basket, she "walked jauntily up . . ., swung her sword three times with both hands, then calmly cut the last flesh that attached the head to the trunk...She then squeezed the blood off her weapon and swallowed it." These terrifying female forces excelled at hand-to-hand combat, frequently decapitated their enemies in the midst of the battle, and included a contingent known as "Reapers" who wielded three-foot-long razors capable of slicing a man clean in two. Typically, after beheading their enemies, the Dahomeys would clean the flesh from the head leaving only the skull. Ghezo had adorned his palace with the polished skulls of the kings of other conquered cities, and he intended to do the same with those who led Abeokuta.

Just hours before, T. J. watched the sick, elderly, and children of Abeokuta escape in weary procession out the northeastern gates. The rest, with nowhere else to go, determined to remain and fight for their lives. Their former towns had been destroyed, and the tribes in the area were unfriendly. Now soaked in sweat, not only from the noon-day heat, but also from the tension, T. J. eyed the dreaded Dahomians advancing across the prairie in heavy squadrons with flying colors. His mind racing, he remembered his experience leading soldiers in the Creek Indian War and as an original Texas Ranger in the early Republic of Texas. Did God have a role for him in this battle?

T. J. Bowen's adventures and explorations in the interior of Africa would make him a national hero. The *Charleston Courier* called him, "that Christian hero, Rev. T. J. Bowen." The foremost newspaper in the nation's capitol, *The Daily National Intelligencer,* unfurled this headline, "A Christian Missionary Explorer is the Hero of the World" and then compared his conquests to those of Alexander the Great. He was frequently compared to his contemporary, the famous British missionary and African explorer, David Livingstone. Eager to hear from such a hero, Congress asked T. J. to testify about his explorations. His celebrity status led to a rare invitation to preach at the House of Representatives in Washington, D. C., and subsequently leading citizens in major cities nationwide urged him to come lecture and preach. T. J.'s account of his adventures became an immediate best-seller and his linguistic work was published by the Smithsonian. His denomination hailed him as their greatest missionary, bestowed on him an honorary degree, and named a regional organization after him. However, less than 20 years later he would be almost forgotten, die alone, and be buried in an unmarked grave.

T. J. Bowen's story unfolds on three continents, involves four wars, and is remarkable, inspiring, and instructive. His greatest adventure began on August 15, 1850, when he attempted the unthinkable. As a white man, he marched alone into the interior of Africa. He would never be the same. Neither would Africa.

"This is the kind of mess I like to get my spoon in."
—Alamo defender Davy Crockett

"David ran quickly toward
the battle line to meet the Philistine."
1 Samuel 17:48

## CHAPTER 1
# Charging Forward

There is something alluring about danger. Heroes are those who are inspired to run toward it and take risks to save others. Such heroes were naturally bred in the rough, frontier life of Georgia in the early 1800s. In 1803 President Thomas Jefferson commissioned Samuel Dale and three companions to identify a route through the wilderness from Greensboro in northeastern Georgia to the Mississippi River. Chopping on trees to mark the path, the explorers found almost no white settlers along the way. By the time Thomas Jefferson (T. J.) Bowen was born in Jackson County, Georgia, on January 2, 1814, most homes were still built of split logs covered with animal hides or tree bark. Most schools and churches consisted of a single log room with split log benches and no backs. American Indian attacks were a constant threat.

T. J.'s son-in-law, historian T. B. Rice, noted that until 1837, "the head of the family carried his gun into the pew when he attended church, so real was the danger of a sudden attack by the Indians." This perilous environment helped shape the man who would dare to walk alone into the heart of Africa.

Early in the nineteenth century, farmer John F. Bowen moved from more civilized Virginia to settle in those wilds of Jackson County, Georgia. There his wife bore him a daughter and two sons, including T. J. In 1810, the entire county only contained 10,569 residents, and like most farmers of the rich red land there, T. J.'s family likely raised everything they wore or ate except salt, iron, sugar, and coffee. Almost all clothing was flax or wool woven and dyed at home. For example, one eyewitness wrote, "Men's summer working breeches were copperas dyed and those plain men-folk were as yellow legged as our choicest breed of chickens." Almost all children went barefoot all year long. Like most other boys in the summer, until he was ten or twelve, probably T. J.'s only garment was a shirt of extra length.

Later T. J.'s father moved the family to Decatur, near Atlanta, where his wife died and was buried. Eventually, he settled near Eufala, Alabama, where he spent the rest of his life. John Bowen appears to have been a committed Christian and faithful churchgoer. Later, he and his missionary son had a strong enough relationship for the son to invite his aging father to live with his family. His father responded warmly, "And with respect to my living with you, I should Be well gratified to live and be with you a part of my time at least. Should my life be spared...So I remain your affectionate Father till death." T. J.'s brother, also named John, moved to Texas, while his sister became "Mrs. Strickland, who is said to have been a physician and lived around Quitman and Bainbridge, Georgia."

Whether due to family circumstances or his own independent spirit, T. J. Bowen appears to have been on his own from an early age. Writing in 1858, he said, "I am very desirous to feel myself located, for I have been adrift in the world ever since I was 17 years old." In his journal, T. J. revealed his early struggles for direction:

> When very young, about twenty-one years old, I debated within myself whether I should labor and strive as other men do to become rich and great. I was thought to be a young man of talents and of honorable character. My relatives and friends (it was in Stewart County, Georgia) had money and influence, with which they were willing to assist me. Jesse Bull, the brother of Judge Bull, offered me his office and practice at law. People held out to me the tempting bait of wealth and honor, as a lawyer and politician. But something within me said: "What is the use? My chief concern ought to be the salvation of my soul.

Thinking he had to renounce his natural ambition to secure eternal salvation, Bowen turned down the offers of his friends and broke an engagement to a worldly-minded girl. However, he confessed, "Notwithstanding all this, although I verily believe I was perfectly sincere, I found it impossible to surrender my heart to God."

---

Six months before T. J.'s birth, the Creek Indians, who lived in parts of Georgia and Alabama, had massacred some 500 settlers at Fort Mims. Like other boys his age, T. J. grew up hearing about the tragedy. After being pushed off their land and forced to live south of the Chattahoochee River, the Creeks would peacefully cross the river to trade with merchants in Columbus, Georgia. But in the spring of 1836 when the whites began moving across the river and settling in their land, the Creeks rebelled. They raided white settlements, burning houses and killing the inhabitants. One day they stopped a stage coach, shot the horses, tied the driver to the wheels, burned him with the coach, and chased the passengers for miles before they hid themselves in a swamp. When the whites rallied to stop the rebellion, twenty-two-year old T. J. quickly volunteered. In his journal, he recalled:

> In the spring of 1836, I plunged into the Creek Indian War. Friends said, "Poor Tommy is sure to be killed." Indeed, on one occasion, May 29, 1836, I escaped by a miracle, running the gauntlet for a hundred yards or more through a shower of bullets from the rifles of about seventy Indians. Those nearest to me were not

twenty yards off. Yet only one bullet struck me, which was the first fired, while I was standing and looking out intently for the foe, whom I had heard. Mr. Jackson, the only man with me, was killed, being shot in eight places.

Neither T. J.'s body nor spirit seemed to be severely wounded by the attack because twelve days later in Jackson County he was elected captain of a troop of soldiers who volunteered to help put down the Indian revolt.

---

While Captain Bowen battled Indians in Georgia, another fight intensified in Texas. In the early 1820s Americans, especially from the South, began to settle in that Mexican territory. In 1823 Mexico encouraged such settlement with the offer of cheap land. Developing tensions between American settlers and Mexican authorities ignited into a skirmish at Gonzalez in October 1835.

When word of this conflict spread across the South, it stirred great sympathy and excitement to join the cause of the Texas colonists for liberty. As Alamo defender Davy Crockett confessed, "This is the kind of mess I like to have my spoon in." Many in Georgia felt the same way. In early November, 1835, the *Macon Messenger* ran the headline, "The cries of our fellow countrymen in Texas have reached us calling for help against the *Tyrant* and *Oppressor*." The article challenged, "Let all who are disposed to respond to the cry, in any form, assemble at the courthouse, on Tuesday evening next, at early candle-light." Newspapers later declared that meeting was the largest assembly ever seen in that town. A committee elected from that intense torch-lit crowd began to enroll those who would "risk their lives, their fortunes, and their Sacred honor" in the noble cause. By the end of the month, 82 well-equipped recruits from Macon had already left for Texas. In fact, the editor of the *Macon Messenger* complained that so many of his employees had volunteered that it was affecting his ability to publish. With rifles borrowed from the arsenal of the state of Georgia, three companies from Macon, Columbus, and Milledgeville united in Texas to form the Georgia Battalion. Tragically, approximately eighty-three of these men were massacred by Mexicans in the spring of 1836.

Now a seasoned soldier and leader of men, T. J. felt the call to join his fellow Georgians and help defend the newly-declared Republic of Texas. He arrived in Texas shortly after his twenty-third birthday in February 1837 at the very time the Mexican Army was invading. He enlisted in the Texas Army on February 14. He recalled:

> In December, 1836, I started alone for Texas, to aid in repelling the Mexicans who were seeking to oppress and subdue our countrymen... Six days after my arrival at the headquarters of the Texas army, I received a commission, which I neither sought nor expected. While in the army, I commanded Company B, Second Regiment of

Infantry; then Company C, First Cavalry; and for a brief time, this latter regiment.

Thus, T. J. Bowen led a company of the famous Texas Rangers. On a later trip to Texas he wrote to his wife, "The other is Col. Ashbel Smith, one of the great men of Texas. I have met with him two or three times. At first he called me Captain, because there are some who remember that I once commanded a company of those amiable men, the Texas Rangers."

Fighting Mexicans may not have been the only responsibility of T. J.'s Rangers. Orville Taylor comments, "Along with guarding the uneasy frontier between Texas and Mexico, Bowen may have also been involved in the pacification of the Comanche Indians in Central and West Texas, for shortly after this he published three poems about the Comanches in the Southern literary magazine, *The Magnolia*." This soldier-poet resigned his commission on August 31, 1838, after serving for over eighteen months. As compensation for his service, Texas granted him 1,280 acres of land in Llano County. Ready to return home, T. J. sold his land five days later in Houston. Just 24 years old, he had already established what would be a life-long pattern—to run toward danger and take risks to save others.

"He is no fool who gives what he cannot
keep to gain what he cannot lose."
—Missionary martyr Jim Elliot

"For whoever wishes to save his life will lose it;
but whoever loses his life for My sake will find it."
—Matthew 16:25

## CHAPTER 2

# Surrendering Everything

Great achievements call for great sacrifice. Reaching for truly valuable things requires letting go of lesser things. T. J. Bowen did not arrive back in Georgia until November 1839, fourteen months later. No record exists of where he was or what he was doing during that time. However, he reveals that he had traded physical battles for a spiritual one. He wrote, "I resigned my commission from a deep-seated conviction that I could not become a Christian while my life and heart were devoted to military service." Evidently, he felt guilty about his lifestyle while a Texas Ranger. Years later in Africa, he confessed, "some of the Episcopalians were laborers in Africa when

I was a wicked young man in the Texas cavalry, ranging the prairies in the western frontier of that country with my sword and yager [rifle]. I deserve the hardest lot of any missionary in Africa."

Yet from the time Captain Bowen resigned from the military, he struggled two more years before he came to faith. When he finally reached that point, he made a total commitment:

> In October, 1840, after a long, long period of seeking, I obtained hope in Christ, and soon after was baptized in the name of the adorable Trinity. My happiness in those days was more than language can express. About September 1841 I began to preach, and about a year after I was called to ordination. I then resolved that, until I should marry, which I scarcely expected to do at all, to give all my earnings, except a bare support, to the poor and to the spread of the gospel.

Facing poverty in his later years, T. J. would admit that he should have saved more money in these early years, but it was never in his nature to make timid commitments.

---

Thus at twenty-seven years old, T. J. became a preacher of the gospel. But it would be years before he would serve as the pastor of a church. Writing to a potential publisher in 1868, he divulged, "In 1841 I abandoned the law and became a Baptist minister. During the next 3 years I was chiefly engaged in traveling in S. W. Ga. [Southwest Georgia], S. E. Ala. [Southeast Alabama], and in Fla. [Florida] as a self-sustained missionary but occasionally teaching." As a Baptist minister in those days, T. J. did not need a formal theological education. Historian J. Edwin Orr explained, "The Baptists excelled in carrying the Gospel to the black man, and both in cities and through the countryside were regarded as champions of the poor and illiterate. They did not stress education, for they believed that the Lord would call whomsoever He wished to preach the Gospel."

Rev. T. J. Bowen made great effort to reach those often black, poor, and illiterate people in what was still rough, frontier country in southwest Georgia, southeast Alabama, and northern Florida. Besides holding several official positions of responsibility near his home in Bainbridge, Georgia, he preached and helped organize Baptist churches and associations of churches throughout the tri-state area. For example, John Nelson, who ran away from his home in Denmark and went to sea at the age of twelve, was farming in Holmes Valley, Florida, when he happened to pick up a stray leaf from a hymnbook left from an outdoor revival meeting. Its words brought him to faith in Christ and he led in organizing the Baptist Church there on July 20, 1846. The church minutes of that meeting stated that the new pastor, "called to his help, Bro. Thos. J. Bowen, sitting as moderator." In November 1847 T. J. preached a series of evangelistic messages at the First Baptist Church of Valdosta, Georgia. The church minutes that month reported, "During the progress of the meeting there were eight received into the church by experience & baptism & seven out of the eight professed conversion during the progress of the meeting and all eight of them are young persons—four males and four females." The church seemed so impressed that the next month they voted to ask T. J. to be their pastor, although no record appears of him accepting the position.

Concerning the early Baptist work in Florida, Gordon Reeves commented, "The earliest churches were established very close to the Georgia and Alabama lines through the efforts of ministers who came to Florida as missionaries. Many of these men were not sent out by a mission board with their expenses paid, but came unsupported, subsisting on the kindness of those to whom they ministered." Evidently, the kindness of these poor pioneers could not completely sustain T. J. financially. To help support himself, he also taught school. On the frontier, a teacher would contract with the parents in a community to hold school for their children for two or three months at a time. Rice related, "The teacher kept school from sunrise to sunset and she taught the three R's, readin', ritin', and 'rithmetic. For her services the teacher received fifty cents for each pupil per month, usually paid in provisions." No doubt T. J.'s frontier missionary lifestyle involved daily sacrifice, hardship, and loneliness.

T. J. Bowen found Florida to be the most needy mission field. Indeed, although in 1843 Baptists numbered 25,621 in Alabama and 43,573 in Georgia, they counted a mere 620 adherents in Florida out of a population of about 70,000. Accordingly, though he continued to minister above its northern border, beginning in 1845 T. J. began to invest more of his energies south of the Florida state line. In 1843 a disagreement on the question of missions divided the Baptists into Missionary Baptists and Primitive Baptists. The Missionary Baptists organized the Florida Baptist Association which had twenty-eight churches in Florida and three in southern Georgia. T. J. aligned his ministry with the Missionary Baptists of the Florida Baptist Association. After he preached on the subject of missions at its annual meeting in 1845, the association voted to hire him as one of their two missionaries at an annual salary of $150. Thus began his professional missionary career.

Few missionaries proved more zealous than T. J. The following year, the Executive Committee reported to the association:

> Bro. Bowen was sent to West Florida...The committee deem it unnecessary to add one word in commendation of the system of missions, or the faithfulness of the Brethren employed in this interesting work; their labors speak for them better and higher praise than we could give them. They have received souls for their hire...our Father in Heaven has blessed our

efforts far beyond our hope...Br. Bowen reports
to have received into the church 32 persons.

Two years later, T. J. played a prominent role in the association's annual meeting. He was elected their clerk and
appointed to preach the missionary sermon and to write
the next circular letter.

The minutes of that meeting also reveal that T. J. was
serving as the pastor of the Hebron Baptist Church. In
this, his first official pastorate, he demonstrated evangelistic fervor. Under his leadership, the previous year the
Hebron church baptized six people out of a total of twenty-six baptisms for the entire association of twenty-three
churches. Unfortunately, those same minutes also dis-
close that the association was in debt and could not pay its
missionaries their full salaries. It owed T. J. seventy-four
dollars, nearly half his annual salary.

The Florida Baptist Association minutes for 1848
demonstrate that T. J.'s ministry had become even more
effective. The records list him as the pastor of four churches
in the association—Liberty, Hebron, and Providence in
Gadsden County, and Lake Jackson in Leon County near
Tallahassee. With thirty churches in the association that
year with a total of sixty baptized, T. J.'s churches baptized thirty-seven or sixty-two percent of the total for the
association. In addition, his churches received thirty-four
percent of all those who joined associational churches by
transfer of their church letter. Evidently, his effectiveness exceeded that of any other pastor in the association. Since most churches in that frontier area only met

twice a month or less, pastors were able to serve more than one church at a time. T. J. needed the financial support of his churches because those same minutes stated, "the Association finds itself under the painful necessity of suspending domestic Missionary operations for want of funds." After 1848 the records reveal that T. J. worked within the newly-created West Florida Baptist Association. Besides his responsibilities as pastor of his own four churches, he assisted other churches in the association which needed help. The new association's minutes record how he and two others helped restore the Sardis church—"Since the commencement of faithful administrations of divine truth by these self-sacrificing 'heralds of the cross,' her prospects have been brightening, and this church, now, is a leading one of the Association."

What were these frontier Baptist churches that T. J. served like? With the same type of construction that they built their own homes, Baptists in Florida typically built simple log church buildings. Edward Joiner commented, "Often those who came to church would travel long distances, bringing their guns and hunting dogs, hunting on way to church and back. Sometimes during the services there would be several deer hanging up near the church." Most of the year the women wore colored calico dresses to church and the men wore homemade jean coats and pants. In the summer, the men either wore suits of light cotton or worshiped in their shirt sleeves. Since churches did not usually meet every week, they often met both Saturday night and Sunday morning. In describing the Holmes Valley Baptist Church, Elba Carswell reports, "They designated the fourth Sabbath and the Saturday before in each month as regular meeting days. The Saturday before the fourth Sunday in August, 1846, was 'set apart for fasting, praying, and feet washing.'" As to worship, Carswell relates men and women sat on separate sides of the church, and the music consisted of familiar hymns lined out by the preacher stanza by stanza without musical accompaniment. The sermons were long and "expounded the fundamentals of faith" with "the basic bread and broth of the law and gospel." These frontier Baptist churches also practiced strict church discipline. Church minutes of the period record frequent actions taken against church members for such offenses as absence from worship services, dancing, drinking, and adultery.

Like his presidential namesake, Thomas Jefferson Bowen could be termed a "Renaissance man" or polymath. Since no record of his formal education exists, he was evidently mostly self taught. Yet before his conversion he commanded soldiers, published poetry, practiced law, and was encouraged to enter politics. Later he would become the acclaimed scholar and linguist on whom Mercer University awarded an honorary master's degree. In his *Central Africa,* he wrote as easily of history, sociology, agriculture, geography, climatology, geology, zoology, ethnology, and medicine as he did missiology. With minimal training, he practiced medicine in Africa and used various scientific instruments to take meticulous weather measurements. He would prove to be a far-sighted missionary strategist whose ideas would be implemented by his denomination for years to come.

Brilliant and talented, T. J. could have done almost anything he wanted. But he gave it all up to spend these prime years of his life serving the poor, marginalized, and unreached on the American frontier.

"I had become willing to live a life of suffering
and die among the heathens, without one kind hand
to wipe the death sweat from my brow.
From the very first, I have never promised myself a
long life."
—T. J. Bowen

"Greet Prisca and Aquila, my fellow workers in Christ
Jesus, who for my life risked their own necks."
—Romans 16:3-4

## CHAPTER 3
# Risking It All

True heroes are willing to face great danger and take great risks. In the mid-1800s few places on the planet involved more of both for white men than West Africa. Philip Curtin explained:

> During the whole of the nineteenth century,
> the most important problem for Europeans in
> West Africa was simply that of keeping alive...
> [T]he coastal experiments of the 1790s brought

an image of West Africa as "the white man's grave" into new focus. The initial death rate for Europeans sent to the Province of Freedom had been 46 per cent. The Sierra Leone Company lost 49 per cent of its European staff, and the Bulama Island Association lost 61 per cent in the first year.

In 1841 the British attempted an expedition in the area traveling up the Niger River. Within two months, forty-one out of 150 Europeans had died of tropical fevers. Fully aware of the risks, T. J. Bowen gradually came to the settled determination to head to West Africa anyway.

Until 1845 T. J.'s Florida Baptist Association connected itself with the General Missionary Convention of the Baptist Denomination in the United States for Foreign Missions. Since it met every three years, Baptists usually called their denomination, "The Triennial Convention." However, on May 8, 1845, 293 delegates from nine states met in Augusta, Georgia, to form a separate denomination, the Southern Baptist Convention. The minutes of the Florida Baptist Association that year stated, "*Resolved, That we highly approve of the Southern Baptist Convention in Augusta; that we commend the great design of that body, in promoting the Redeemer's kingdom.*" Slavery proved to be the hotly-contested dividing issue. Those same minutes noted, "*Resolved, That this body recommend to the ministers and churches, whenever persons come among them representing themselves as Baptist ministers, that they require them to present satisfactory* credentials, and to define their position on the great question that has divided Baptists of the North, and South."

Baptist historian William Estep commented, "While it is undeniable that the primary cause of division between the northern and southern Baptists was the slavery issue, it is also evident that the missionary spirit was the new convention's breath of life." Thus Article II of the new denomination's constitution established two mission boards, one for foreign and one for domestic missions. The Convention determined that their Foreign Mission Board (FMB) would be located in Richmond, Virginia, and be led by a corresponding secretary, who would be the executive officer. (The FMB is now known as the International Mission Board or IMB.) Within months the FMB had elected the pastor of Grace Street Baptist Church in Richmond, James B. Taylor, to serve as corresponding secretary.

**James Taylor**
(Photo Courtesy of IMB)

In September 1848, Taylor received a letter and an article from T. J. Bowen proposing a mission to Central Africa or Yoruba (present-day central and southwestern Nigeria). Excited, Taylor shot back, "Permit me to say that your letter and article...have awakened in my bosom the most inspiring hopes." The FMB's first periodical, *The Southern Baptist Missionary Journal,* published Bowen's article, "Central Africa," in its November issue. In it T. J. argued that the climate in the interior might enable missionaries to survive longer and that the people might be more receptive to the gospel than on the coast, revealing his extensive research about the region.

The land of T. J.'s missionary hopes had recently received a few British Anglican and Wesleyan missionaries whose efforts were focused primarily on the city of

Abeokuta. These missionaries were recruited by heart-
felt pleas from ex-slaves, converted in Sierra Leone, who
had returned to their homeland in Yoruba. One wrote,
"For Christ's sake, come quick. Let nothing prevent you...
Come and see God convert the [unbelievers]...Do, do for
God's sake, start at this moment; do not neglect me with
all this burden; it is more than I can bear." T. J. probably learned about the work of the missionaries who
were moved to respond to such pleas from the FMB's
*Southern Baptist Missionary Journal*. An article in the
January 1848 issue claimed, "And in Central Africa, as
it appears from the missionaries at Abeokuta, the same
principle of toleration is recognized, and presents an open
field to the teachers of the Christian faith." In the June
issue of the same journal, T. J. would read about Africa,
"100,000,000 immortal spirits there lift up an imploring
cry for the bread of life. Not 1,000,000 of these have ever
heard the name of Christ." The statement that only one
percent of Africans had heard of Christ would have moved
a man with a missionary spirit like T. J. to go to them.

Baptists had sent white missionaries to West Africa
before, with terrifying results. In 1821 African-Americans
Lott Carey and Collin Teague were appointed as missionaries to Liberia by the African Baptist Missionary
Society, yet they were assisted financially by the Triennial
Convention. In 1830 that convention sent their first white
missionary family to serve with them. They died in less
than a year. Speaking of West Africa, missionary historian
Travis Collins wrote, "By 1846 fifteen other white missionaries had been sent by the Triennial Baptist Board,

but nine of them and two children had died, while the rest had returned home due to illnesses from which some never recovered."

---

Despite the danger, T. J. Bowen was determined to go. The FMB explained, "This brother...had for some time been looking at the probabilities of a successful entrance into this thickly-populated region, and becoming satisfied of its feasibility, his thoughts were turned to the question of personal duty in the case. He decided to attempt the difficult task. An offer of himself was made." T. J. knew the high probability that he would die in Africa. In his second letter to James Taylor he wrote, "If I should only live long enough to plant the Redeemer's standard on those bulwarks of heathenism as an ensign for others I trust that my labor would not be in vain." Two months later he commented, "I have not offered my services without mature deliberation, and a fixed resolution to live and die in my field of labor notwithstanding all the hardships and danger which may await me."

At the request of the FMB, T. J. traveled to Richmond to be interviewed on February 22, 1849. The minutes of that meeting read:

Board met at the call of the President to attend to the examination of Brother Thomas J. Bowen in relation to his religious experience, call to the ministry, and particular views in regard to

Central Africa as a field for missionary labor...
After the examination...the Board unanimously
appointed him as their missionary to labor in
Central Africa...On motion, Brother Thomas
J. Bowen was appointed as an agent of this
board to collect funds in the states of Florida
and Georgia for the mission in Central Africa
at a salary of $50 per month.

Thus T. J. had to raise his own funds for the mission. But
who else could match his passion for it? The Central Africa
Mission was his vision and it was his impressive influence and leadership that moved the FMB to act. Their
annual report that year stated, "The Board have been led
to contemplate Central Africa as a most inviting field of
missionary labor. Their attention was first called to it by
Brother T. J. Bowen, who has since been appointed to
commence its exploration, and to institute measures for
its cultivation."

The newly-appointed FMB missionary spent the next
several months wrapping up his pastoral responsibilities
and promoting the Central African Mission. That April,
Georgia Baptist paper, *The Christian Index,* published
a list of twenty-five churches where T. J. was scheduled
to preach and raise substantial funds for the project. He
wrote, "The whole expenses of the outfit for four or five
missionaries will probably be about two thousand dollars, which I trust the brethren of Georgia and Florida
will contribute before our departure next fall." FMB
Corresponding Secretary Taylor requested him to try to

get a contribution from every member of every church he visited and to write articles for *The Christian Index* and the FMB's new magazine, *The Commission*. African-American Baptists were especially interested in T. J.'s work. One such pastor wrote, "Since I have heard of Brother Thomas J. Bowen's appointment as a missionary to Central Africa, I have concluded to take up a collection in my colored congregation...I preach to a large black congregation in Palmyra...They appeared to think it a great privilege to aid in spreading the gospel to their own race."

One African-American volunteered to go to Central Africa with T. J. The October 1, 1849, FMB minutes record a remarkable situation:

> Brother Robert Hill in accordance with the above recommendation was present and after giving an account of his religious experience, etc., the following resolution was adopted, Whereas, Brother Robert Hill expresses his earnest desire to accompany Brother Thomas J. Bowen to Central Africa, therefore, Resolved, that when Brother Robert Hill shall have procured his freedom by purchase from his present owners that he be appointed an assistant in that Mission.

With fund-raising help from T. J., Hill did purchase his freedom for $750, and at twenty-two years of age was appointed a Southern Baptist missionary.

Hervey Goodale also joined T. J.'s team. In his early twenties, Goodale had spent a year serving with the Young Men's Tract Society of Louisville as a colporteur, or distributor of religious literature. Later, as a college student in Kentucky, he began writing James Taylor about his desire to be a foreign missionary. He was appointed by the FMB as a missionary to China and married shortly before his scheduled departure in May 1849. Tragically, his wife of one month died of typhoid fever before they could sail. Since Goodale was not inclined to marry again soon, and T. J. as a single man himself needed another companion, the FMB reassigned him to the Central Africa Mission.

James Taylor's Richmond church held a commissioning service for T. J. on November 7, 1849. The church took up a special collection to help purchase Robert Hill's freedom. Taylor addressed T. J.; T. J. addressed the congregation. They knew he was attempting something extremely dangerous. *The Commission* reported, "The congregation was large, and appeared to be deeply interested. The remarks of Brother Bowen can never be forgotten."

After picking up supplies in New York, T. J., Goodale, and Hill sailed from Providence, Rhode Island, on December 17 and arrived in Monrovia, Liberia, on February 8, 1850. When T. J. caught his first view of Africa from the deck of the ship, he was awestruck. He wrote, "[T]he exuberance...the intensity of tropical vegetation...the white foam of the surf...the wall-like forest...the smoky horizon...all presented a scene of mingled beauty, wildness, and somberness." Embarking from the ship, T. J. and his companions found themselves in another world. He said, "Our first employment ashore, was to look at everything within our reach, and to inquire into everything we could think of. It may be presumed that we were not inattentive observers. We were in a new country and climate where every beast, bird, and plant bore the impress of novelty."

When their ship's captain informed them that he would not be able to transport them down the coast to Badagry as planned, the men determined to wait in the Monrovia area a while, taking advantage of temporary missionary opportunities and acclimating to West Africa's inevitable tropical fever. Already weakened from the trip, that fever hit T. J. immediately. He wrote, "I have been sick much of the time since I left New York, with indigestion. Was weak when we landed, and soon broke myself down with baggage and other affairs...I am too weak and nervous to write much."

As it often did, T. J. Bowen's determination overcame his physical weakness. The day after writing the above statement, he and his associates set out on a 150-mile march into the interior. They were headed for Bo Pora, a large Golah town where the king wanted missionaries. Goodale wanted to visit the town and T. J. would not let him go alone. Liberian missionary H. Teague accompanied the new missionaries part of the way, to Vonzwaw. Writing to Taylor, he said, "Mr. Bowen's health was rather feeble while here; so much so that I felt considerable anxiety as to the issue of an attempt at the time to go to the interior, and endeavored to shake his purpose, but all of no avail. To go he was determined...He bore the walk, about ...seven miles, much better than I expected." Delayed at Vonzwaw for seventeen days, T. J. wrote, "[D]elivered my first message to the heathens of Africa. Only one woman present...On the following Sunday we both preached to a congregation of Deys, Vies, and Mandingoes, and other strangers from the interior."

After learning that the king of Bo Pora had died and the government had moved to Sama, the missionary team traveled sixty-five more miles through the territory of cannibals to that city. Once there, Goodale enthusiastically began a school and T. J. began to study the Vy language. He relates, "Our first and last public discourses were on Sunday after our arrival in Sama. Mr. Goodale was taken sick on the same day." For a time both Goodale and T. J. were ill. Writing to Taylor from Sama, Hill said, "Brother Bowen and Goodale both are sick with fever. Brother B. is very sick at this time...I am the only Dr. here." T. J. recovered and encouraged Hill to stay in Sama and study the language. Instead, Hill chose to return to Monrovia, leaving T. J. alone to tend to Goodale. Because of their isolation and having not received any word from America, they keenly felt their loneliness. T. J. wrote, "We are like men cut off from all life and yet living. Our hope is in God...Home is very dear to us and we are anxious to hear from it."

A few weeks later T. J. told the agonizing story of Goodale's last days: "About the 10th of April on feeling his feet, I found them for the first time becoming cold. This was a heart-rending discovery. I thought he might not live through the day...He often spoke of the poor heathen and exhorted us not to falter...the 13th of April, when he breathed his last. Surely no one can conceive of the awful loneliness of our mud hut in that sad hour." T. J. later described this extreme heart-break: "Almost everyone knows what it is to mourn the death of a friend; but there are not many who can fully appreciate the sorrow and loneliness of a man who buries his beloved and only companion in the wilds of Africa."

Nonetheless, finding himself alone in the interior of Africa did not turn T.J.'s heart back to the coast. Instead, he tried to go even further into the interior. However, the king of Sama stopped him. Determined to get deep into the heart of Africa, T. J. made the long, difficult journey back to the coast and as soon as possible boarded a ship headed toward Badagry.

With his doubts growing about Hill's maturity, T. J. did not take his assistant with him to Badagry. In an introspective, lengthy letter from Sama, he told Taylor, "I may as well now tell the unwelcome truth that I have doubt of Robert. During the voyage and since, I have found him lighthearted and vainheaded." Hill also seems to have been resistant to T. J.'s leadership. T. J. added, "Before we knew that we should be unable to proceed to Badagry he had resolved not to go with us, but says he would have followed next fall. I have not been pleased and thought of dismissing him...However...he has good qualities which have kept me in hope that he would yet be useful."

Before he left for Badagry, T. J. sent Hill to school at Bexley, Liberia, under the influence of missionary John Day. T. J. then left the decision of what to do about Hill in the hands of the Board and said, "I have written Robert a kind but candid letter." After T. J.'s report and counsel from its Liberian missionaries, the FMB dismissed Hill as their missionary on December 4, 1850. However, the following summer they received an earnest letter from Hill appealing their decision, complaining of no opportunity to answer the charges against him and being "left upon the cold charity of strangers with a dollar." From that point until the American Civil War, Hill was supported (with some interruption) by the FMB. Evidently, he did mature and became a respected missionary pastor and teacher in Liberia.

After fighting sickness, delays, and discouragement, T. J. finally arrived at the coastal town of Badagry on August 5, 1850. There he met "Old Simeon," a Wesleyan convert he had read about in America. Simeon's appeal for missionaries to reach his hometown of Igboho had inspired Bowen's goal to reach that city first. However, learning that wars in Yoruba had closed the road to Igboho, Bowen aimed for the only place he could reach safely, the city of Abeokuta. Finally, on August 15, with eight men to carry his baggage and a young boy to serve as translator, T. J. Bowen risked everything by setting out on his dangerous journey as the only white man on the sixty-five-mile trek into the interior of Africa.

"Twenty years from now you will be more disappointed by the things you didn't do than by the ones you did do. So throw off the bowlines. Sail away from the safe harbor. Catch the trade winds in your sails. Explore. Dream. Discover."
—Sarah Francis Brown

"And thus I aspired to preach the gospel, not where Christ was already named...but as it is written, 'They who had no news of Him shall see, and they who have not heard shall understand.'"
—Romans 15:20-21

# CHAPTER 4
## Enjoying Adventure

E xploration is not adventure unless it carries some risk of danger. But that sense of adventure can heighten the explorer's excitement and enjoyment. It did for T. J. Bowen. After traveling through a dense forest for three days, he said, "[W]e suddenly emerged into an open country, and my eyes were greeted with a more lovely scene than I had ever expected to behold in Africa—a vast expanse of undulating prairie, scattered over with palms and groves, and bounded in the distance by blue, mountainous looking hills." The next day, August 19, T. J. arrived at Abeokuta, where he was hosted first by the Wesleyan and then by the Anglican missionaries. He arrived in Central Africa not only as the first Southern Baptist missionary, but as the first American missionary there. In 1852 FMB Corresponding Secretary James Taylor wrote to him, "As no American Christians have yet attempted an entrance here, I see not why Southern Baptists should not expend largely in the occupancy of this field."

Always the adventurer, T. J. had always intended to go much further than Abeokuta where missionaries were already at work. The Yoruba country did not even begin until twenty miles north of Abeokuta. In April, the previous year, he wrote that he intended to establish a mission in Central Africa—"a land which no missionary has yet seen." Accordingly, just three weeks after his arrival, on September 9, 1850, he set out on a missionary journey to Iketu, sixty-five miles west. He carried his luggage with him, because he did not expect to return, hoping to get permission to pass on from Iketu to Igboho. At the town of Aibo on the way, a young man ran up to him, eager to hear the word of God. He later explained that he had long wanted to learn it and one night he had a dream that a white man came to his town to teach them. That, he said, "is the reason I was so glad to see you." Unfortunately, near Iketu T. J. received word that the chiefs were opposed to him coming there and the king had rescinded his invitation. Disappointed, he returned to Abeokuta.

Writing to Taylor a week later, he explained:

> I have arrived in Yoruba, but have found its conditions unfavorable to my design. The nation has been dismembered by civil war, and the divided provinces are still more or less unfriendly. Besides, the people in the most have imbibed a foolish notion that if a white man comes into a town, it will be destroyed by war, as some places were not long after the visit of the Landers...Several towns were quite unwilling to give me shelter for a night.

T. J. concluded that there was nothing for him to do but wait in Abeokuta for doors to open to the interior. While there, he busied himself learning the Yoruba language.

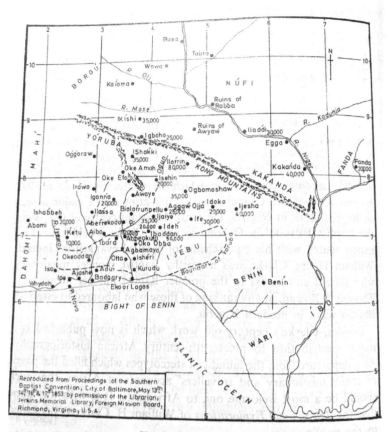

*Yorubaland in the 1850s*

(Photo Courtesy of IMB)

When he arrived in Abeokuta, T. J. was shocked to discover that all the missionaries still used interpreters. To Taylor, he wrote, "None of the English yet preach in the Yoruba language, although some of them have been here four years. They brought interpreters and monitors with them from Sierra Leone or from the West Indies." A year later he wrote, "I find it is a bad plan. The force of the preacher's thoughts is almost sure to be weakened by the interpreter, and sometimes the true meaning of a sentence is lost." Expressing his disgust, he wrote, "Vast amounts of preaching are thrown away by missionaries... What the interpreter calls 'high English,' or 'deep English,' is often an unknown tongue to him, and of course he can not tell the people what the preacher has said, though he is sure to tell them something."

Accordingly, T. J. gave himself to studying diligently the Yoruba language and in eighteen months was speaking without a translator and was "tolerably well understood." At the same time, he was developing a grammar. In November 1851 he wrote, "I have compiled a considerable grammar which will facilitate the progress of my future colleagues." By December 1854 he was able to write, "I have finished the rough sketch of a vocabulary, containing 6,596 words. The grammar is on hand." Nonetheless, two years later he was close to doubling the number of words. He became a superior Yoruba linguist, translating the gospel of Matthew and eventually seeing his grammar published by the Smithsonian Institution.

In addition to language study, T. J. did all he could to immerse himself in the Yoruba culture. Describing this season in Abeokuta he wrote, "To acquaint myself with the language, intellect, feelings, and every-day life of the natives, I used to visit them on their farms, ten or fifteen miles from town, and remain two or three days." Doing so, he learned that the Yorubas were not polytheists as was previously believed. He discovered that they "believe in but do not worship one great and universal God, called Ollurrun (owner of heaven). Their orishas [idols] are mediators who are strictly substitutes for the one mediator Jesus Christ. The devil is worshipped not as a mediator but to propitiate his favor and escape his malignance." He added, "I have many solemn conversations with these people."

T. J. found much to appreciate about the Yoruba culture. He was impressed with their morality which was inculcated through teaching proverbs, mentioning that many of their manners and customs were similar to those of Jews. He remarked, "[A]lthough the women do not marry till they are eighteen or twenty years of age, I have never known a case of an illegitimate child. The law and public opinion are too strongly set in favor of virtue to allow the frequent occurrence of such things in Africa." He also valued their industry, commenting, "The Yoruba and other tribes in Central Africa are far from being lazy people." In addition, he spoke favorably of their energy of spirit, their common sense, and their optimistic and social nature. The more he learned from them, the more he grew to respect them. Defending them, he wrote, "Tell me not of their sins, their ignorance, or their barbarism. They are more virtuous, more intelligent, and more civilized than many suppose."

Although he had limited interaction with missionaries from other societies, T. J. found himself increasingly lonely. He admitted, "I sometimes feel very keenly the loss of Christian society. A familiar hymn or tune or passage of Scripture often recalls the happy, happy days I have seen in the sanctuary, and I am ready to exclaim how can I bear this long and painful exile from all my brethren." He also began to express his need for a wife, "Do not send unmarried men. They <u>must have</u> wives, not only for their own happiness but for the success of the work." Later, he told an FBM member of his growing desire for a wife, "I want a holy and amiable woman, of sterling sense, and sound body, not less than 28 or 30 years old. Perhaps you know one of the thin kind?" Evidently, T. J. believed that slender women were attractive and also better suited for Africa.

———

In early March, 1851, something dramatic happened to break T. J. out of his lonely, tedious routine of language study. The 60,000 citizens of Abeokuta got word that the dreaded army of Dahomey under King Ghezo was advancing against the city with 16,000 warriors, including 6,000 vicious females. Determined to wipe out opposition to the slave trade, Ghezo aimed to be rid of the city and the missionaries there who opposed it. The defeat of Abeokuta would not only be a bloodbath for its people, but an enormous setback both for the anti-slave-trade forces and for the missionary cause.

In preparation, the main citizens of Abeokuta, the Egba tribe of the Yoruba people, had constant patrols in every part of the city and surrounding countryside. Tension was high, and several times at night there were false alarms with women crying "Ele! Ele!—to arms! to arms!" Christians were fervently praying, and unexpectedly, just hours before the battle, 12,000 musket balls arrived from Sierra Leone.

Finally, early on the morning of March 3, patrols brought word that Ghezo's army was almost upon the city. The other missionaries moved to a safer distance at the top of a near-by tower of rock where they set up a first-aid post and observed the battle through a telescope. Captain Bowen stayed in the thick of the fight. Lending his military expertise, he challenged the people to stand firm, reserve their fire, and take good aim. About noon, 15,000 Egbas marched quietly out the gate to meet the enemy. T. J. said, "I could plainly see in their firm and solemn countenances, as the thousands and thousands passed by, that they were prepared for the occasion." Across the prairie, Ghezo's larger army dramatically appeared with flying colors, divided into two parties, and quickly launched a loud and furious charge. At first one of the closest Egba divisions gave way in retreat, but helped by those behind them, they soon rallied and the battle reached a fierce intensity.

Seeing the ferocious battle, some of the Egbas who had remained by the gate, ran back into the city and disappeared. T. J. tried in vain to stop them. However, others who fled back to the city mounted the wall and defended the gates with rifles. T. J. remarked, "The guns were roaring along the wall for a mile or more." It soon became apparent that the city was safe. When T. J. returned to the wall after dinner, he saw the Egba troops quietly resting in the field with the king of Dahomey's soldiers holding up at a safe distance. Despite occasional skirmishes, things were calm enough for both armies to sleep in the field. While his army slept, Ghezo evacuated, and discovering this, at dawn his army followed. After the Egbas chased them for 15 miles, the Dahomians turned to fight them, but were again soon put to flight and the battle was over. While the enemy was being pursued, T. J. and another missionary, Samuel Crowther, surveyed the local battlefield on horseback. Over 1,200 bodies of enemy troops were counted.

Historian Biobaku commented, "The Egbas owed their victory...to the tireless energy and example of the missionaries. Bowen of the Baptist Mission employed his military training to direct and encourage the Egba fighters upon the walls...'[T]he Egba were vociferous in their gratitude to the missionaries.'" T. J.'s role in the improbable victory of the Egba was a recognized deciding factor. This good will toward the missionaries opened previously-closed doors, especially for T. J.

In fact, King Ghezo's defeat changed history. His attack on Abeokuta was widely reported in England, as many churches and Christians there had been praying for the missionary work in the city and its protection. Taking advantage of the moment, English missionary leaders exerted pressure on the government to act in that part of Africa to protect the missionaries and end the slave trade. Missionary Crowther was quickly brought from Abeokuta to England where he gave first-hand reports in various meetings, including with Sir F. Baring, the First Lord of the Admiralty. Crowther even had a lengthy meeting with Queen Victoria and Prince Albert. In November, when T. J. traveled to the coastal city of Badagry for supplies, he met Consul Beecroft and several of his naval officers who were a part of a British squadron who had been sent to make a treaty to end the slave trade.

Days later, T. J. wrote, "Six men of war are at Lagos... Lagos was bombarded this morning. We heard the guns for six hours." After further conflict in December, the British soundly defeated the pro-slavery forces of Dahomey. This paved the way for a treaty with the anti-slavery Egbas which opened the door for missionary expansion. In his journal, T. J. recorded the historic occasion:

> January 5, 1852. Today Capt. Forbes, R. N., who has been here for six weeks, concluded a treaty between the British government and the Egbas, or people of Abeokuta. They agreed to abandon the foreign slave trade, to suppress the practice of human sacrifices...to prevent all further persecution of Christians, and to give white people free permission to visit the interior. In conversation Capt. Forbes mentioned me particularly, and they said I should go.

About this treaty, J. E. Ajayi commented, "two additional clauses were added at the instigation of the missionaries, guaranteeing freedom of movement about the country for themselves and for the emigrants." The signatures of four witnesses are listed on the treaty. Thomas

J. Bowen's is one of them. Evidently, through helping to negotiate the terms of this treaty, he played a key role in opening up Central Africa not only for himself, but for future missionaries.

———

However, even before the treaty was signed, new doors had opened for T. J. Just weeks after the battle of Abeokuta, he received a fresh invitation to visit Iketu. He wrote, "On the 28th [of April 1851], with rather sad feelings, I bade farewell to the last speck of civilization in this region, and departed to go still further into the moral desert. My journey extended about 70 miles."

This new adventure proved to be filled with danger. Though invited by the king of Iketu, the city's Muslim-influenced chiefs opposed him. Those chiefs even burned down the king's house to distract attention from T. J.'s house so they could burn him alive, but the plot failed. Later, he reported another attempt on his life:

> One day my boy came from the milkman's, with a bottle of milk as usual, but...affirmed, with some appearance of excitement, that the man had slyly taken a large leaf out of the milk before he poured it into the bottle. As he is a Mohammedan, I made a toximeter of my dog. He drank the whole bottleful, which produced vomiting...Next day I sent the man a red cap as a present.

T. J. added, "I drank no more milk in Iketu."

Despite these dangers, T. J. discovered more opportunities to share the gospel. He wrote, "I cannot preach yet, but I talk a good deal, and my young man interprets. Many of the common people hear me gladly. Some have come to my house and asked to hear the Word of God. Both here and in the streets some listen with great attention."

Despite the dangers, T. J. was enjoying his African adventures. But the hardships began to weigh upon him.

"I am nearly barefooted and my clothing are failing.
I have only about $40.00 left and don't even know if my
former letters have reached home."
—T. J. Bowen

"Suffer hardship with me,
as a good soldier of Christ Jesus."
—2 Timothy 2:3

# CHAPTER 5
# Enduring Hardship

A missionary's greatest battles are not found on the outside. They are the inner battles against loneliness, frustration, and discouragement. How much more was that true of pioneer missionaries like T. J. in the mid 1800s. His miserable living conditions in Iketu sometimes overwhelmed his gratitude for ministry opportunities. He found himself struggling with sickness in a hot, stinking, damp, windowless hut. He wrote, "If I die, it should not be attributed to the climate, but to this horrible filth which I am obliged to endure for a few months if I can."

"But," he said, "bodily afflictions are small compared to what I have suffered on account of my exile from home, and friends, and Christian privileges. For me, there is no sympathizing friend, with whom I can take sweet counsel." His loneliness only exacerbated the normal temptations of human existence. He confessed, "Besides all my other troubles, I have many painful conflicts with the flesh and with the devil." In his suffering, T. J. found comfort in his strong sense of God's sovereignty. He wrote, "If he has chosen ones here, he will reveal them; if not, my labors shall glorify him in some other way. Mine is no uncertain work which depends on chances or accidents, but all things are 'ordered and sure.' I rest and rejoice in the sovereignty of God my Father."

However, when T. J. began to preach in Iketu openly, after only one month there, the prime minister told him he had to return to Abeokuta. As he left the city, T. J. "heard the firing of guns and beating of drums, which I supposed was the rejoicing of my enemies." Since his horse was too weak to carry him, he walked the seventy miles along rain-soaked roads and through swollen streams, well aware that his second attempt to penetrate the interior of Africa had failed.

Back in the Anglican compound in Abeokuta by June 1, 1851, T. J. continued the lonely study of the Yoruba language, waiting for some breakthrough into the interior. But he was waiting even more for letters from home. By September, after 21 months alone in Africa, he had not received a single letter or dollar from the FMB. In desperation, he wrote that month to the FMB treasurer, "I am nearly barefooted and my clothing are failing. I have only about $40.00 left and don't even know whether my former letters have reached home." Three weeks later, on October 11, he finally received some letters from home.

Yet more than money, T. J. felt the burden for missionary associates. Appealing to Taylor from Iketu in May, he wrote, "A continent lies before us, millions of men are here who have never heard the name of Jesus. Who is the laborer who refuses to leave the cool shade, while others are toiling to gather sheaves for eternity. We have not time to rest and take our pleasure now." Such passion led him to donate his anticipated salary—"My whole expenses this year up to this date, on behalf of the Board, are not charged, because I want to give that much to the cause of missions. I had rather see a missionary any day than to have $500."

With the signing of the Treaty of Abeokuta and new doors opening for missionaries, T. J. gladly welcomed an invitation to visit Biolorunpellu in the beautiful mountains of the interior. Arriving there on February 1, 1852, he found himself a novelty to the town's 2,000 citizens. They had never seen a white person before. Yet he reported that a number of them proved open to his message:

> During my stay here I have preached to people
> from various parts of Yoruba. Bioku the chief
> has learned something of the gospel which he

frequently repeats to others. Several persons have expressed a desire to follow Christ...On the 24th inst [instance, a term for the date] a woman came and told me that she desired to serve God...Her countenance, words, and manners are strikingly earnest, humble, and Christianlike. There is joy in heaven over one sinner that repenteth.

This woman, Oyindala, requested baptism, but T. J. hesitated because he thought, "who would feed her on the sincere milk of the Word? I will instruct her, however, as much as possible, and wait till I see what the Lord will do for her." After listening to T. J. for a while, a man named Alaiju said to him, "I have no idols; I am not a Mohammedan; I have nothing of this kind to lay down, but I am a sinner and I want to be saved." This man also made a commitment to Christ as well as others in that same village. Years later T. J. admitted that he should have baptized Oyindala and others who were ready and tried to establish his first mission station there. However, he was thinking that he should explore the country and establish work in some of the larger cities. He confessed, "In fact, I was just too curious to see the country." Indeed, T. J. loved adventure and challenge. When the residents of Biolorunpellu told him that a precipitous mountain nearby was impossible to climb, he promptly reached its summit.

Nevertheless, the response of the people of Biolorunpellu moved its missionary deeply. He wrote,

"The circumstances by which I am surrounded make a deep impression on my mind. When I look round on these thousands of people ever ready to listen to the gospel...I feel at times as if this world with its pride, power, and opinion was fading away and that I am already in the twilight of eternity." In the postscript of that same letter he pleaded, "I beg the Board to send men, if some of them have to come themselves." Reading this comment in a denominational publication so moved twenty-four-year-old William Clarke that he volunteered for Central Africa where he later became T. J.'s associate.

Leaving Biolorunpellu on March 12, T. J. traveled toward Ishakki to which he had received an invitation. However, the king of Ijaye, Kumi, had sent orders throughout the area to prevent him from going further. Kumi wanted him to come to his city instead. Thus, T. J. found his way blocked at the cities of Ishakki, Awaye, and Okeefor. Much of this time he was very ill. He wrote, "I was sick 40 days at Awaye in April and May." However, the little preaching he was able to do on these journeys did make an impact. Three years later he wrote in his diary for March 8, 1855, "A man from Ishakki informs me that I preached to him in Abeokuta in 1851, and again at Awaye. He remembers well, and declares he has never worshipped an idol since. His appearance and conversation are hopeful."

After recovering from sickness, T. J. made his way to Ijaye, arriving there in May, 1852. King Kumi eagerly listened to the gospel and gave him land to build a mission station. Back in Abeokuta, T. J. wrote Taylor of his historic decision:

> My tidings are good. Much of the Yoruba country is ready to receive us...I have selected Ijaye as the place for our first station, because it is only 7 days from the sea, & because Kumi the prince refused to let me go further unless we would begin in his town first. Ijaye is about 8 miles in circuit, densely populated, very cleanly and pleasant, and is situated in a beautiful prairie country. Within from one to five days journey of Ijaye are several large cities...Ijaye being in a central position and the almost independent head of western Yoruba will probably be our headquarters.

While T. J. was exploring Africa alone, back in the American South, FMB Corresponding Secretary James Taylor was desperately trying to recruit missionaries to join him in Central Africa. Taylor wrote to T. J., "We have endeavored by correspondence, and by frequent appeals through the *Journal* and *Commission,* as well as appeals at public meetings to excite attention to this necessity, and thus to procure candidates for appointment to this mission. But hitherto all has been vain." After hinting for months, Taylor finally told T. J. that the Board wanted him to come home to recuperate and recruit. At the same time Taylor was writing these things in America, T. J. had come to the same conclusion in Africa. Without money or associates, he had no hope for establishing the Ijaye mission station. He had explored the land and laid the plans. His initial mission was accomplished.

T. J. left most of his baggage in Ijaye, and since the road to Abeokuta was closed due to fighting and robbers, he set out across country for the coast. As it was the rainy season, he and his two bearers marched for miles through tall, wet grass and waded chest-deep streams. Reaching the Ogun, he rented a canoe to go down river through hostile territory. He related, "Hosting the stars and stripes on a bamboo staff, and laying six loaded guns at my feet, we pushed off into the rapid current, and were soon gliding through the hostile district. From time to time, the canoe men pointed out places on the bank from which the Igebus had recently fired into canoes." T. J. sailed for London on August 8, 1852, and a miserable 103 days later finally arrived. In December, he left Liverpool for New York, probably arriving in late January 1853, completing his initial missionary journey.

He had survived and succeeded. His Foreign Mission Board summarized this first expedition with remarkable words:

> The beloved brother who spent nearly three years in conducting the enterprise was beset with difficulties which would have driven ordinary men from the field. He remained more than a year on the borders of Yoruba, unable to enter the kingdom in consequence of fierce and bloody wars...These wars having terminated, mainly

through his instrumentality, he embraced the earliest opportunity of penetrating further into the interior, discovering large cities, before unvisited by white men, and preached in them to multitudes who had never before listened to the words of salvation through Jesus Christ. During his stay in the interior, his exposures and sacrifices were extreme. Wading rivers, sleeping in the open air, with all his supplies cut off, and depending often on the kindness of the natives for daily food, with scarcely a change of raiment, and frequently barefooted, he was in continual danger of being cut off by death. For twenty months he received not a solitary line from home, to cheer his wanderings. But God was with him—his faith failed not. The hearts of people were opened to receive the word from his lips, and not a few rejoiced in the salvation of the Lord.

T. J.'s endurance was remarkable, in part, because he had prepared himself beforehand for hardship. Writing from Iketu, he said:

My mind was made up for the toil before I ever wrote to the Board. I had counted costs for months in the midst of conflicts, between selfishness and duty. I had become willing to live a life of suffering and die among the heathens, without one kind hand to wipe the

death sweat from my brow. From the very first,
I never promised myself a long life.

"Georgia alone, kindled to enthusiasm by the example of one of her noblest sons, will qualify and send out and sustain an army of missionaries to bring all Central Africa into subjection to Christ."
—R. R. Gurley after hearing T. J. speak at the Georgia Baptist Convention

"And He said to them, 'Follow Me, and I will make you fishers of men.' Immediately they left their nets and followed Him."
—Matthew 4:19-20

CHAPTER 6

# Inspiring Others

Passion inspires passion. Fire catches fire. Sacrifice stirs sacrifice. And because T. J. Bowen lived and breathed fiery passion and sacrifice for missions in Central Africa, upon his return to America, he inspired multitudes for the cause. He threw himself into a flurry of traveling, writing, speaking, recruiting, and fund-raising, even though he would later write, "During the short period of my stay at home I was several times sick and never well." But his passion for Africa and to be back there in nine months, gave him no real time to recuperate. He later confessed:

> To have restored my health I should have retired to some quiet place where I could have seen but few persons and I should have remained in America several months longer than I did. Still I do not regret the labor that I performed while at home. I knew what the consequence was and would be, while doing it. Above all I do not repent of returning to Africa prematurely. I feared much sickness as the consequence, but if I had retired to the most quiet and pleasant place in the U. S. I would have found no peace and no health there while my feelings were so intensely fixed on establishing the Yoruba Mission...I should hate myself if I could rest and fatten while my portion of the Lord's vineyard were left a prey to thorns and thistles.

Traveling first to Richmond, Virginia, T. J. met with the Foreign Mission Board. He led them in prayer, reported on his work, and received an appointment as their agent to raise funds for his mission. In a second meeting with the FMB, they determined, "that this Board will endeavor to secure at least five men, some or all of whom may be married, to accompany Brother Bowen to Central Africa, at the earliest practical period." Evidently, the Board's confidence in T. J. and their enthusiasm for his work led them to make bold plans for expansion. Their confidence in T. J. was extraordinary. Taylor wrote to him, "And now, I will say that the Board have the utmost confidence in the soundness of your judgment, as well as the integrity of your aims, and they prepared to second, and to cooperate with you in any distinct and feasible line of operations you might strike out."

Accordingly, the FMB depended upon T. J.'s judgment and persuasiveness during the recruiting process. They wanted him present for their interviews with potential candidates whenever possible. He also interviewed candidates in his travels. Writing to Taylor from Alabama in March he reported, "There can be no manner of doubt that Bro. Clarke is well qualified for the work and we now regard him as one of our number." T. J. had strong opinions even about the physical appearance of potential candidates. Later, he would write, "Fat, juicy people, those with a lymphatic temperament and those who are easily knocked up by sickness or exposure should not come here for they have the sentence of death or banishment written in their constitutions. A tough leather string of a man is the man for Africa."

T. J. gave special attention to one candidate, who no doubt had been recommended to him by her brother-in-law, who was the current chairman of the FBM Committee on African Missions. On March 23, he wrote to Taylor from Greensboro, Georgia. While there, this tough, thirty-nine-year-old adventurer must have spent quite a bit of time with refined, barely-twenty-one-year-old Lurana Davis. She found him somewhat reserved, but intense. He would write to her later, "I was never demonstrative but if I say little, I think & feel much." Lurana saw him as a dashing missionary hero and fell for him quickly. He proposed; she accepted. A few weeks later she wrote to him a love letter expressing her confidence in their engagement:

> It seems a long time since I saw you...<u>One</u> week has dragged heavily away. Absence has taught me the true depth & sincerity of my affection for you. I know now, that, 'I love thee and I feel that in the fountain of my heart a seal is set, to keep its waters pure and bright for thee.' Not a doubt has crossed my mind since I first gave my heart to thee; on the contrary I feel happier with the exchange we've made...I believe too that our Heavenly Father approves the step and will show us His favor. I feel grateful to Him for directing such a great and good man to regard me with favor and to select me to assist him in his noble work. Ever yours—Most affectionately, Lurana

**T. J. AND LURANA BOWEN**
(Photo courtesy of the IMB)

Lurana's father, Samuel Davis, was a wealthy and influential planter who had moved to Greene County, Georgia, from North Carolina sometime before 1817. After living on a farm for years, he moved his family to a home in Greensboro in 1832. Born the seventh of eight children on March 6 that same year, Lurana was raised in an atmosphere of Southern aristocracy. Her father's farm was tended by 33 slaves. Six days a week those slaves worked from sunup to sundown, and on Sunday Lurana worshipped with many of them at the Greensboro Baptist Church which had more slave members than white members. At meal times in her family's home the table was covered with the bounty of their fields. The best magazines lay on other tables and the best of English writers filled their bookshelves. The family was surrounded by well-trained, polite, and attentive servants. Lurana's life up to this point embodied refined culture and privilege.

The wealth and influence of her family proved extraordinary. The Georgia Railroad reached Greensboro in 1838 and began transporting the area's cotton to Augusta. Lurana's father bought stock in the railroad and thus gained wealth not just from raising cotton, but transporting it. The railroad also brought to Greensboro's merchants large stocks of goods at low prices. These merchants soon grew wealthy and influential like the planters. Foremost among them were two of Lurana's brothers, Charles and William, who in 1860 built a huge, two-story store of more than 12,000 square feet. It was nicknamed "the big store" and was the largest retail establishment between Augusta and Atlanta. One of Lurana's sisters married one of the most influential men in Georgia, Judge Thomas A. Stocks. One of the original settlers in the county, he became a wealthy planter. He served as a Greene County Justice on the Inferior Court or as county commissioner for 30 years, in the Georgia House of Representatives for eight years, in the George Senate for 12 years and was president of that body for eight years. Stocks also became an influential leader in Baptist life. For over 40 years he served on the Georgia Baptist Convention Executive Committee, and he attended the National Triennial Convention on three occasions.

The wealth and influence of Lurana's family afforded her an education that few young women in her day could experience. After being privately tutored at home, at

14 she enrolled at the nearby Penfield Academy. Three years later she entered the newly-formed Georgia Female Academy in Madison. She was one of two women to graduate in November 1850. Her rigorous studies included political economy, moral science, trigonometry, geometry, geology, and astronomy. Her three-day commencement consisted of examination questions from the faculty and audience. Lurana's proud father gave her a piano as a graduation present.

Her education proved not just academic. Spiritual matters dominated the students' lives. Historian Cliff Lewis writes, "At a weekly student evening prayer meeting in September 1850, when she was eighteen years old, Lurana delivered a statement dedicating her life to 'renewed Christian piety.' A missionary calling became her prayer." Two weeks before their wedding, Lurana wrote to T. J.:

> I often feel very unworthy of so high a calling—but the duty of becoming a missionary has been so long and deeply impressed on me—and I feel <u>so sensibly</u> that my happiness depends upon the performance of a duty so plain—that I cannot doubt that such is the will of God concerning me. And I sincerely thank Him for directing me so early in life to my field of labor. They tell me I am making a great sacrifice! It may be so in the eyes of the world or those who do not comprehend the feelings of a missionary...

it is a poor sacrifice compared to that which our blessed Savior made for us.

Lurana was not the only one in her family who was willing to sacrifice for the cause of missions. When she spoke to her parents about going with T. J. to Africa, they replied, "It is a severe trial to give up a daughter to go so far away; but if you feel that the Lord calls you to the work, we dare not refuse. God will be as near you in Africa as here, and we can pray for you just the same." Also, it seems that Lurana's missionary calling inspired her younger sister, Cornelia. She too married a missionary and they moved to the Indian Territories (now Oklahoma) and ministered to the Native Americans there for many years.

Willing to give up her charmed Southern life for one of sacrifice and suffering, Lurana was commissioned as a FMB missionary at the Baptist church in Greensboro on May 30, 1853. Her fiancé, T. J., preached the sermon. The next morning they were married and immediately began the journey toward New York from which they would sail to Africa.

But they would not sail alone. T. J. had been busy raising funds and recruiting. His passionate letters from Africa to the FMB had, for the most part, been printed in its publications, along with reports from the other famous African missionary explorer of the day—David Livingstone. Southern Baptists read about these two inspiring missionaries side by side in the pages of their magazines. Both were considered heroes and widely admired. That fame opened doors and opened hearts for T. J.'s speaking and recruiting.

In demand as a speaker, he preached in churches and lectured at in various cities across the South. At FMB Corresponding Secretary James Taylor's direction, he focused especially on college students. Taylor wrote, "It is desirable that we should go up to the university & spend three or four days at Washington [D. C.]...Can you attend a meeting at Penfield [Mercer College] before you return, conferring especially with the students? It is to be hoped that many may there be prepared to follow you to Central Africa."

Thirty-five-year-old J. L. Dennard had wept over the letters T. J. had written from Africa. A lawyer in Houston before his conversion in October 1845, he had pastored five churches in Alabama, near Eufala where T. J.'s father lived. When T. J. interviewed him about joining him in Central Africa, Dennard jumped at the chance. In fact, Dennard began traveling with Bowen so they could recruit and interview candidates together. Writing to Taylor, Dennard comments, "Bro. Bowen and I met at this place on last evening...We have just had an interview with Bro. Clarke and he has determined to go to Africa with us if the board will send him." The Board did accept Clarke, and at times he joined T. J. and Dennard in speaking and recruiting.

These three courageous adventurers made a deep impact on the attendees of the Georgia Baptist Convention in Atlanta in April 1853. On Sunday the 24th in mid-afternoon, T. J. spoke to a great congregation of African-Americans, some of whom had traveled a great distance to hear about the work in their country of origin. That evening at eight he, Dennard, and Clarke were the featured speakers at a great missionary meeting. One observer wrote, "Mr. Bowen's statements are the most interesting of anything which has been brought to light from the interior of Africa; that they made a profound impression on the Convention." The Convention's Committee on Missions reported:

> [W]e should record our fervent gratitude to God that we have been cheered, during our present session by the presence and labors of our returned missionary, brother Bowen, of the Central African Mission. We have no doubt that the great Shepherd has sent him to our meeting for good. We moreover rejoice that two others, brethren Dennard and Clarke, native of this State, have been designated to the same important and inviting field.

Thirty-one-year-old, Virginia-born J. H. Lacy was serving not only as a preacher, but also a teacher of Greek. T. J.'s call to Africa became God's call to him. Writing to Taylor in January, he said:

> The long and earnest appeals, which have been made for Missionaries to join Bro. Bowen and the millions of benighted Africa dwelling in the region and shadow of death have for some time

been subjects of deep interest to me...I feel that, (if the board send me) I peril my health and life, and may lose both. It is painful to sever the ties which bind me to friend, brethren, home, and a loved widowed mother...I would count all these lost for the excellency of the knowledge of Christ.

In the end, it was Lacy and Dennard who would accompany T. J. Bowen to Africa. The plan evolved for Clarke to come a few months later, hopefully bringing other recruits. Shortly before their voyage, the three adventurers were honored to appear at the national Southern Baptist Convention in Baltimore in June. On that Sunday, T. J. presented a passionate message about the needs of African Yoruba territory, stirring the hearts of many.

All three missionaries married shortly before they left for Africa. The FMB pressed them to find a willing wife, but wanted them to wait for marriage until close to the voyage to prevent them from being distracted from their work of fundraising and recruiting. Taylor wrote Lacy in March, "In regard to your question, I will say that the unanimous opinion of the Board...is that the missionary ought to no means marry until just before his embarkation...Have you found a <u>helpmeet</u>? Please let me hear from you soon." Nevertheless, Lacy married first—to Olivia on May 1, 1853. Next, Bowen married Lurana on May 31, and Dennard married Fannie on June 18. On July 6, 1853, these three newly-wed couples set sail from New York on their honeymoon cruise to Africa for the adventure of their lives.

"I live to show his power, who once did bring
My joys to weep, and now my griefs to sing."
—George Herbert

"Weeping may last for the night,
but a shout of joy comes in the morning."
—Psalm 30:5

## CHAPTER 7
# Overcoming Tragedy

I n this broken world, tragedies and heartache come to everyone. Some people become immobilized by them. Others grieve deeply, but keep moving. On their missionary adventure to Africa as a couple, T. J. and Lurana Bowen would face hardships and heartaches that would have caused others to turn back.

The adventure began sooner than expected for the three honeymooning missionary couples. Writing from England, T. J. reported, "One night in the midst of the ocean, the ship caught fire, and some of the inner planks were burnt through before it was discovered." However, the fire proved to be a benefit. T. J. continued, "On arriving at London July the 19th, we despaired of being able to make our purchases and get the articles aboard ship before she left on the 21st. It chanced however, that she was obliged to go to dry dock for about seven days, which enabled us to ship most of our things."

Leaving Plymouth, England, on August 1 aboard the steamship Hope, the adventurers stopped briefly at two islands off the coast of Morocco. Then once again their ship caught fire. In his journal for August 11, T. J. noted, "Ship on fire—serious time for two or three hours—much gunpowder on board." After stops at islands off Senegal, they traveled up the Gambia River to the settlement of Bathurst. Of this, the team's first time to step foot on African soil, T. J. wrote, "Our party had the pleasure of spending several hours on shore at Bathurst, where, to most of us, everything wore the charm of novelty."

Earlier, while he was in London, T. J. purchased medical supplies and equipment. His son-in-law, T. B. Rice commented:

> Mrs. Bowen told the writer [that]...Mr. Bowen, during his first visit to Africa, learned much about the native diseases, treatment, etc. He had studied medicine and had a fairly good medical library; so, when he reached London on his second trip, he laid in a supply of such drugs as he felt he would need, including prescription scales, bottles, graduated measures, mortars and pestles, spatulas, microscope, etc. Therefore, in addition to

teaching the gospel, he did what he could to heal the sick; and according to Mrs. Bowen's statement he was frequently called upon to visit other tribes in the capacity of a physician... Mr. Bowen did not graduate from a medical college, but was thoroughly conversant with such medical words as Dr. James Ewell's "Medical Companion," published in 1816, and similar works.

Later, T. J. would write in his diary, "Today we removed to our new house which when finished will contain...a medicine room 8 by six." His diary affirmed that his medical skills were appreciated. On January 24, 1854, he noted, "People continue to call on me for medical assistance."

Unfortunately, T. J.'s medical abilities and supplies were tested almost immediately. The team landed in Lagos on August 28, 1853. That very day the Dennards came down with fever and were in bed for a week. When they had sufficiently recovered, the party traveled three days by armed canoes up the Orgun River to Abeokuta, where the rest of the party came down with fever. Perhaps because he never took time to fully recover in the States, T. J. became sicker than the rest. Lurana wrote, "Mr. Bowen has not been very much affected by fever, but what is much worse in this country, suffers a great deal with dysentery. He has been quite sick with it for the past two weeks, and for a day or two, he has well as myself, had some fears as to the result."

The first-time missionaries fell in love with the beauty of Abeokuta and its surroundings. Writing to her sister, Lurana confesses:

> With the country I am pleased. Mr. Bowen did not give an extravagant account of its beauties and luxuriance; where we are now is the most romantic place you ever saw; the city is built among hills, or mountains (they might be called) all covered with shrubs, flowers and grass, looking as green and luxuriant as any portion of the temperate zone; and as far as the eye can reach you see one range of hills rising above another in one direction—while in another, a dense forest, like a widespreading plain, meets the eye; and nearer round where you stand there are thousands of houses built some in the valleys and plains, some on the sides and others on the very top of these beautiful hills.

After six weeks of "acclimations fever," the missionaries seemed better and ready to press on. Bowen had been preaching daily in Abbeokuta, but was eager to move to Ijaye in the interior. He received word that Kumi, the king of Ijaye, was eager for them to come. The plan was for the Lacys to join the Bowens in Ijaye and, against T. J.'s preference, for the Dennards to move back to Lagos on the coast to facilitate the shipment of supplies to those in the interior. They were all full of hope for the future.

Lurana wrote, "Our brightest anticipations of Africa have been fully realized."

* * *

On October 31, 1853, the Bowens set out on the three-day journey to Ijaye in a caravan of 25 to 30 Africans who were carrying their luggage. A significant amount of it was sea shells—coweries whose smooth and shiny shells were used as money by the natives. Lurana was carried in a hammock suspended between the heads of two strong men, while T. J. rode a horse most of the way. When they camped at night, their food supply was suspended in nets to protect it from ants, and watched by a guard to protect it from monkeys.

The missionary couple were warmly received in Ijaye. The king gave Lurana enough blue and scarlet "bride's cloth" to make a dress, which only royalty were allowed to wear. For the first five days they stayed in Adolphus Mann's house, an Anglican missionary who had moved there a few months earlier.

For the next two and half months the Bowens rented a tiny native house—eleven feet long, six feet wide, and six feet, six inches high. Because the house had no windows and only a four-foot high door, it was dark, hot, and stuffy. Lurana, who had grown up in an expansive, comfortable house, must have felt the claustrophobic conditions keenly. But she never complained. A few years later, T. J. described her as "more ardent than myself, a woman who has never faltered at any difficulty, or uttered a word of complaint against any of the troubles we have encountered in that country."

That poorly-ventilated 66-square foot house no doubt contributed to almost two months of sickness for both T. J. and Lurana. Since he was already weakened by never really resting in the States and the severe dysentery of the previous month, T. J. was facing death. Writing on November 19, he described "indescribable bodily anguish which I have felt since last Friday." On top of the fever, the dysentery returned. On December 6 he confessed his fear, "I feel I am too weak to survive a severe attack." Eleven days later, Lurana wrote that T. J. was "just recovering from the severest attack of sickness he has ever had in Africa...For many days he was so ill that we had strong fears as to the result...For I have often thought him to be near death's door."

Lurana was also often sick and, to complicate things, was pregnant. T. J. urgently felt the need to provide a healthier living situation for his family. So as he was able, he began building a house. The work was arduous—clearing the land, making mud bricks, setting the joists, thatching the roof—it took about three months. Though he hired workers, he did as much work himself as he could.

Whenever T. J. felt strong enough, he was also evangelizing. On December 10, he mentioned the man who would become the first he would baptize in Africa. "There is a man here named Tella, the son of an Ilorin general... This man seems to have no doubt that every word of the gospel is true." Two days later he described a typical street preaching scene:

A crowd soon collected to whom I proclaimed salvation through the sacrifice of Christ. A young man asked if it had not been long since the whites had received the gospel. I replied, "Yes, but the devil has hindered us from coming to you before. A woman spoke with animation for some minutes approving our design to improve the morals of their country, but alleging that their fathers from time immemorial had worshipped *orisha* (l-ri-sha—idols). To this I answered that my forefathers also were idolaters, but when they heard the gospel they threw their idols away and embraced Jesus Christ as their Savior. The objectors being silenced, I spoke again of salvation and the love of God. Finding them greatly interested, I saluted them and went home. Such are the scenes daily repeated, with many little incidents too minute to describe.

By mid-December he was preaching twice a day in the Ijaye streets or marketplace. Beyond that, on the little porch in front of their house where they would frequently sit and take their meals, many visitors came by asking questions about Jesus. The Bowens were encouraged by the receptivity of the people and were eagerly awaiting the arrival of the Lacys from Abeokuta.

But they never came. Lacy's eyes, which had never been strong, were significantly weakened by the fever, to the point he could not write. Fearing he would lose his sight completely, he and his wife traveled to Lagos where he found an English physician on a ship in the harbor. After examining him, the doctor told him, "that the disease was amaurosis with which the natives sometimes suffer, resulting in the total destruction of the optic nerve." When he recommended returning to America as Lacy's only hope to preserve his sight, they promptly did so on December 6.

Since the Lacys did not write the Bowens to tell them the whole story, they felt abandoned. Lurana confided, "Mr. Lacy, who was expected to occupy this station, has deserted us; so we are alone...We deeply regret his affliction and that our ranks are broken so soon." Three days later, T. J. wrote, "I suppose he never will return and I feel sad at being left alone in Yoruba." Normally gentle and patient, FMB Secretary James Taylor was deeply upset about Lacy's sudden departure. He wrote to him sternly, remarking that several of the Board's missionaries in China had the same thing and stayed at their posts.

To some extent, the Bowens also felt deserted by the rest of their team. Against their original plan, instead of moving with them to the interior, the strong-willed J. L. Dennard had moved to Lagos on the coast for the purpose of forwarding supplies. He appears to have a decidedly different view of African missions than his team leader. He spoke of not rushing into the interior, of not taking the country by storm, but gradually. And writing to Taylor, he asserted, "We cannot live in this country unless we have comfortable houses."

T. J. had repeatedly warned his associates of the health danger of living on the coast. Dennard paid a dear price for not listening; his wife died of fever in early January 1854. In agony, he wrote to Taylor, "The Lord gave her to me; in the short space of six months and a half he took her from me...I feel that the last and dearest tie that bound me to earth has been severed." It was another devastating blow to the little team of missionaries. Now alone, sick, and struggling, the Bowens doggedly pushed forward in their work.

Lurana proved to be extraordinarily effective. Though she was very sick the last half of December and into the new year, on January 22, 1854, she began the first Baptist school and Sunday School in what would become Nigeria. In her diary that day, she noted, "Sabbath began a school with our servants, 5 in number, and five others employed as laborers during the week, with some few drawn by curiosity. Formed three classes: one beginning the alphabet; a second for those advanced in spelling; a third reading in the Yoruba testament."

The school grew quickly. Her diary for February 12 read, "Sabbath, large school. Some appear anxious to learn, but many attend through curiosity." A week later, she wrote, "Sabbath—very many persons young and old attended our school." Evidently, by March the school grew to the point where they used other teachers besides Lurana. In his diary for March 5, T. J. recorded:

This has been a good, not to say glorious day. The attendants on the Sunday School are so numerous, that each of our few teachers are thronged by the press of adults and children, and yet not all can get near enough to learn. They listen to the gospel with deep attention, and the countenances of some indicate not only interest, but emotion. I have felt today, as sometimes I did at home, just before revivals.

In large measure, the school owed its success to the fact that the people adored Lurana. Three years later, missionary Clara E. Warner Priest wrote to FMB Associate Corresponding Secretary Poindexter, "I saw this manifested in Ijaye. Sister Bowen has a warm place in the hearts of many persons there. Their countenances brighten with joy at the mention of her name."

Nevertheless, during this time Lurana found her hands full with other matters besides her school. Her diary for January 28 recorded, "Sick with a chill and fever all day. Notwithstanding, we moved to our house, though half finished, thinking it more comfortable than the small dark rooms we have been in so long and hence more healthy for us." Yet about that new house, T. J. later wrote, "The floor was made of beaten clay, and neither it nor the clay walls were fully dry, which endangered our lives." On February 23, he wrote in his diary, "For some time I have been much concerned about the state of Mrs. Bowen's health. She is now again attacked with ague, attended with symptoms which appear to me to be highly dangerous." Yet just two days later, the couple welcomed into the world a "fine, healthy" daughter, Mary Yoruba Bowen. T. J. commented,

"Today we have had an addition to our family, to whom I have given the name Mary Yoruba, she being the first white child born in this kingdom."

Although that spring the Bowens found joy in their baby and the responsiveness of the people to their message, sickness and circumstances often discouraged them. On March 16 Lurana wrote, "Came out of my room for the first time in three weeks. Very feeble but improving gradually. Mr. Bowen's health very bad, suffers exceedingly with headache and enlargement of the spleen." Besides ill health, T. J. found deep frustration that they were not receiving desperately-needed supplies from home. By March 19 he gave evidence of depression, writing, "But the fact is hope from any quarter is very near extinct...To pass month after month without receipts of anything, and to need and expect help all the time is a situation which can not be appreciated by anyone unless he would come here to this remote region and experience it."

T. J.'s physical and emotional struggles continued to worsen. By April 18 he complained of a painful and enlarged liver and spleen. He added, "Sometimes when asleep my heart appears to have a sudden spasm, a sort of whizzing darts through my ears, I leap up while yet asleep and on waking find myself gasping for breath and my heart palpitating violently...Some days ago I was seized with acute inflammation of the liver with great pain in the part and in the right shoulder."

By far the greatest health concern of the Bowens soon became that of their infant daughter. She took ill on April

25 and her health continued to decline. Lurana's diary recorded their agony as they watched their child suffer:

> May 26—We are alarmed about our babe. She is almost choking with phlegm. May 27—After a watchful, sleepless night we find our babe no better, but rather worse...Our anxiety and distress is inexpressible. We hardly know what to do. May 28—This morning about 9 o'clock the spirit of our only earthly treasure took its flight to the heavenly worlds. Our dear child is dead!...Stillness and loneliness fill the house, and we are *very, very* sad, but hope in the Lord...We submit to the affliction and draw nearer to him who inflicts the stroke.

Though devastated, the Bowens remained determined to carry on their work. The next day Lurana wrote in her diary, "Today I have commenced the language with double diligence." T. J. himself kept busy with building and preaching. By June 2, he had completed not only the house for his family, but another for a kitchen and servants, both surrounded by a clay wall six feet high, all for about $130.

In January of that year when J. L. Dennard's wife, Fannie, had died of fever, he had written, "But in my grief I must not forget that I have duties to perform...I know not how soon I may fall a victim to this inhospitable climate." It happened sooner than Dennard wished. He did move away from the coast to Abeokuta, but he contracted fever there in June. Bowen reported:

> Bro. Dennard is dead. He was attacked [by] severe fever on the 7th inst. [instance, a term used for the date]. After being considerably out of danger he was seized again on the 17th and expired the next day. During his illness he was carefully attended to not only by the missionaries but by an excellent physician, Dr. Irvine of the Royal Navy. He died in the faith. I may also add to his credit that he died at his post, like a good soldier of the cross.

Just a few months earlier, Dennard had written, "If my dear brethren at home will only hold the rope for me I will descend this dark well of Heathenism and dig and toil and suffer until my master calls me home, and then again I will hold communion sweet with my own dear sainted Fannie in that land of eternal love."

Thus in the space of six months, the Bowens had suffered repeated, severe sickness and grieved the loss of the Lacys, the deaths of the Dennards, and the death of their only child. Many others would have given up and gone home. T. J. and Lurana stayed and saw their greatest fruitfulness.

"There is no magic in small plans.
When I consider my ministry, I think of the world.
Anything less than that would not be worthy of Christ,
nor of His will for my life."
—Henrietta C. Mears

"Now to Him who is able to do far more abundantly
beyond all that we ask or think, according
to the power that works within us"
—Ephesians 3:20

## CHAPTER 8
# Dreaming Big

S mall ambitions lead to small results. Men and women
who dream and plan for great things are much more
likely to see great achievements. T. J. Bowen was such a
man. Pushing past the tragic losses of the previous few
months, he kept toiling toward the goal of bringing multitudes in Central Africa to Christ. The response to his
preaching in Ijaye began to grow. On June 10, Lurana
remarked, "We are now receiving full compensation for
our troubles and trials, since we have been in this country.

The light of the gospel seems to be breaking upon the darkened minds of these benighted people. They come of their own accord and ask to hear more about the Word of God." By mid-July T. J. had completed another major building project—a thirty-by-twenty-foot chapel. At that point he was preaching up to twenty times a week.

His efforts bore fruit. On July 23, Lurana wrote, "Tella baptized and the Lord's Supper administered for the first time among us in Africa." Of that historic occasion, years later T. J. wrote, "It fell to my lot, under the providence of God, to be the first to consecrate the steams of Sudan by baptism." He was referring to the first baptism by immersion in that large area of Africa.

Yet T. J. still found himself hounded by lack of supplies, illness, and depression. Lurana's diary from July 7 read: "Dark and raining. Mr. Bowen very despondent, has little hopes of his recovery and often speaks of dying and feeling certain that he cannot live. This is trying to my faith and hopes, but I believe God will not forsake his cause in this place, but will sustain it and will use my husband as the first means." Lurana's faith and prayers carried her husband through his darkest days.

The surprise arrival of new missionary associate William H. Clarke on September 29, 1854, brought the Bowens significant joy and encouragement. Clarke abounded with energy and enthusiasm. T. J. had the highest regard for him. He would write later, "Want of discretion arising from too much energy and self-esteem is the only fault I have ever seen in Brother Clarke." In another letter he commented, "Bro. Clarke is a sterling man who lacks nothing but experience and a little less impetuosity."

October found T. J. performing a wedding ceremony in the church and baptizing a woman. But by the end of the month he slipped into his worst time of illness in Africa. On October 29, Lurana wrote, "Mr. Bowen very ill, attacked yesterday with congestive chills which returned today with something like collapse of the lungs or heart. For several hours, death seemed to be inevitable, but the Lord graciously spared him."

The illness lingered and affected T. J. mentally. On December 21 he wrote:

> Of late my disease has affected my heart and head, and on several occasions has produced alarming symptoms...In my feverish hallucinations, I have mused upon it [his disease] as a great monster, rushing upon me, and I was armed with a sword, hastening to meet it. If I roused up for a minute, I would probably sink back into the same reverie. This state of mind did me no little injury for months...to divert my disease of personality, and willful indignity, appeared impossible.

Improved health in January 1855 spurred T. J. to dream of a dramatic expansion of their work into the interior. As the three missionaries busied themselves learning the language, endeavoring to make Yoruba as familiar to them as English, T. J. was itching to make a move into the Muslim stronghold of Ilorin. He wrote to Taylor, "My own ultimate station as I have often said is to be further interior. One man should go to Abeokuta & build for himself. Two married men should come to Ijaye, two men should go to Ogbomosho, myself and another to Ilorin." The next month he wrote, "My direct and indirect calls to Ilorin, and my inclination to go still continue. So as soon as you think it prudent, I hope you will send me...First of all, however, we must have a station at Ogbomosho. Bro. Clarke at my request is gone on a visit to that later place, and writes back that he is much pleased." Although at this point, he could only speak "in broken Yoruba," in Ogbomosho Clarke preached to eager crowds of "hundreds and thousands."

To make his dream a reality, T. J. began building accommodations for new missionaries and kept pressing Taylor to send them. He wrote, "Surely Bro. Phillips will be sent without delay even if he has to come alone. The demand for preaching is so urgent that we begrudge the loss of every day." Evidently, overwhelming physical and mental difficulties did not dim T. J. Bowen's missionary vision and motivation.

On February 17, Clarke came back from Ogbomosho sick. The first part of March he grew worse, vomiting blood. T. J. spent much of his time caring for him and for a time doubted that he would live. On March 8, he wrote, "This morning the drivers (black ants) invaded our bedroom which we had given up to Bro. Clarke, and we were obliged to carry him to his own room in the other end of the house." Had they not moved Clarke, the ants would have eaten him. Of these ants T. J. commented:

> They march forth by the million and feed on nothing but flesh. No living creature can stand before them. When they invade a house which is generally at night, we are obliged to retire, and every mouse, roach, cricket, scorpion, etc., which cannot escape is soon to be devoured. On one occasion they killed a parrot in its cage. Their visits, though disagreeable, do not last more than an hour or two, unless they should find a piece of meat or the like to detain them.

By March 13, Clarke was well enough to sit up and by the next month was eager to start a mission station of his own in another city.

That spring a number in Ijaye were professing faith in Christ. On May 20 Clarke baptized two converts whom T. J. was convinced were ready, a man and a woman. The following Sunday T. J. baptized another man. Lurana summed up their progress to her mother, "I wrote in my last of three more being added to our small band of Christians, whereof I know you will rejoice. There are other serious inquirers, and we think hopeful over one who is a Mohammedan, who has been living by making charms, but has now given it up, and gone honestly to farming."

The Bowens felt deeply the spiritual needs of those around them. After mentioning that she heard a crowd of idol worshippers passing by to make sacrifices, Lurana wrote, "My first impulse is always to follow them, take away their orishas [idols], and preach to them, then and there, of Christ who died to save them, but prudence holds me back...but oh! How we long to see it! And what a joyful sight it would be to see these people turning to God, with their whole hearts."

———

From the beginning of his call to Central Africa, T. J. was focused on reaching the Muslims there, in particular, the Fellatah people. In his first published article about Central Africa, before his appointment, he enthused, "The Mohammedan Fellathas are so different from other Mohammedans that they might prove a 'people made ready for the Lord.' They might embrace the gospel and go forth as missionaries to every part of Africa." Later, in his *Central Africa,* he made his target group clear, "My own intention had been to study the Puloh or Fellatah language...Should the gospel be established among these people, who are known to be the most intelligent and energetic tribe south of the Desert, they might become active missionaries, and subdue more nations by the Word, than they have by the sword." An examination of FMB publications from 1845 to 1860 revealed that T. J. was the first Southern Baptist missionary to write and publish the fact that he was targeting a Muslim people group. Further, he appears to be the first missionary in Central Africa to focus on reaching a Muslim people group.

T. J.'s passion to reach Muslims was fueled by frequent positive responses from them. On his first expedition, two Muslims from Ilorin had visited him in Biolorunpellu and were eager to hear the gospel. One Muslim *alufa* or scribe asked to spend five months with him. On his second expedition, Muslims frequently attended their worship services. On July 24, 1854, Lurana noted, "Several Mohammedans who became offended yesterday and left the church came today and brought others with them who had never heard the Word of God." In fact, the Bowens saw a number of Muslims put their faith in Christ.

T. J.'s passion to reach Muslims in the interior became unstoppable in April 1855. Writing to Taylor, he insisted, "I have never felt satisfied here and I suppose never shall. Let me wait until all things are ready, but do not deny me the privilege of going to the interior. I am called and must go." The next day Lurana wrote in her diary, "Mr. Bowen making preparation to travel, his bad health demands a change." William Clarke told what happened next, "[M]y colleague [T. J.] expressed his conviction of the absolute necessity for a change for himself and wife. He proposed to go to...a high mountain point west from Ijaye [Biolorunpellu]...but at my suggestion he changed his place for a temporary residence in Ogbomosho with an eye on Ilorin, and left me in charge of Ijaye."

T. J. set out without Lurana on an investigative trip to those cities on April 14. Few wanted him to go, especially to Muslim-controlled Ilorin. He remembered, "I believe that almost everybody in Ijaye disapproved of my going. The Mohammedans were vexed, and the heathens frequently expressed their fears that the bad people of Ilorin would murder me." For safety purposes in Yoruba, traders would travel in large, guarded caravans from city to city. T. J. wrote, "A great company were going from Ijaye to Ogbomosho, and I fell in among them without ceremony, as if I had been a native." He traveled with this caravan two days, preaching to them some, all the while getting warnings not to go to Ilorin. He then traveled two days alone, sleeping in the prairie before reaching Ogbomosho on April 17.

He was delighted with his reception, recording in his journal, "Well received in Ogbomosho, a pleasant, healthy town; population about 25,000. Chief and elders said they would turn to God." Two days later he wrote, "Spent two days in looking over the town and preaching. Mohammedans still molest me. Heathens beg that I would go no further."

Undeterred, T. J. traveled on to Ilorin. Arriving, he rode on horseback through the first and second gates before he was asked by the gatekeepers why he came without permission. T. J. preached Christ to them. They gave him water and took him to the house of the prime minister, who, in turn, put him in the custody of the king's executioner. He could not go out, but received, "a good many visitors." He preached; they listened in silence. Finally, the king sent for him. T. J. described the scene, "He was sitting in state behind a screen; many of the nobles in front on his left hand. Questioned as to my faith. They controverted nothing. After half an hour's talk the king said, 'Go home and rest. Our consultations are not finished.'"

After meeting with the king, T. J. had the freedom to leave the executioner's house at will. He preached widely and found great delight in the people and the city. He commented, "Much pleased with the Pulohs, (Fellatas). They are mostly black, but some are nearly white...They have good European features." He found many of them responsive to his message, writing, "They are surprised and impressed by the doctrine of the new birth...The people have a great respect for the New Testament and desire to see it." On April 27 T. J. went to one of Ilorin's large markets. He remarked, "A wonderful sight. Ilorin is about the largest town I have ever seen, except London." He later estimated the city's population between 70,000 and 100,000. The next day the king gave T. J. a private interview, asking the missionary to read part of the Bible to him. The Muslim king then commented, "I am afraid that your religion will spoil ours." Nonetheless, the following day T. J. received word that the king was pleased with him and was going to grant him land on which to build a house for himself and also a chapel.

T. J. returned to Ijaye full of enthusiasm about the possibilities of the interior. He shared his vision with Taylor:

> I have seen much and have returned with enlarged views and feelings. If it can be so I beg the Board to send me at once to Ilorin. Two or three others should come out immediately for the same place...I trust we are now about to

> lay the foundation of a mighty work in Central
> Africa…The Fulah's, the people of Nufi, Hausa
> and Kanike, whom I met are more intelligent
> and civilized than I expected. Most of them
> desire missionaries though they know our
> doctrine and designs. The energetic spirit of
> change which pervades other parts of the globe
> has come hither also. The whole seems to be
> approaching a great social revolution. Now is
> the time for missions.

The climate further into the interior also gave T. J. reason
to be encouraged. Its dry air and warm nights made him
feel better physically, something he desperately needed.
Thus he and Lurana made plans to move. Yet they had
to wait because summer brought the rainy season and
expected missionary recruits had not yet arrived.

---

While they waited, their ministry in Ijaye continued
on. That rainy season brought much sickness and death,
resulting in smaller crowds. Clarke left in late July for
a thirty-eight-day missionary tour and left the Bowens
working in Ijaye alone. However, by September the
Bowens were seeing increased response. T. J. had developed a systematic preaching plan for the city, preaching
in a different district every day. He explained, "Have
been laying off Ijaye into districts, one for each day of

the week...I have 7 roads through the town from wall to wall along which I travel every day to tell of Jesus."

His diligent labor brought results. After preaching to an unusually large congregation, he remarked, "I could see the word tell upon them as it reached them. The fact is we seem to be bordering on revival feelings. The cloud mentioned some time as resting on us is gone...I expect to be as happy in preaching here as I ever was at home." Two days later, he added, "Wonderful effect of truth. Though it happens daily now I must again record the wonderful effect of the word. Even Mohammedans appeared borne down like reeds before the wind. Surely God is in this place."

The Bowens' success in Ijaye was due in part to their wise adaptation to the culture of those around them. In a day when most missionaries attempted to plant Western culture as well as Christianity among their hearers, T. J. took a remarkably different view. In *Central Africa* he observed:

> It is not wise, however, to commit the too common mistake of supposing that our form of civilization is the exemplar for the whole earth. It is not even the best for ourselves, and is not adapted to Africa at all. The climate and the moral and mental conditions of the people, are unanimous in demanding an African civilization for Africa, such as that which the people of the interior have already originated, and which only needs to be developed on its own basis,

in conjunction with pure Christianity... Every attempt to force our full-grown civilization upon barbarians, serves only to stupefy and paralyze them ...The wise instructor of Africa is content to begin with the elements of knowledge, both religious and secular; and he continues his course by attempting a diffusion of such principles of Christianity, science, art, and social improvement as the people can appreciate and reduce to practice.

Writing in 1966, Nigerian historian E. A. Ayandele commented, "This was a remarkable opinion in the middle of the nineteenth century."

Accordingly, like pioneer missionary Hudson Taylor was doing at the same time in China, T. J. and Lurana sought to adapt to culture in Africa as much as possible. They did not impose Western hymns on the Yoruba. In his journal, T. J. noted, "Baptized a man who was received two weeks ago. Administered communion. We have suitable hymns for all these services, in good Yoruba meter, idiom, and rhyme, if they are not good poetry." They also tried to adapt to the Yoruba diet for the sake of identifying with the people. T. J. professed, "I had rather live on yams and palaver sauce than to make the displays we all make at our stations."

Next to the use of native language, missionary housing proved to be T. J.'s biggest cultural concern. He believed Western-style housing and furnishing were a hindrance to the acceptance of the gospel. A month after he landed in Africa, he wrote, "I am surely convicted that mission-aries cannot do well in Africa with a load of goods around them. Oh that God would be pleased to send me who can leave all and be content to suffer hunger, nakedness, and peril as did the apostles." Later, when he brought Lurana, he did build houses, but confessed, "I look upon such houses as I have built as a serious obstacle to the gospel. Our unbending foreign customs and our display of what appears great wealth to the natives cause them to feel that we are aliens and excite their cupidity and envy." He added, "Give me a plain native house, and trim me around till nothing is seen in me but myself and the Bible in my hand."

So why did T. J. build nicer houses? He felt it neces-sary to draw other missionaries to Yoruba. Speaking of his work to build a missionary compound, he explained, "Why then am I doing here just as others do? Because I cannot labor alone, and have no hope of seeing men who will do as I desire to do. ...I have been toiling for others."

Despite the encouraging response in Ijaye, T. J. could wait to move no longer. He laid out their plan to the FMB, "I am to remain in Ogbomosho some two months or more. By that time two or three other brethren will be here, and no doubt two will come to Ogbomosho. If I go on to Ilorin and no one comes to Ogbomosho, I am to preach at the latter place about once a month." Leaving the work in Ijaye with Clarke, the Bowens set out for Ogbomosho on September 20, 1855. Lurana felt some sadness in leaving. To her parents, she wrote, "I left Ijaye with many regrets and many attachments to draw me back. It being the place of the birth and death of our dear Mary, our little church, and my school, besides many and kind friends, all tended to hold me there. But these ties were willingly and easily broken through when the importance of the furtherance of God's work was considered."

The highlight of the journey proved to be Lurana crossing a river floated by large gourds, T. J. swimming beside her. Those gourds were two large calabashes cut in half, cemented together, forming a cushion-shaped "African sailing vessel" that could support hundreds of pounds of cargo. Traveling on from the river through the rain, they arrived wet and unwell on September 23. The people of Ogbomosho regarded light-skinned Lurana with amazement. She told her parents, "[W]hen I venture in the streets. Crowds of fifties and hundreds follow me, some with open mouths in utter astonishment; others laughing, running, jumping, screaming, hollering, and calling out to those in the house to come and see!" Despite her novelty, Lurana began a school one week after they arrived, with a class of fifteen.

That same day T. J. preached at an assembly of the city's chiefs. He minced no words:

> I replied, I have said nothing about your wars. That is only one sin. You must believe in Jesus or go to hell. He will pardon our sins, and give you a clean heart, and then you will sell slaves no more. Take him for your Master; your king, your all, love no one else. After hearing patiently they inquired, "How shall we serve

Jesus?" I told them again to believe and be baptized; and gave them an outline of Christian behavior. The governor said, "We (can) do it." (The word might be "will").

T. J. Bowen despised the development of African Christianity that was not self-supporting. Therefore, with this first presentation of the gospel to the king of Ogbomosho and his court, with stunning boldness he demanded that they build their own chapel building with their own funds:

> "Now," said I. "Arise and build you a meeting house. He that first believes and loves Christ will first be baptized." They thought that we would build the meeting house (a bad precedent) (a real hindrance to the gospel). "No," said I, "if you cannot stand alone without somebody to prop you up behind you, you can't serve God. Remember how much money you have spent on your orishas (idols)—how many houses you have built for them? From Jesus you may receive all that your orishas can not give you. If you love him you will build the house." They said they would do it.

Their response to his courageous challenge to follow Christ greatly encouraged T. J. He appeared to have a keen ability to read people and situations. There in Ogbomosho he sensed that things in Yoruba were moving toward a tipping point. He wrote, "I am sure from the nature of their minds and feelings that they must be moved as masses if moved at all. There will be a deepening and widening of gospel influence—the crisis will come—some towns will renounce idolatry, and the example will spread like a contagion, through the nation."

After nearly a month of ministry in Ogbomosho, feeling that his wife was well situated there, T. J. made another trip to Ilorin to see if the door was still open for him to establish a mission there. Upon entering the city, he wrote, "I soon discovered that something was wrong." During the months since his previous visit, opposition to him had been building. When T. J. appeared before the king and he asked him to preach, a crowd of about two or three hundred soon gathered. T. J. wrote, "When they were seated I proceeded to preach with all my power... No one spoke till I had finished. The king then said, 'We do not reject God, but we are Mussulmen [Muslims].' He told me further to go and build a house in Ogbomosho and come occasionally to see him." Disappointed, T. J. returned to Ogbomosho where the city's chief gave him a nice building site.

Although T. J. found himself somewhat occupied with building a home and preaching in Ogbomosho, he spent most of the last two months of 1855 nearly incapacitated by serious illness. On November 12, Lurana wrote, "Sick, Mr. Bowen suffering from apoplectic [stroke-like or convulsive] symptoms—had his hair shaved." Six days later she noted, "Mr. Bowen sick, symptoms variable, sometimes indicate an attack of African fever then some cutaneous disease with the normal complaints of liver and spleen." She revealed how seriously ill he was in a letter to her parents on December 18, "Mr. Bowen's health, which has never been good in this country, is now in such a state that he writes to the Board this month to advise him what to do. He thinks he cannot be of much service any longer here, and a change of climate seems the only alternative for the prolongations of his life."

T. J. himself wrote similar things. To the FMB treasurer he expressed, "here lately I have been almost dead." To the Associate FMB secretary he confessed, "I have... been unusually sick for several weeks...My health is too bad to do anything except hold on. Before long I must beg leave of absence till my liver is restored to a better condition." Evidently, during this time he also faced symptoms of serious mental illness. He admitted:

> Truly I have suffered torture, and have frequently been almost crazy, so much so that I was afraid sometimes to go out alone with my gun, owning to the temptation of the devil. I never dreamed of suicide before, but my nerves have been so wrecked for months that it could not be banished from my mind. Although I have kept going most of the time, I have now and then had the horrors—no man can estimate or describe such feelings.

In the midst of these enormous struggles, the Bowens kept working as much as possible. On January 30, 1856, they moved into their newly built home in Ogbomosho.

It had twelve-foot-wide rooms, one for them, one for the expected missionary associate John F. Beaumont, and one for storage. Although ill, T. J. still preached. For the first Sunday in February, Lurana noted, "Attendance large and attentive, morning and evening." On February 27, they received word from Ijaye that three new missionaries had joined their band—Rev. and Mrs. A. D. Phillips, and John Beaumont. The trio had sailed together from New York the previous October. Before their appointment, Phillips had been a pastor, Beaumont a teacher. As was typical, Phillips had married his wife, Fannie, just a few weeks before leaving for Africa. To their sorrow, on March 12 the Bowens received a note that Fannie Phillips was sick and dying. Leaving Lurana in Ogbomosho, T. J. traveled thirty miles that day and arrived at Ijaye the next day about noon. He reported, "Sister Phillips died on Friday the 14th. Bro. P. was well distressed and he is going home with me tomorrow if the Lord permit...for a change of scene."

Evidently, John Beaumont had joined the Bowens in Ogbomosho around the first of March. Seeing Phillip's wife die seemed to have made T. J. fearful for his own wife's safety. On March 18 he wrote to her from Ijaye, "But if you or Bro. Beaumont should get sick, you must send a runner with a letter without a moment's delay. Be sure to do so if either of you should be taken with ague or fever or dysentery, for these things require immediate attention."

Beaumont, a single layman, had come to the mission to serve primarily as a teacher and preparer of books. T. J. gave his opinion of him—"I fear that Bro. Beaumont is too nervous. It gives me great uneasiness—still he is sound in body and exceedingly quiet and prudent. He preaches well—nothing so much surprised me—and he loves solitude."

Beaumont got along well with T. J., but not at all with Phillips. Later, in a letter to Bowen, Poindexter quoted Beaumont, "As I have no person here of the same mind as me, it is my request to be permitted to operate by myself until Brother Bowen returns. If he does not return and I cannot be permitted to operate by myself, I beg you to have me recalled...instantly." When Poindexter sought T. J.'s insight about this, he replied that Beaumont "has a great aversion to Bro. Phillips which I labored in vain to heal...Bro. B. has no confidence in Bro. P. and I am now convinced that they will never work together in the same station." He called Phillips "chappy" because he had supposedly repeatedly insulted Beaumont on their voyage. Nevertheless, T. J. commented, "It appeared to me that Bro. Phillip's faults as stated by Bro. B. were not so great as to give incurable offence." Evidently, they did seem incurable to Beaumont, because later that year he did leave the mission suddenly. One of the FMB secretaries wrote, "It is true that the sudden flight of Brother Beaumont & his abandonment of the mission work on his own responsibility, has painfully affected many minds."

Before his return to his wife and Beaumont in Ogbomosho, T. J. had eight days to reconnect with Clarke and become acquainted with Phillips. There in Ijaye, the three missionaries convened a formal meeting of their mission on March 20 and adopted nine resolutions regarding the work of the mission for the FMB to consider. The first of those resolutions stated that missionaries should return home about the end of every fourth year to rest and recoup their health.

T. J. probably listed that resolution first because it was something he himself was seriously considering. The next day, March 21, he wrote to Taylor telling of his health struggles and saying, "If I can I want to stay here till next winter and get home (if the Board approve) in time for the May meeting 1857. But three weeks later a change for the worse in his wife's health hurried his plans. He wrote:

> When I last wrote I did not expect to leave for America till instructed by the Board...I am now packing up to leave immediately. My wife's health has been deranged for some time and it is now evident that she must have the benefit of a colder climate. No consideration could induce me to keep her here when both Bro. Beaumont and myself are convinced that delay might be fatal. I do not feel justified in trifling with her case as I have done with my own.

Years later, T. J. explained to Poindexter, "My own wife would have been a corpse in three months if I had not left as I did six months before I intended. She was already laboring under dropsy [edema], that infallible precursor of death, and it did not leave her full till 12 months after leaving Africa." T. J.'s own health was failing too. About this time he wrote, "I have always fallen back, sinking lower and lower with each relapse...I have never recovered from the attack of November 1853. At first my spells came every month or two; now I am sick by the month and well by the week."

As T. J. and Lurana Bowen left Ogbomosho on April 13, a crowd of people followed them some distance expressing wishes for safety on their journey. They needed safety. On that journey they faced a severe storm, a poisonous snake invading their camp, and swarms of mosquitoes before they reached Lagos on the coast on April 30 exhausted and sick. On May 11 they boarded a steamer to travel up the African coast. The canoe ride to the ship in the harbor proved dangerous. Twenty months earlier Clarke described those harbor canoe rides as "harrowing," commenting that "sharks as big as horses preyed on those who fell into the turbulent water." After steamer stops at Acra, Cape Coast Castle, and Monrovia, another experience with on-board fire occurred. Lurana journaled, "A very narrow escape from fire. My clothes caught on deck from the coals of a cigar." Landing at Freetown in Sierra Leone, the Bowens stayed for three weeks. Still, Yoruba continued to fill T. J.'s thoughts. He wrote, "In spite of my efforts to the contrary I have suffered so much anxiety about the work in Yoruba."

To his joy, T. J. found Yoruba people there in Sierra Leone. He reported, "So soon as the Yoruba and Egba people discovered that I had come from their country, they gathered around me like bees. Every one had something to say and something to ask, if it were only for the sake of hearing me speak their native tongue. I felt a great desire to remain and preach to them." T. J. did preach in the Baptist church on his last Sunday in Freetown. A week later they boarded a ship for New York, arriving there thirty days later on July 15, 1856. While there, he worked to arrange passage for the next group of missionaries headed to Central Africa and awaited instructions from Taylor about meeting with them before they embarked. The Bowens came to Richmond on August 5, and spent two days reporting, interviewing missionary candidates, and making recommendations on the Central African Mission. Then they headed for Lurana's family in Greensboro, Georgia. Arriving there on August 9, 1856, T. J. completed his second missionary journey to Africa. In spite of overwhelming obstacles, he and Lurana had accomplished the enormous task of establishing the first pioneer Baptist mission stations and schools in Central Africa.

"A Christian Missionary Explorer
is the Hero of the World."
—Headline in *The Daily National Intelligencer*

"So I answered them and said to them,
'The God of heaven will give us success;
therefore we His servants will arise and build."
—Nehemiah 2:20

## CHAPTER 9

# Capturing the
# Imagination of a Nation

P erhaps nothing captivates and inspires the public like
a person who demonstrates extraordinary courage
and attempts daring adventures. As he shared his exploits
in the mysterious and dangerous heart of Africa, no one in
mid-nineteenth century America captivated and inspired
its citizens more than T. J. Bowen. Although he was
quickly propelled to celebrity status, he single-mindedly
used that status to promote the cause of reaching central
Africa for Christ.

Of course, T. J.'s accomplishments were already celebrated by his denomination, the Southern Baptists. They had been reading many of his letters from Africa that had been published in their missionary journals and state papers. As a result, of the 30 missionaries sent out by the FMB, he was hailed as their greatest and most beloved. While he was still in Africa, after attending the Georgia Baptist Convention in 1854, Taylor wrote to him:

> Perhaps it will not be improper for me to say that God is blessing the influence you have exercised in this state, for good to his cause, and the extending of the empire of his Son in this dark & guilty world. The Yoruba mission is obtaining a deep hold upon the hearts of the people in Georgia...I may mention that you were frequently alluded to in the addresses and conversations of the meeting & our dear Sister Bowen too was mentioned again & again with affectionate tenderness. You both have a large place in the hearts of the disciples, and are often remembered in their prayers.

Associate FMB Corresponding Secretary A. M. Poindexter told him that "no missionary that the Board has ever sent out has taken so strong a hold upon the feelings of the denomination as you have done." The editor of the Georgia Baptist state paper, *The Christian Index,* exclaimed:

I must utter a commendation of our own Bowen of the Central African Mission. For devotedness, practical judgment, far reaching plans of usefulness, dauntless heroism, and strong faith in God, where shall we find one who surpasses him? No discerning man can be in his presence for any length of time, without feeling that God has raised him up for forming and executing noble plans.

The FMB's own magazine, *The Commission,* echoed such praise, "From his known character as a zealous missionary, and a bold and persevering explorer...who seems to have but one purpose in life...the advancement of his race...He is no visionary enthusiast. His representations of the wants and prospects of Africa are those of a man of strong practical sense." After speaking of T. J.'s appeal to Congress for the exploration of the Niger River, the article continued:

And should it be successful, he will necessarily take rank among the noblest of the world's benefactors. But Mr. Bowen's character does not rest on any doubtful contingency. His direct labors in the cause of religion and humanity, and his indirect advancement of human knowledge, have not only endeared him to his own denomination of Christians, but have given him a name which all his countrymen will delight to honor.

Southern Baptists did not hesitate to compare their Bowen to the greatest missionary heroes. *The Commission* compared him to the honored Adoniram Judson of Burma, calling him, "Brother Bowen, that Judson of Africa." Far more frequently, he was compared to the famous British missionary and African explorer, David Livingstone. Robinson's *History of the Georgia Baptist Association* stated:

> In 1856 the Association adopted the missionary to Africa, Rev. T. J. Bowen, paying his salary in full. On his visit home in 1857 Brother Bowen met with the Association. Rev. Scott Patterson, himself a returned missionary from Africa, and well acquainted with the work of the Bowens there, says, "I believe the work done by Bowen in Africa out-reaches for permanent good all the work done on the Dark Continent by David Livingstone."

T. J. Bowen and David Livingstone lived and served at the same time. Missiologist Cal Guy remarked, "If the gravemarkers...were placed side by side one would read: David Livingstone, 1813-1873; the other: Thomas J. Bowen, 1814-1875." Southern Baptists esteemed them both as heroes. As a result, it is not surprising that shortly after T. J. returned, Georgia Baptists honored him by forming a new regional group of churches in Southwest Georgia named in his honor—the Bowen Association.

When T. J. and Lurana arrived in Greensboro in early August 1856 they found it much like they remembered—a quiet, prosperous Southern town of about 1,000. It was the main city in Greene County whose free inhabitants' wealth was about twice that of the rest of Georgia. That wealth was evident in the large Greek Revival courthouse and similar college chapel at nearby Penfield. This affluence originated from the production of cotton which depended upon the exhausting toil of the nearly 8,000 slaves in the county. The Bowens moved in with her parents in their comfortable Greensboro home built in 1797. The neighborhood had a curious communication system. Lurana's son-in-law notes, "Long before the telephone was invented, neighbors used Conch shells to convey messages to each other. A code was worked out whereby each blast had a definite meaning."

Since restoring their broken health was key to their return to Africa, after a short visit with Lurana's family in Greensboro, they boarded a train headed toward Montvale, Tennessee. The mineral springs there were famous for their healing properties. Like many other Georgians escaping the summer heat, Lurana and T. J. would have recuperated at the newly-built Seven Gables Hotel and spa. They found a great interest in their work in Africa among the other guests. And after several weeks of rest and treatments, they began to feel better. Because their return trip was punctuated with stops to speak about their work in Africa at associational meetings, they arrived back in Greensboro on October 1.

Although his health continued to relapse in cycles, that fall T. J. spoke in various church and denominational settings, and was occupied with correspondence with the FMB and its missionaries in Yoruba. But he primarily gave himself to writing. His first book, *The Rise and Progress of the Baptists,* had been published while he was in route to Africa the first time. To this small volume which traced the history of Baptist beginnings, T. J. now added his major work, the 359-page *Central Africa. Adventures and Missionary Labors in Several Countries in the Interior of Africa, from 1849 to 1856.* He had actually prepared a partial manuscript of the work in 1853 before his second expedition. T. J. completed this early effort and by December 1856 had sent a manuscript to a Charleston publisher. *Central Africa* was published in February and sold for a dollar. The volume quickly became a best-seller and by August had been published in seven editions. In the book T. J. gives an account of his explorations and missionary efforts, along with detail about the geography, people, animals, and vegetation of Central Africa. He ended the work with his plan for the regeneration of Africa and a passionate appeal for missionaries.

Although T. J. believed that he had written "too rapidly for good composition," others considered his writing extraordinary. In an early review, Poindexter remarked:

It is written in that lucid, easy-gliding, and graphic style which marks all the writings of the author. The energy of a deep, quiet, but powerful enthusiasm nerves the whole volume. Without any parading of learning, the author displays a large acquaintance with languages and philology, familiarity with the leading authorities regarding Africa, and large powers of comprehension and analysis.

Others agreed. The *Savanah Georgian* stated, "It is rare, indeed, that we meet with a book more beautifully written than that before us." The *Daily National Intelligencer* commented, "This work is one of the most scientific ever written on an unknown country just explored, bearing, as it does, the marks everywhere of a thoroughly analytic mind, guided by years of personal observation and inquiry on the ground." *The Christian Chronicle* concluded, "It is probably the best book on Africa for the people of this country which has ever been published."

Although praise for *Central Africa* came from every quarter, Southern Baptists especially liked it. They saw it as a powerful tool to call out missionaries, especially to Central Africa. Indeed, T. J. filled the volume with statements like, "Now is the time to invade Africa with swarms of missionaries." *The Commission* observed, "Mr. Bowen has given us a most valuable book [which]...will, no doubt, hasten the regeneration of that land to which M. Bowen has devoted his life." *The Southern Baptist* pronounced,

"The great demand for this book seems to be a special indication of Providence. No book has ever appeared which will give such determination to the interests of missions... [I]t will doubtless decide many to look upon this field as their own personal duty."

T. J. also labored hard to complete his second major work during this period—his *Grammar and Dictionary of the Yoruba Language: with an Introductory Description of the Country and People of Yoruba*. The *Grammar* was a project he had been working on since beginning to study the language seven years earlier. The Smithsonian Institution agreed to publish it, but its printer wanted T. J. on site in Washington to review each form before it was printed—a process which took six months. Then he had to go to New York and supervise the printing of the dictionary portion of the book, a procedure which lasted off and on for another year! Long months into this arduous ordeal, T. J. confessed, "It seems a pity that I undertook this book for if I had rested for the last eight months instead of toiling night and day I might have had better health. But I was afraid I might die and leave it unfinished."

T. J.'s toil proved not in vain. For nearly a century it brought great benefit to the missionaries of Yoruba. In 1917 missionary S. G. Pinnock said that T. J.'s *Grammar and Dictionary* was "a work of such value that missionaries of all societies would like to have it republished." Writing in 1936, FMB missionary C. Sylvester Green stated, "A product of this period was the splendid and now-famous 'Grammar and Vocabulary of the Yoruban

Language.' This is still regarded as the outstanding work."
As late as 1940 T. B. Rice noted, "Mr. Bowen's grammar
and word book are still being used in the schools of that
country [Nigeria], and were used to translate the Bible
into the Yoruba language."

Besides these two major works, during these years T. J.
did various kinds of other writing. He revised a British
book entitled *Meroke; or Missionary Life in Africa*. In
addition, he contributed numerous items to Christian
publications. He composed lengthy theological articles
on the nature of the church. He provided thoughtful book
reviews. He also wrote a number of other articles and letters to editors, especially on the topic of missions.

History has proved that T. J.'s written thoughts on
the organization of missionary funding during these years
were prescient. In June 1859 he proposed to Taylor that
the FMB institute an annual or semi-annual offering for
foreign missions. He wrote, "There is one measure which I
should wish to recommend everywhere, and that is a uniform efficient plan of taking up an annual, or semi-annual
collection in every church, without waiting for future visits
from an agency. I have had this plan in mind for years."
Nearly thirty years later Southern Baptists would adopt
a similar plan which became known as the Lottie Moon
Offering for Foreign Missions. Further, T. J. encouraged
Southern Baptists to set aside an annual week of prayer
for foreign missions. This pattern was also adopted in
1888 along with the Lottie Moon Offering. In addition,
T. J. wrote to advocate a uniform, systematic budget
plan for giving to missions. He encouraged churches to

designate a certain percentage of their budgets to missions, then to send that money to the convention or association to be distributed to various mission causes. He touted the cost advantages of the plan and predicted it would generate far more revenue. In fact, T. J. led his Greensboro church to set aside a certain percentage of its budget for missions. Sixty-six years later the Southern Baptist Convention would adopt such a plan called, "The Cooperative Program."

The popularity of *Central Africa,* propelled T. J. Bowen to the height of celebrity. His daring adventures led more than one newspaper to proclaim him a hero. One of them, the foremost newspaper in Washington, D. C., *The Daily National Intelligencer,* declared T. J.'s exploits greater than those of Alexander the Great:

> Mr. Bowen in his youth was a bold and hardly soldier; but in his manhood and his Christian devotion the qualities of a hero born in him have found a field which no soldier ever has a chance to enter. To penetrate alone into an extremely unknown and hostile region; to go straight through the gates of a city peopled by hundreds of thousands who looked on him with the same wonder as they would an angel or a fiend dropping down from the clouds; to say before the court and king of a great nation,

in whose presence he stood arraigned as Bowen did, 'The God of Heaven is my King; I am a soldier, and this book (referring to the Bible) is my sword, and thus to conquer his way from city to city, is an achievement such as an Alexander never would have dreamed of undertaking. It is comparative cowardice to be a conqueror shielded on all sides by an invincible army.

Requests for this acclaimed hero to speak poured in, especially from church and denominational groups. On a trip to regain his health in June 1858, he told Taylor, "I am preaching frequently." Sometimes churches would schedule special weeknight meetings for T. J. to "lecture." For example, the Alabama *Southwest Baptist* noted, "The Rev. T. J. Bowen, author of the interesting work on 'Central Africa,' will lecture at the Baptist Church on that country, on Thursday evening the 23rd inst., at early candle lighting." And T. J. found enthusiastic reception in churches beyond his own denomination. He commented, "Two or three weeks ago I addressed a Methodist meeting of perhaps 250 persons. They expected to take up a collection [for the Central African Mission] of two or three hundred dollars, but it ran up to about $1,250.00. They were so much pleased that they offered me a liberal donation and when I refused to accept it, they sent it after me."

T. J. also spoke frequently at large Baptist gatherings at associational meetings or state conventions. Shortly after his return to the States, he told Taylor that he had spoken at the Fleet River Association and then said, "I plan to attend the Georgia Association, the Bethel, the Florida Convention, and visit Charleston." Since the Georgia Association had supported him, he repeatedly preached the annual missionary sermon at their meetings. Hearing his exploits made Georgia Baptists want to honor their missionary hero. Thus, Mercer University conferred upon him an honorary master's degree in 1858.

The admiring public demanded that T. J. also speak in nontraditional settings. He lectured at universities. Speaking of potential new missionaries, he said to Taylor, "From the manner in which the students at the University listened, I should not be surprised if we hear from that quarter also." He even received the rare honor of speaking at the Capitol building in Washington, D. C. *The African Repository* reported, "His recent visit to Washington afforded him the opportunity, on the Sabbath, first in hall of the House of Representatives, and subsequently in several of the city churches, of presenting before the public... the results of his careful inquiries and observations [in]... Central Africa." T. J. also entertained many requests to speak in public settings. For example, twenty-six leading citizens of Philadelphia formally wrote to request that he present lectures in their city. Among other cities, T. J. gave a highly-publicized and well-attended series of lectures in a public hall in New York. Evidently, he had an engaging lecture style. One reviewer remarked:

> You attend some lectures, and what do you get
> but staleness, vociferation, and gesticulation...

> Not so with Mr. Bowen; he rivets your attention
> to the facts he develops, to the positions taken,
> and to the arguments to sustain them. He gains
> upon you as he advances in earnest, candid,
> clear, simple manner, seldom failing to make
> a decided impression in favor of his cause.

During his visit to the nation's capitol in February 1857, his just-released *Central Africa* stirred considerable interest in the Congress. T. J. met with the Chairman of the House of Representatives Committee on Commerce and was invited to testify before the committee. There he argued persuasively that the U. S. government should appropriate money for an expedition to explore the Niger River with a view to future commercial development in Central Africa. This and other meetings led to the Senate passing a bill for "the appropriation of 25,000 dollars, and the appointment of some competent officer of our navy, for the exploration of the Niger." But in the mind of Congress, T. J. Bowen himself should be the leader of the exciting endeavor. The FMB magazine, *The Commission* stated, "We sympathize with the sentiment which has been expressed privately to us, from high sources in Washington, that Mr. Bowen should accompany the expedition, as the master spirit, and be appointed a commissioner to negotiate treaties with the chiefs and nations of Central Africa." However, the Senate's bill failed to pass the House of Representatives and the pro-posed expedition never happened. Nevertheless, T. J.'s heroic courage and persuasive writing and speaking had captured his nation's imagination of what could be done for Central Africa.

"The spiritual condition of a person's soul
is infinitely more important than any
political transaction on the face of the earth."
—John Piper

"Jesus answered, 'My kingdom is not of this world.
If My kingdom were of this world, then My servants
would be fighting so that I would not be handed over to
the Jews; but as it is, My kingdom is not of this realm.'"
—John 19:36

## CHAPTER 10
# Mixing Politics and Ministry

When those who are called to proclaim the perfect gospel of Jesus adulterate their ministry with a necessarily imperfect political message, it inevitably brings harm to the kingdom of God. Like many others in his day, T. J. Bowen fell into the same snare. Speaking before the Congressional Committee, he testified that he believed that Africa could best be evangelized by being colonized. He had found affinity with an organization which held the same belief—the American Colonization

Society (ACS). Established in Washington, D. C., in 1816, the ACS proposed that a colony be established in Africa where free African-Americans could reside. Society members and supporters included many prestigious politicians and educators, including Henry Clay, Daniel Webster, Francis Scott Key, General Andrew Jackson, and U. S. President James Monroe.

However, the ACS had not just a political, but also a Christian foundation. Since the British Chapman sect had spent vast sums to establish the colony of Sierra Leone between 1791 and 1807, many evangelicals were keenly interested in African colonization for the purpose of bringing the gospel to that continent. In fact, at the organizational meeting of the ACS, Elias B. Caldwell said, "But Mr. Chairman, I have a greater and nobler object in view in desiring them to be placed in Africa. It is the belief that through them civilization and the Christian religion would be introduced to that benighted quarter of the world." It comes as no surprise then, that Samuel Mills, Jr., perhaps the greatest foreign missions activist of the day, was not only instrumental in founding the ACS, but went as their agent to West Africa in 1817.

With such Christian and missionary sentiments, in 1823 the ACS began a successful campaign to enlist the support of the churches of many denominations. The year before, the society had hired Rev. R. R. Gurley to be its agent and for the next eighteen years he was the dominant figure in the organization, giving its work a strong Christian emphasis. Gurley spoke in many churches and denominational conventions. He met T. J. Bowen at the

Baptist General Convention of Georgia in 1853. Since T. J. was fresh from observing colonial life in Liberia, Gurley found him a sympathetic supporter of colonization. From that point forward, T. J. turned into an ardent promoter of the ACS cause. He became one of the main contributors to the Society's journal, *The African Repository,* which published at least thirty-six articles by him or about his work.

Besides writing, T. J. preached the colonization message passionately in churches up and down the Eastern seaboard. He often spoke to African-American audiences. A New York newspaper reported about one such instance in Alexandria, Virginia:

> Rev. T. J. Bowen, who had been an adventurous missionary in Africa...addressed at length a large assembly of colored people, bond and free...He spoke of Liberia...as a radiant point of light on the borders of the long-benighted continent. Upon the system of the American Colonization Society, upon the whole colonial enterprise...he had a pronounced a decided opinion, and he considers immense blessings wrapped up in this germ of civilized empire.

Beyond ACS, T. J. also connected with the African Civilization Society which had similar colonization goals. Interestingly, T. J.'s FMB not only approved his connection with the ACS, they strongly encouraged it. Taylor repeatedly counseled T. J. to make efforts to connect with the ACS and Poindexter wrote publicly, "The United States must colonize, and Christianize Africa."

T. J. Bowen tended to think big. The colony he hoped to plant in the interior of Africa was only the start of a continent-wide strategy of evangelization and colonization. Speaking of "the friends of colonization," he wrote, "Their single object and motive is to plant a great negro nation in Africa, which shall be a means of diffusing civilization and Christianity throughout the whole continent: thus making an immense addition to the moral power and commercial wealth of the world...[T]his gigantic scheme is yet in the feeblest days of infancy." He frequently spoke in glowing terms of African colonization as "creating nations and founding empires."

To be clear, however, T. J. advocated a distinctly Christian colony. He spoke specifically of "Christian colonization," the creation of a "Christian colony," and "the commencement of a glorious Christian Republic." Did he mean that the newly-created state would by law support the work of the church? Yes. His proposed colony was modeled on the Liberia that he so often praised. He specifically liked Liberia's government. In *Central Africa* he wrote, "Liberia is full of well-attended churches and schools. She has a good government, well administered under officers elected by the people from among themselves."

The ACS did indeed establish Liberia as "a Christian state, which from the nature of its institutions, the development of its principles and resources, and the discipline of its circumstances must strengthen and elevate the moral character of its citizens; by example and endeavors plant and propagate civilization and Christian doctrine in Africa." So wrote ACS agent R. R. Gurley after he had been to Liberia in 1834. Speaking of what he saw there, Gurley observed, "Nowhere is the Sabbath more regarded, or divine worship attended with more apparent devotion."

Yet it was not Christian devotion alone that made Liberian church attendance great. Liberian law mandated that those who did not strictly observe the Sabbath could be stockaded or whipped. Gurley made no secret of the fact that he and the ACS were out to "give existence and form to a state—to enact and administer laws—to send out among uncivilized and untamed men the voice of instruction and authority...to mark and seal the institutions of the newly-organized society with indelible characters of wisdom." In other words, the ACS, of which T. J. was a chief promoter, aimed specifically at creating colonial governments whose constitutions and laws supported the work of the church—a combination of church and state.

Because he had explored and lived in Yoruba, no one saw a proposed colony there in his mind more clearly than T. J. Bowen. He envisioned where the first towns would be established, that it would be an American trading post so that it would be protected by the U. S. flag, the terms by which both American and African negroes would have rights and respect, even the name for the colony, "Nigritia." Some suggested that T. J. play a significant role in the founding of the colony and become a Consul of the United States there. However, in a letter to Taylor, he confessed, "I can not think of trying the coast for the sake of planting a colony and being U. S. Consul both put together. I should be glad to accept these proposed schemes if I could, but I am getting too old and my constitution is too much impaired." Nevertheless, T. J. put forth significant effort to secure a charter for the colony.

But his dream of an African colony never materialized for three primary reasons. First, when the U. S. Congress failed to appropriate the funding for the exploration of the Niger, there was no sure means of transporting commerce, making a viable colony impossible. Second, no one more qualified than T. J. could be found to lead the colony, and his broken health continued to deteriorate. Third, the U. S. Civil War and resulting emancipation of slaves removed one of the driving forces behind African colonization. T. J. had written earlier about the possibility of "the crushing of the slave-holding power which, of course, would put a stop to emigration."

Absolutely convinced that civilization must accompany the gospel to Africa, T. J. Bowen did everything in his power to make it happen. Why? He believed that Christianity would not be established firmly enough to reproduce itself without a measure of civilization. For by "civilization," he meant not the replacement of the beneficial native culture, but "the power to perpetuate the gospel among them." He explained:

> No Christian will deny that men may be converted without civilization...But our designs and hopes to Africa are not simply to bring as many individuals as possible to the

knowledge of Christ. We desire to establish the gospel in the hearts and minds and social life of the people, so that truth and righteousness may remain and flourish among them without the instrument of foreign missionaries. This cannot be done without civilization. To establish the gospel among any people, they must have Bibles, and therefore must have the art to make them or the money to buy them. They must read the Bible, and this implies instruction. They must have competent native pastors, and this implies several things which can not exist without a degree of civilization.

T. J. could not envision such civilization without commerce, which he called a "promoter" of civilization and thus an "auxiliary" of the gospel. In a published letter to the corresponding secretary of the African Civilization Society he stated, "I have long believed that...civilization, including the powerful stimulus of commerce, must... accompany the evangelization of the heathen countries. A settlement in Yoruba...for the joint purposes of preaching, planting, and trading...would be an embryo, yet real nationality, composed of independent, self-sustaining men." T. J.'s exuberance for commerce spilled over into statements like, "No one denies that schools and the industrial arts would be useful in Africa, and helpful to the establishment of the gospel. But the greatest of all these secondary means for the extension of the gospel is commerce with Christian countries."

Seeing Muslims at work in Africa helped convince T. J. about the effectiveness of commerce to assist in the spread of civilization and the gospel. He complained, "All the interior traders being Mohammedans, are indirectly missionaries of the false prophet, and their influence is beginning to be felt even among the rude tribes of Guinea." If Muslim traders could spread their doctrine, how much more could Christian traders spread the true gospel? Where their traders went, the Muslims also planted schools which proselytized the people. In promoting a plan for his own proposed school, T. J. remarked, "Mohammedans extend themselves in a great measure by their schools. Thus they have spread over half the continent." Along that line, T. J. felt keenly that commerce would do more than anything else to stimulate education in Africa, thus in turn stimulating the spread of the gospel. He commented:

> The extension of civilized commerce to Central Africa, attended, as it would be, by the pure gospel, could not fail to have a powerful effect on the minds and institutions of the people. The various branches of business called into existence by commerce would require education, and the people would be anxious to obtain it...As a consequence, missionaries would no longer preach to illiterate barbarians who will never be able to perpetuate the gospel among them, but to men who can learn their duty by reading the Bible, and, of course, would

be able to sustain their churches and pastors from generation to generation, like other Bible-reading people.

T. J. did not stand alone in this view. In 1858 *The African Repository* noted, "We observe that his [T. J.'s] views of the importance of commerce and civilization as mighty auxiliaries to Christianity, agree with those of the great traveler and missionary, Dr. Livingstone."

Always a man of action, T. J. took practical, sacrificial steps to implement this vision for Central Africa. He encouraged the building of "a railroad from Lagos to Raba." To aid both commerce and the travels of missionaries, he proposed the building of a fifty-mile road from Abeokuta to Ijaye which could serve wagons and carts. Near the end of *Central Africa,* he appealed for funds for this road, writing, "The missionaries have commenced raising a road fund, by contributing from fifty to one hundred heads of cowries each, a head of cowries being nominally one dollar. All the profits of the present volume, which may accrue to the author, have been turned over to the same fund."

Could gospel-promoting civilization be engendered by commerce and education alone, without colonization? T. J. thought not. He argued:

> Conquest, colonization, or some other stringent means must be employed to raise the people of Guinea to humanity, before the gospel can elevate them to Christianity...Some persons

> believe that schools are the means to prepare
> people for Christianity; but schools cannot
> create the wants to drive men to civilization…
> Desires to stimulate, labor to supply, and the
> strong arm of the law to direct and restrain,
> are indispensable to the improvement of any
> barbarous nation.

T. J. had found Africa to be full of tribal wars. These wars had gone on for many generations and he saw nothing that could stop them in the future except the imposition of colonial rule. In his mind, colonization could bring the necessary stabilization to establish civilization, which, in turn, could promote self-sustaining evangelization. He saw that progression happen in Liberia where several hundred native Africans had become citizens of that republic. He remarked, "Some of these I am personally acquainted with, and their present condition as civilized men and Christians is one of the most pleasing things I have ever seen in Africa. What glorious results may be reasonably expected if Christian nations and Christian churches will do their whole duty to the African colonies!"

Other missionaries would join T. J. in the belief that the force provided by colonization was a necessary step. When T. J.'s colonization attempt failed, the early missionaries in the interior of Africa were left to struggle against tribal wars for many years. Ayandele commented, "It was not long before all the pioneer missionaries in 'Central Africa' discovered that the Yoruba would not willingly accept the gospel, nor surrender their customs and institutions tamely." As late as 1892 Southern Baptist missionary C. C. Newton complained to the FMB secretary Tupper, "Tribal wars that lead to kidnapping and obstruction of roads are constantly recurring hindrances to our work here. It has been plain to me that nothing permanent can be accomplished by us in our interior missions until there is a change in the political relations and government of the tribes." As a result, Newton and other missionaries supported British military efforts to bring peace. That backfired on them by bringing scorn on the missionaries from the population. Nevertheless, Newton would write, "A sword of steel often goes before the sword of the Spirit." Nigerian historian Ayandele defends T. J. and other missionaries who thought this way saying, "They believed that they were working in the intrinsic interest of the Yoruba. If intra-tribal warfare could be terminated, human sacrifice suppressed, technological improvement carried out, and the Christian faith introduced into the community, then the society would be transformed in a wholly beneficial way."

T. J.'s appreciation for education was another influencing factor in his push for colonization. His porters lugged about 150 heavy books with him into the interior of Africa. In a letter to the FMB in 1859 he mentions some of them—erudite titles of history, culture, geography, geology, mineralogy, zoology, and more. From such reading T. J. became convinced of the importance of developing civilization among "barbarous" peoples if Christianity was to last among them. He remarked, "[H]e that expects to evangelize the country without civilization will find like Xavier in the East, and the Jesuits in South America, and the priests in the Congo, that his labors will end in disappointment."

Beyond the influence of education in his own life, T. J. had seen first-hand how it could civilize the lives of others. During his time of teaching school in the American South, he developed a keen appreciation for the transforming power of education, especially as it helped people read the Bible for themselves. He saw even more dramatic transformation in Africa. Speaking of the English missionary schools in Sierra Leone, he noted that some of their students who had made "progress in science and literature, including Latin, Greek, and Hebrew" were "willing and even anxious to return to their distant homes, and diffuse the light of Christianity and civilization among their countrymen." He also admired the civilizing results of education in the English missionary schools of Abeokuta, remarking, "Mr. Crowther and Mr. King, both natives, have translated several books of the Old and New Testaments, which are handsomely printed and bound in separate books. Hundreds of people have learned to read in their native tongue, and the whole tribe has advanced considerably towards civilization." With his own planned schools in his proposed colony, T. J. intended to help build Yoruba civilization one student at a time.

T. J.'s experience with more civilized tribes in Yoruba also motivated his colonization efforts. Intelligent, educated Muslim Fellatahs traveled many miles from Ilorin expressly to hear the gospel from him. Writing from the English Channel in November 1853, he remembered, "At

Abeokuta six Mohammedans from Ilorin, learning that I had arrived, sought me out saying that they had heard of me in the interior and had called on me to inquire about my doctrine." Most of these Muslim inquirers were in their thirties and could read and write Arabic. Moreover, when T. J. visited Ilorin he commented, "The number of people who can read and write surprise me. I see more plainly than ever that Central Africa should be our field of labor." He exulted, "They claim kin with me, and seem to be pleased that I propose to write books in their language. We must write in Arabic characters, for then our books will be intelligible to millions of people from Senegal to Lake Tsad." These experiences led T. J. to claim:

> The influence of a Christian colony would be far greater in Yoruba and other parts of Sudan that it has been in Liberia, because the Sudanese generally are almost prepared to receive civilization and the gospel. They are just that state of society, in which they cannot naturally recede, or remain long stationary. All the regions of the interior are almost sure to come under the influence of Mohammedanism or of Christianity, within a comparatively short period...Under these circumstances, I am rejoiced to see that several active friends of colonization are looking toward Yoruba.

T. J.'s plan to stop polygamy also urged on his colonization plans. In his day, polygamy ruled as the social norm in Africa. He found that upon conversion, Africans would give up their idols, but were naturally reluctant to give up their extra wives. He knew that changing this cultural phenomenon would take years, but he saw four reasons why the cultivation of commerce as a part of civilization and colonization was integral to making the change. First, the extension of commerce "would erect new standards of respectability, and thus remove one of the props of polygamy." Second, it would provide money for the remodeling of African homes. Those homes were "a gloomy square of twenty, thirty, or fifty rooms, one or two of which is assigned to each of a man's wives." Fewer wives would mean those extra rooms would be taken over by rats and scorpions. the necessary extensive remodeling of those homes demanded money which could only be obtained from commerce. Third, increased money from commerce would help poor bachelors to be able to take a wife. Finally, the increased money and respectability by commerce would raise the feeling of refinement and respect within the Yoruba family, thus aiding the demise of polygamy. Such astute observations of Yoruba culture repeatedly reinforced T. J.'s political plans for Yoruba.

Of course, T. J.'s colonization was flawed by its underlying Western perspective. Like most human beings, he was a man of his time who tended to see things the way the people and culture of his day did. In T. J.'s day, the culture of the West as it pertained to the rest of the world was colonialism—claiming a people's territory, exporting their natural resources, and imposing on them a "better," Western way of life. Most Western missionaries, including

T. J., had difficulty seeing that this violated the rights, resources, and cultures of native peoples. Thus, as missiologist David Bosch said, "Whether they liked it or not, the missionaries became pioneers of Western imperialistic expansion."

T. J. wholeheartedly accepted the paradigm of what became known as the three "C's" of colonialism: Christianity, commerce, and civilization. But in his glorification of commerce, he failed to mention the very real possibility that through taking advantage of native peoples, crooked Western businessmen might turn them away from Christianity rather than toward it. In his exaltation of colonialism, he never spoke of the loss of freedom for the people of that territory. However, to his credit, Ayandele mentioned, "[T]here is no evidence that, unlike the Anglican and Methodist missionaries, he ever directly asked British agents to subjugate any people." In addition, T. J. carried a respect and sensitivity for the native culture like few missionaries of his day.

Another great flaw of T. J.'s colonization plans was its underlying assumption of force. As a nineteenth-century colonial advocate, he saw nothing wrong with a judicious use of force to help establish his proposed Central African colony. Such colonization did force doors open for the gospel initially. As Andrew F. Walls wrote, "The era of imperial expansion is, of course, the era of missionary revival. Hundreds of new missionaries from the West pushed forward, seeking—in the eloquent title of a popular series of books at the time—the Conquests of the Cross." Although presumably the Central African colony would purchase its property like the founders of Liberia did, T. J. envisioned that it would be established and protected by American military power.

However, this kind of imperialistic colonialism associated with Christianity erected enormous persistent barriers to the gospel. At the Chicago Conference on World Religions in 1893, Swami Vivekenanda, who was not one of the program speakers, stood up, went to the podium, and said:

> We who came from the East have sat here on the platform day after day and have been told in a patronizing way that we ought to accept Christianity because Christian nations are the most prosperous. We look about us and see England, the most prosperous Christian nation in the world, with her foot on the neck of 250 million Asiatics. We look back in our history, and we see that the prosperity began with the invasion of Mexico. Christianity wins its prosperity by cutting the throats of its fellow men. At such a price, the Hindu will not have prosperity. I have sat here today, and I've heard the intolerance. Blood and sword are not for the Hindu whose religion is based on the laws of love.

The ill effects of colonialism lingered long. The Crusades were an earlier, similar demonstration of force by Christians and are still resented by Muslims today. Fuller Seminary professor J. Dudley Woodberry observed, "[F]or many Muslims, colonialism represented a crusading spirit that also manifested itself as support for Zionism and Israel." As a result, of his speaking in the Middle East in 2000, one evangelist commented, "Half of the challenge is removing the prejudice of Christianity's baggage across the centuries." Ajith Fernando gave a similar witness:

> In Sri Lanka, opponents of evangelism are saying that the current evangelistic emphasis of Christians is a "new colonialism" or "new imperialism" in which the West is trying to dominate and control people through religion. They say that earlier the Western imperialists came with the Bible in one hand and a gun in the other. Now they come with the Bible in one hand and material aid in the other.

T. J. Bowen would be horrified to see that the seeds of colonialism he helped plant would grow up to erect formidable barriers to the gospel.

"I have a dream that my four little children will one day live in a nation where they will not be judged by the color of their skin, but by the content of their character."
—Martin Luther King, Jr.

"But the Lord said to Samuel, 'Do not look at his appearance or at the height of his stature...for God sees not as man sees, for man looks at the outward appearance, but the Lord looks at the heart.'"
—1 Samuel 16:7

## CHAPTER 11
# Struggling with Racial Bias

Sometimes even the best people can have the worst blindspots in their vision of their world and their own heart. T. J. Bowen stumbled at times because of his blindness to his racial bias. At first that seems hard to believe. In the early years of his ministry in the American South he preached and ministered often to enslaved African-Americans. He developed an all-consuming passion to reach Africans for Christ. He raised money to buy a black man's freedom so he could accompany him to Africa as a fellow missionary. There he willingly suffered incredible hardships and frequently risked his life to bring the message of Christ to its dark-skinned inhabitants. He wanted to spend the rest of his life among them because he loved them and wanted to help them.

More than that, even though he was raised in a culture where enslaving Africans was the norm, T. J. hated the slave trade and crusaded against it. In fact, one of his motivations for colonization was to stop the slave trade. He had read about its evils before leaving America, but was shocked by what he saw in Africa. Tribes went to war for the sole purpose of capturing and selling members of other tribes. In March 1855 he bemoaned about the king of Ijaye, "Areh and all the strength of the town have been gone for some days to the west of Yoruba to kill and capture their countrymen...If the few misguided advocates of the slave trade who still lurk in Christian countries could reside one week in Africa in time of war, it would open their eyes."

Speaking of the area near Abeokuta, T. J. lamented, "Fifty years ago this small territory could boast of nearly three hundred towns, some of which were considerably prosperous; but now the village of Oko-Obba, in the southwest of the kingdom is the only one remaining; all the others have been utterly destroyed by war." He continued, "It is not improbable that these wars destroyed some two hundred thousand people. Multitudes were captured and sold to the slavers." Later, when a proposal to renew the slave trade was circulated in the American

South, T. J. wrote a fierce letter opposing it to the *Augusta Constitution:*

> The opening of the French traffic in apprentices immediately produced the slave-catching wars, which had almost ceased in every part of Western Africa. If the Southern States should adopt the French policy, this evil would, of course, be augmented. Having resided and traveled in different countries of Western Africa for six years, I can testify, what no one can deny, that the battles and sieges which supply Europeans with slaves, or apprentices, <u>destroy from two to four persons</u> for every laborer who reaches the plantations of America.

In the same letter, T. J. championed his own solution to the slave trade—colonization. He argued, "The true policy of the civilized world is to develop the vast resources of the great continent by commerce and civilization, to cover its plains with tropical plantations and populous towns, and to make its numerous rivers so many highways of an active and valuable commerce." He even specified the main crop for those African plantations, "The little palm nut is one of the greatest foes to the slave trade."

As well-meaning as T. J.'s colonial vision was, it was tainted with the stench of racism. Yes, his passion to evangelize Africans primarily motivated him to preach colonization, but the fact that this involved a fundamental philosophy of racial separation and false classification of the black race as inferior remains. American blacks recognized this prejudice immediately in the ACS's colonization strategy. On the one hand, they heard some Christian leaders like T. J. promoting a "missionary colony," while on the other, they heard other ACS leaders talking about seeing "all the free colored people transferred to their own country" with the result that "we should be cleared of them." Albert G. Oliver concluded, "The impetus for the formation of the American Colonization Society had its roots in a racist and historical attitude that blacks and whites could not and should not function together in the same society and, therefore, government or individual organizations, should actively assist in the colonization of free blacks and those who would become free."

Sadly, T. J. himself demonstrated racist beliefs. Beyond the goal of evangelization in Africa, he believed that the emigration of American blacks to Africa would be "the best and only solution to the race problem in the United States." In a letter to the *New York Tribune,* he wrote, "I suppose that the present inferior races would be for ages dependent on the European race if they were today elevated to the highest point of civilization of which they are constitutionally capable." In *Central Africa* he made clear which races he thought were inferior, "Let it be granted that the dark races are constitutionally inferior to the white." T. J. also believed in the "Hamitic Hypothesis—the theory that any evidence of advancement in Africa was to be attributed to outside influences." Thus in his travels he claimed to observe that the more European blood an African tribe seemed to have, the more handsome and intelligent they were. Of those without any supposedly European blood, he remarked:

> The true or typical negro, as everyone knows is distinguished by his low organism. His jaws are progmathous or monkey-shaped...His intellect, and especially his reasoning facilities are weak, his moral perceptions low, and his animal feelings strong. He appears to be a stranger to modesty...I doubt whether any negro of this class has ever felt disgust or ever will. They are incapable of refined feelings.

In accordance with these outrageous views, T. J. saw colonization as the natural duty of the white man to the black. In 1859 a reporter attended his lecture in Macon, Georgia, entitled, "Ethnology of the Negro Races." He noted, "Mr. Bowen concluded with some remarks on the social position of the Negro races—spoke of their degradation, and the duty of those who were more highly gifted to take them under protection, and if necessary, rule them for their good and for the glory of God."

However, such strikingly-biased thinking permeated much of European and American culture in T. J.'s day. It even became accepted science. For example, while T. J. was in Africa, several respected scientists published a thick volume titled *Types of Mankind*. The book contained horrifying sketches of various African tribal members compared to sketches of either chimpanzees or orangutans. This volume was the culmination of a "scientific racism" movement that dominated major literary quarterlies and erudite publications.

Although T. J.'s thinking was infected with racism, he vigorously denied the more extreme racist views common in his day. Ayandele explained, "He opposed the suggestion that Negroes matured earlier than Europeans—an idea fostered by the Anthropological Institute of London to show that there was a relation between Negroes and animals. He recognized Africans as a part of the human species, with skills, mental capabilities, and a culture on a level comparable to other human societies."

T. J. also spoke strongly against the common racist belief that black Africans could not be truly civilized. Early in his ministry in Africa he wrote to the *New York Tribune,* "At the present time I think it would be premature to decide that any race of man is doomed to perpetual barbarism." He stood convinced that the barbarism of Africa was not due to the inferior race of its inhabitants, but the isolation of "physical geography." In *Central Africa* he made this penetrating statement, "But we are met by the objection that the Africans are mentally and morally incapable of civilization. I have sometimes expressed the opinion that while opponents are perplexing this question by vain arguments, there are other men who will solve this problem by doing the work." T. J. continued his argument, "Let it be granted...1) That man is everywhere capable of improvement. The most enlightened races were once barbarians...2) The limit of man's improvability has never been ascertained...there might be

negro nations fully as much civilized as we are at present."
In the same letter to the *New York Tribune* above, T. J.
concluded, "For my own part, I respect them far more
than I did, and I am convinced that they are capable of
being Christianized and civilized. In this belief I consecrate my life, strength, and talents, and all that I have and
am to their instruction."

T. J. so esteemed blacks that he became convinced
they would make the best missionaries for Africa. Writing
to Taylor from Ogbomosho in April 1856, T. J. enthused,
"All the rest of my time [in America] I should like to spend
in Baltimore instructing a class of colored men in the Bible,
the Yoruba language, and the various details of the missionary work that they may return with me to this country.
It is my settled conviction that such men are nearly or
quite indispensable." After his return from Africa, T. J.'s
letters are filled with such plans for such a missionary
training school. For example, he told Taylor in 1858, "If
the Board should make a constant and well directed effort
to train Black men for the work, I have scarcely a doubt
that they might have twenty or even fifty such laborers in
the field in the course of ten or twelve years." T. J. also
wrote extensively about developing schools for future
leaders in Yoruba.

Beyond his opposition to the slave trade, was T. J.
opposed to the entrenched institution of slavery itself?
First, it is important to realize that slavery was cultur-
ally accepted nearly everywhere he went. In Georgia, the
state of his birth, slavery had been common for centuries. Before the arrival of Europeans, Native Americans

enslaved members of other tribes or even their own tribe. This practice continued in T. J.'s day. Early white colonists in Georgia bought and traded captured Native Americans as slaves. When the penal colony of Georgia was established in 1732 by social reformer James Oglethorpe, he banned slavery of Africans, but not Native Americans. In 1751, the English government opened Georgia to African slavery again. During this period, some Native Americans bought African slaves and used them to work their fields.

But T. J. also found slavery woven into the fabric of African culture. Many victims of the slave wars were exported to the coast where they were sold to slave traders, but thousands were kept by Yoruban kings and chiefs to be used locally. When T. J. and Lurana moved to Ijaye in 1853, King Kumi there had "thousands of slaves who worked his farms, served administrative functions, fought in his army, and bore his children." When the king loaned the Bowens some of those slaves to help clear the land he had given them, they encouraged them to redeem themselves with the money they paid them. But they shortly felt uncomfortable using Kumi's slaves and began to hire free day laborers instead.

Further, T. J. and Lurana were members of a denomination that in large measure was born to support the practice of slavery (although it has since repeatedly and vigorously renounced racism in all forms). They were sent to Africa by the mission agency of that denomination. They were members of a church that had more slave members than free. Lurana was raised in a home where her parents owned slaves who worked their fields and served their meals. All around them, nearly everywhere the Bowens went, they breathed the cultural atmosphere of slavery. Yet there is no evidence that they themselves ever personally owned slaves. Instead, as in the case of T. J.'s first missionary associate, Robert Hill, and Kumi's slaves, they made efforts to help slaves gain their freedom.

Beyond that, there is evidence that people of African background sensed love and acceptance from the Bowens and reciprocated that love. African-American congregations and audiences frequently requested T. J. to come and speak. After observing one of his lectures at the invitation of a black audience in New York, a reporter for the *Daily National Intelligencer* wrote, "His long and intimate knowledge of the people, his indomitable energy, together with his sincere and earnest love for that race which has won for him the love alike of the free-black in New York and the slave of Georgia...and of the refined Yoruba on the African coast, give promise that a great work is before him." In May 1851 an African-American congregation in Milledgeville, Georgia, sent an offering for T. J.'s work in Africa to the Georgia Baptist Convention, calling him, "our beloved brother Bowen."

Did Lurana Bowen display overtly racist thinking like her husband? For a refined white woman raised in the antebellum South, she demonstrated remarkable unreserved acceptance and appreciation for black men and women. Yes, growing up she was attended by her father's household slaves, but she demonstrated great affection for them. In fact, in 1856 she wrote them from Ijaye, beginning, "I often think of you all, and pray for you." In the letter, she vividly describes the pagan worship around her and passionately encourages them to take advantage of the gospel preaching they have in America and to give their lives to Christ. She says, "You don't know how much it would grieve me to hear of one of you dying in your sins and going to hell." She names some of them specifically and encourages them to remain strong in their faith, ending her letter endearingly, "With much affection I bid you, for a time, farewell."

Throughout her life, Lurana seemed to sacrificially love the people of all races around her. In Africa, when she had to leave Ijaye, it pained her to leave "many and kind dear friends." Those Ijayens sensed her love. Three years after she left, a missionary serving there commented to the FMB about Lurana, "And nothing can give the converts more delight than to talk to them of her." Years later, when she was living as a widow in Greensboro, she saw a vicious dog attacking a black woman, and in trying to save her fell and broke her hip. As a result, her son-in-law said, "Mrs. Bowen remained a cripple for many years prior to her death."

Like all people, the Bowens were shaped by their culture and therefore at times struggled with racial bias. But their love for people of other races was real and led them to be willing to sacrifice everything for them. For as T. J. wrote from Africa in 1853, "The essence of the missionary spirit is love."

"We must let go of the life we have planned,
so as to accept the one that is waiting for us."
—Joseph Campbell

"Hope deferred makes the heart sick,
but desire fulfilled is a tree of life."
—Proverbs 13:12

# CHAPTER 12

# Accepting Change

Life does not always go as planned. An unexpected detour can take us down a road to a place a long way from where we hoped to be. And sometimes there's no road back. During the years 1856 to 1860 T. J. Bowen found himself struggling desperately to find a way back to his beloved Africa. He had returned to America as an employee of the FMB, planning on a temporary furlough to regain his health and write and speak for the cause of the Central African Mission. However, as the months and years wore on, he continued to experience severe illness. He had left his heart in Africa, but his body prevented his return, leaving him torn. In July 1857 he wrote, "I am growing so anxious to get back to Africa that I dream of being there frequently. Unless I do get well it would be folly to go." Though at times when he would feel better his hopes would rise, gradually the heart-rending realization sank in that he would not be able to return to the land and the people he cared for so much. In August 1857 he admitted, "If my health should not permit my return before the close of the year, I must resign and turn to some other field of labor." Accepting this change seemed harder to him than all the difficulties he faced on the field in Yoruba.

Two months later he and Lurana faced another change. America experienced a major financial crisis. J. Edwin Orr explained, "On the 14th of October, the extensive banking system of the United States collapsed, a far-reaching disaster bringing to ruin hundreds of thousands of people in New York, Philadelphia, Boston, and industrial centers of the nation." Many banks stayed closed for two months. Because they were closed, they couldn't lend to farmers in the West to transport their crops. Factories closed their doors. Cold and hungry, the unemployed staged great protests, some of which turned into riots. Because the economy of the South was primarily agricultural rather than industrial, the crisis there proved less severe. However, it added to the financial pressure which T. J. and his family felt during those years.

The Greensboro Baptist Church had been pursuing T. J. to be their pastor for several months. In November 1857 he confided to Taylor, "At present, I scarcely think it would be right to enter into an agreement with the church at Greensboro, Georgia, because I should there be cut off from all labors which could have any direct bearing on missionary work." T. J.'s reluctance led the church in January 1858 to call another man as their pastor. On April 10, the church minutes read, "After a warmhearted & practical sermon by Bro. T. J. Bowen conference was opened. It being inconvenient for Bro Tucker to accept the call of the church, Bro. T. J. Bowen has finally committed to serve us...henceforth as the pastor of this church."

Intense financial pressure in March 1858 helped push T. J. to accept the pastorate in Greensboro. He frequently mentioned his money woes in letters during this time. Early that month, the church offered him a salary of $250 a year, only one third of what he had been receiving from the FMB. A few weeks later, the church upped their offer to $300 a year. Less than a month after he agreed to serve the Greensboro church, he received four well-paying offers from four other churches, two in Georgia and two in South Carolina. As a result, by September, his church increased his salary again, to $400 a year. But that still was not enough to make ends meet, so in addition to the church in Greensboro, he accepted the pastorate of the Baptist Church in Beech Island, South Carolina. That was manageable, since, as was typical in those days, Greensboro Baptist met only twice a month, on the second and fourth weekends—usually Saturday evening and Sunday morning. Traveling by train about 25 miles an hour, no doubt T. J. had every inch of the approximately 85-mile journey between those two churches memorized.

But another pressure motivated T. J. to lay aside his hopes to return to Africa and take the Greensboro church. Lurana was pregnant and due in a month. They had already lost one infant in Africa; they could not bear to lose another. He confessed to Taylor:

> I have never pretended to be [torn] of natural affection. Humanly speaking I might now have a child [torn] on my knee, as well as other men, were it not for the African climate, [torn] should return next July...I should deprive myself of another. It is impossible for me to set so lightly a value on [torn] —an life...I desire to settle down, either as a pastor to build up some church, or as a missionary in some field where I can be at home frequently, without neglecting my duties. I desire a healthy place.

Happily, he and Lurana welcomed a healthy daughter into their family on May 12, 1858. She bore her mother's name, Lurana, but they called her Lulu.

T. J. found himself the pastor of a church where Lurana's family were the dominate members. In a town of about a thousand people, they were living in her parents' home with a new baby and serving in her parents' church as a new pastor. Her prosperous merchant brothers were prominent members. But Lurana's brother-in-law, Judge Thomas Stocks, was by far the most influential person in the church. A well-respected political and denominational leader, he would accompany T. J. to regional and state-wide meetings. He made key reports and motions in the church's conferences or business meetings. Such intertwined family and church relationships would prove precarious.

Something dramatic happened that affected T. J.'s ministry during this time. A major spiritual awakening—"The Layman's Prayer Revival"—swept the nation during late 1857 and 1858. Thousands of laymen gathered together at noon in cities all across the country to pray for revival. God was moving, many churches opened every night for the preaching of the gospel, and hundreds of thousands were coming to faith in Christ. Although revival initially broke out in Canada, in the U. S., surprisingly, it started in the South among enslaved blacks who proved to be the more spiritual members of their congregations. For example, at the Anson Street Presbyterian Church in Charleston, South Carolina, the 48 black members outnumbered the 12 white members and initiated fervent prayer for revival. As a result, their pastor, Dr. John L. Girardeau, "preached to crowds that numbered 1,500 to 2,000 for eight full weeks nightly" and "large numbers of white and black converts joined the various congregations of the city." In Beaufort, South Carolina, Baptist pastor J. M. C. Breaker reported that he had baptized 565 people before the end of 1857, only eight of them being white. This brought the membership of his church in that small town to 3,511, only 108 of whom were white.

In 1858 the awakening hit Georgia with extraordinary power. Every day at noon, every church in Atlanta was open and filled with people seeking God in prayer.

In Columbus, a town of 9,000, 500 professed conversion. That summer the Georgia Baptist state paper, *The Christian Index,* exulted:

> Never since we entered upon the state of action has there been so generous and so glorious a work...Our souls have been greatly refreshed, our brethren have been revived, the churches have appeared as an army with banners; our children, friends, and neighbors, and even our enemies have been converted to God, and are together rejoicing in hope.

The awakening did not leave T. J.'s church untouched, especially during the fall of 1858. On September 11 seven people were received into the fellowship of the church on profession of faith. At their next meeting two weeks later, the church received four people by profession of faith and appointed them to be baptized the next morning at 9 o'clock. On these baptisms, T. J. commented, "Before leaving home I baptized 13 converts, and I have received a letter today expressing hope that I will soon baptize others. This also is a matter of joy." Two months later he mentioned, "I expect to baptize several others in Greensboro in January when I return from Ala. wither I am about to go visit my father." In December several "servants of others" came for membership in the church.

T. J.'s evangelistic efforts played a part in the church's increase in baptisms. In August the next year he remarked, "Two or three weeks ago, while out fishing for men, I got wet and had a spell of sickness." As his Greensboro church prospered, it solidified its ministry. The church met in a "union house building" which was owned by the Presbyterians. On January 8, 1859, under T. J.'s leadership, the Greensboro Baptists purchased the building from the Presbyterians for $1,000. That seems to be a fair price since in May 1858 whiskey in Greensboro cost between fifty and eighty-five cents per gallon. T. J. continued to serve the Greensboro church until the end of 1859, although he gave notice of his resignation on November 12. Evidently, he ended his pastorate at the Beech Island church at the same time, for on December 2 he told Taylor, "It is only about 3 weeks now till I shall be free from my churches, which I leave with joy and sorrow."

---

T. J. Bowen resigned his pastorates to accept another major change in his life—to serve as a missionary in Brazil. Although he had formally resigned from the FMB in a letter dated August 20, 1858, his missionary desires never abated. He knew that his health would not permit a return to Africa, but in January 1859 he wrote the FMB inquiring about the possibility in some other field. Poindexter, who was known to be plain spoken, yet loving, replied cautiously:

> [I]f you wish the Board to consider the propriety of appointing you to another field, I will send you an application in time. I will lay

it before them at their next meeting...But...I repeat the condition of my own mind, that without...health, to attempt to start a new mission would be unwise. Should you, however, apply to the Board, I will say nothing to defeat the application. My dear brother, I sympathize deeply with you.

During the next several months T. J. considered missionary work in such various places as San Antonio, Texas, and Japan. However, on August 29 he confided to Poindexter, "Brazil is the only place which has appeared to enter into my heart. I should find there perhaps thousands of Yoruba people, and the climate of the South, at or above Rio, is far from being a bad one." In October, he wrote Taylor, "I desire to offer myself formally as a missionary to Brazil...My health is better now than it has been in nearly five years."

The FMB responded favorably. Taylor admitted, "It had occurred to me that you might, in the providence of God, go to Brazil and there lay the foundations for evangelical movements in that interesting country." The FMB Minutes for November 9, 1859 stated, "A letter was read from Brother Thomas J. Bowen offering himself for appointment as a missionary to Brazil. After a free conference on this subject and it having been stated that the members of the Committee on New Fields favor the appointment, he was on motion appointed accordingly." When T. J. heard the news, he became ecstatic. He exuded to Taylor, "Your favor of the 11th inst. has given me unspeakable joy. The dark cloud, the crushing weight, which has rested on my soul for three years seems to be suddenly removed."

Full of enthusiasm, T. J. began preparing to pioneer not only a new field, but a new continent for Southern Baptists. He became the first missionary the FMB sent to either Central or South America. After his work there, it would be nineteen years before the FMB would enter Mexico and twenty years before they would re-enter Brazil. Yet for nearly a decade before T. J. was sent, the SBC had been passing resolutions and encouraging its FMB to send missionaries to Central and South America. In fact, in 1859 the SBC adopted the following state- ment regarding Brazil, "Perhaps the missionaries of no other part of Christendom can operate so effectively in that region as the missionaries that might be sent from Southern churches [because Brazil permitted slavery]. A mission should be opened there the coming year, if possible."

That pressure from the Convention may have moved the FMB to appoint T. J. to Brazil even though they knew he was not in good shape physically or mentally. His health had actually declined from the time he first offered himself for Brazil. In February 1860 he admitted to Taylor, "My health is not as good as it was last fall when I proposed to go to Brazil. Still it would look too much like instability to back out. My varying health has already made me too variable in purpose." After this letter, Taylor conceded to other missionaries, "Bro. Bowen will soon go to Brazil...He is yet in precarious health." Two months later, the FMB acknowledged in the most public way, in its annual report, that their newly-appointed missionary to Brazil was not altogether stable mentally. They revealed, "He feared a return to Yoruba, in the shattered condition of his nervous system." "A shattered nervous system" was the terminology of the day to refer to serious mental or emotional problems. Moreover, the FMB knew they were sending this weakened volunteer to pioneer a difficult field. Speaking of Brazil, the same annual report noted, "The Board regard this as a hard field. The superstitions of a spurious Christianity have embedded themselves in the minds and hearts of the people." Further, the FMB sent this wounded Christian soldier into this difficult battle alone, without any missionary associates besides his wife.

Nevertheless, upon his appointment, T. J. began preparing for his new missionary assignment. He searched unsuccessfully for a missionary candidate to go with him, writing three days before his departure, "I am sorry that I see no prospect of finding a colleague in the Brazilian work. But surely a good and proper brother will be found before long." He read all he could about Brazil, noting, "I have been reading Kidder and Fletcher's 'Brazil and the Brazilians.'" He devised strategy:

> If I settle in a commercial town, I can probably do good service by forming an English-speaking congregation and a Sabbath school. The so-called Mina Negroes, who are very numerous, are said to be from the Slave-Coast,

and if so, there is a great probability that I can form a Yoruba congregation, or at least labor daily among the people. In the meantime I will learn the Portuguese language as rapidly as possible. Much of my influence will depend on personal character, and consequently on the quiet labors of every day intercourse.

Realizing that he would face Roman Catholic opposition, T. J. tried to equip himself by studying the writings of the early church fathers. He commented to Taylor, "I must have at least some of 'the fathers' in my library as it will not do to be contemptible through ignorance. At the same time I am not inclined to display knowledge. I merely wish to be ready for any attack which I may receive from the monks and clergy." A pastor in his Georgia Baptist Association, H. A. Tupper, gave T. J. $100 to purchase a set of the early church fathers. Tupper later became the FMB corresponding secretary after James Taylor and because of their friendship, would deal with T. J. and Lurana with extraordinary kindness.

James Taylor accompanied T. J. and Lurana to their ship, which departed from Norfolk, Virginia. Lurana's diary recorded many days of sickness, slow sailing, dead calms, and an occasional storm. As they approached their destination, she wrote, "We are now opposite our African home, Lulu's second birthday on ship, May 12, 1860; eating the last of the ham mother gave us for our voyage. Abreast of Cape Frio, Sugar Loaf in sight; came in the Bay of Rio de Janeiro at 3 o'clock." Immediately, they discovered that the city was in the grip on an epidemic. Lurana saw their slow voyage as providential, writing, "Yellow fever prevailing. How merciful of the Lord in detaining us upon the sea!" A Christian merchant, Mr. Wright, showed them hospitality and helped them get settled. Taylor had been told that living in Rio was cheap. Therefore, the prices the Bowens discovered there shocked them—double what they expected.

Ever the evangelist, T. J. began sharing the gospel almost immediately. But he experienced instant and extraordinary opposition. Two weeks after arriving he wrote, "There are thousands of Yoruba people here. They swarm around me like bees and seem delighted that I have come to teach them. I have forgotten little or none of their language." Perhaps one of the reasons T. J. so wanted to reach them is that most of them were Muslims. The next day after he wrote that letter, the opposition began. The May 26, 1860 edition of the newspaper, *Diario de Rio de Janeiro,* published a story about 'suspicious' conversation between T. J. and Yoruba slaves, noting that he could speak their language well. It expressed concern that he might be an abolitionist who was seeking to incite an insurrection among the slaves and called on the authorities to investigate. T. J. went to the newspaper to explain the facts, but the story it published as a correction also contained mistakes.

The paper's attack brought a dramatic reaction from the authorities. They arrested and imprisoned T. J. Months later, he told Taylor, "I exposed myself to danger of imprisonment, and of being tried for my life, simply by telling the Mina or Yoruba negroes that Christ is the Savior. I did this in private conversation sitting in the Wrights' counting room." Rice related the extraordinary details as he heard it from his mother-in-law, Lurana Bowen:

> The Brazilian authorities thought he was stirring up an insurrection, and had Mr. Bowen put in prison. He immediately got in touch with the American Consul and explained the situation. He immediately cabled Washington and asked the authorities there to get in touch with the Baptist Foreign Mission Board; which they did. The Board and the War Department got busy and demanded an immediate release of the prisoner. The Commander of the American fleet at Rio was also sent instruction to send a formal demand for his release; and the time limit was six hours. The War vessels were lined up and the decks cleared for action. However, it was not necessary to fire a gun, as the prisoner was released immediately.

In part because of such opposition, T. J. discovered that Protestant mission work in Brazil was very limited. A few weeks after arriving, he observed that of the thousands of Germans, English, and American citizens in Rio, scarcely 100 attended German and English chapels there. Moreover, no missionary had attempted a work among Brazilian citizens, "lest they cause a premature disturbance." T. J. found this timid missionary approach intolerable. He attempted bolder moves. He reported, "Since my arrival I have preached two Sundays at the hotel. The landlord dislikes it & on the next Sunday I went to the city but could not get up a congregation."

T. J. soon discovered, however, that it was actually illegal for him to preach to Brazilians. He informed Taylor, "The law expressly forbids all <u>public worship</u>, except that of Catholics, 'in any place whatever,' under the penalty of...a fine from two to twelve mil reis for each person assembled. Foreigners are permitted to have indoor worship, but if Brazilians should meet to hear me preach, we would all be liable to the penalty." T. J. had experienced opposition in Africa, but nothing like he was experiencing in Brazil. He concluded, "To establish the gospel in a heathen country is like clearing a heavy forest and raising a crop, but to establish it in a Catholic country is like entering the same forest full of fierce savages who must be subdued before you can clear the land."

Frustrated with the prohibition to his work, high prices, and rampant yellow fever in Rio, the missionary pioneer moved his family to a rented house in a rather remote area of the near-by town of Tijuca. Although he found prices less expensive there, he commented, "Current expenses are at least twice as great as N. York." By October 10 he had developed a plan to rent a room in Rio where he could sell Bibles, speak to those who were interested, and hold Bible classes. Yet the plan never materialized. During the following six weeks in Tijuca, T. J. and his family struggled with sickness, including cholera.

They struggled even more with discouragement. The unresponsiveness of the people of Rio to the gospel increased to the point that even the other missionaries ceased to hold worship services. T. J. wrote, [T]he brethren in town have discontinued their preaching for want of hearers...Such things are truly discouraging and painful." He then confessed:

> I have been sorely tempted to regret that I ever came here...Shunned as heretics, condemned to silence by penal laws, hated by a people who are merciless in speaking evil of each other, without society or associates, and a gloomy prospect before us, we both feel that we have never been so unhappy before in our lives...[W] e force ourselves to hope for better times.

In that same letter, T. J. explained that they were packing up to prepare to move to a hopefully more promising location—the city of "Desterro, on the island of St. Catherine's, but *very* near the coast." T. J. desperately missed preaching and other active ministry. He was feeling useless. He admitted, "I am very anxious to be regularly at work. Then I hope to feel better satisfied. At present I feel more feeble, ignorant, and worthless than I ever did in my life. Still I am not out of heart." But his doubts about the work in Brazil grew. He confessed, "I do not know whether I should remain in Brazil or not. At least I shall never express a desire to leave, and I am willing to bear all the troubles that come upon me."

Such reports from Brazil gave the FMB and other Southern Baptists doubts about the continuance of T. J.'s efforts there. Taylor began to echo T. J.'s doubts in early December. The FMB minutes that month noted, "Recommended that it is the opinion of the Committee that the condition of Brazil does not justify the continuance of the Mission there, but as a South American mission was undertaken after repeated instructions from the Convention and as the next meeting of that body is now so near at hand, it would be better for the Board to refer the question to that body." After providing quotes from T. J. about the living expenses and the illegality of preaching in Brazil, the editor of *The Christian Index* commented, "The prospects of success are, to say the least, very small... In our opinion the Board should seriously consider the recall of Bro. B. or at least a change of locality."

Three sources of financial pressure influenced the FMB's inclination to bring the Bowens home. First, philosophical opposition to the FMB was growing within the Southern Baptist Convention. Taylor observed, "The miserable dispute...is distracting the mind of many good men who take no part in it, and funds are withheld by them. Our loss in this respect is heavy. Though we have assumed new & large responsibilities, our receipts are $6,000 less than the corresponding part of last fiscal year." Second, a major drought in the primarily agricultural economy of the South had seriously affected contributions.

The approaching Civil War proved to be a third, far more ominous, source of financial pressure for the FMB. Taylor gave T. J. the alarming news:

South Carolina will go out of the Union in a short time, and others will follow, perhaps all the Southern States...all the banks have suspended, and even war...fearful in its character, is apprehended. This is lessening our accounts every day...Congress is now in session, but the spirit of conciliation is diminishing. But little hope of compromise remains. The cloud thickens. Only God can save this land from a war the most fearful on the records of time.

A few weeks later, Taylor added, "Suspensions in business are occurring, operations by thousands are thrown out of employment, & where it all is to end, no human mind can foresee." By February 19, 1861, Poindexter wrote T. J. that it looked as if the FMB might have to break up or at least move from Richmond. He admitted, "I feel that we are in great peril in our missionary work." Indeed, by the end of the Civil War, the FMB only had $1.78 in its bank account.

Another pressure for the Bowens to return was building. Lurana's parents needed her help. Her father had lost his sight and her mother's health was failing. On January 24, Lurana's mother pleaded:

[M]ust ask you both to come home and stay with your father is anxious for you to do it and you know the desire of a mother we have no one else to ask and we are dependent I feel that it is a duty you owe us if you will come you will never regret it for we feel that your work is here you can do no good there we shall not be here long and in that time the Lord may open a door some where else...your father says come he will gladly give you both a home as long as he lives... don't you want to come.

One further pressure for the Bowens to return home proved to be the deciding one. T. J. had a major physical and mental breakdown. Writing in early February, Lurana explained to Taylor, "My poor husband, who has suffered so much and so long, is rapidly failing, failing in mind as well as physically. His brain is so much affected that he is seldom entirely rational." In the light of these developments, Lurana made the arrangements for their return to America without her husband's knowledge or consent. T. J.'s physical problems seemed as severe as his mental illness. Lurana felt uncertain about his survival on the voyage home. The FMB's annual report that May summarized the tragedy:

> The mission commenced by Brother Bowen at Rio de Janeiro has been abandoned. The complete prostration of his health compelled him to leave. He arrived about the first of April. We deeply sympathize with our dear brother and his excellent wife in this second disappointment of their desire to labor in the foreign field.

"No wound? No scar?
Yet as the Master shall the servant be,
And pierced are the feet that follow Me.
Yet thine are whole, can he have followed far
Who has no wound or scar?"
—Missionary Amy Carmichael

"But the Lord said to him, 'Go, for he is
a chosen instrument of Mine, to bear My name
before the Gentiles and kings...for I will show him
how much he must suffer for My name's sake."
—Acts 9:15-16

## CHAPTER 13
# Fighting Physical and Mental Illness

A ll too often soldiers return from an overseas war wounded mentally as well as physically. Though he had been fighting for a heavenly kingdom rather than an earthly one, T. J. Bowen also returned as a shattered soldier. Yet he returned to a nation that was also shattered and distracted with talk of war. In response to Abraham Lincoln's election as president and fearing conflict, the citizens of Greene County, Georgia, organized a militia, "The Greene Rifles," "to defend the rights of their Sunny South." One faction of the county's leaders sought compromise with the North. The other faction, led by Lurana's brother-in-law, 75-year-old Thomas Stocks, called for immediate secession.

Those feelings prevailed throughout the South and by the time the Bowens returned home to Greensboro to live with Lurana's parents in early April 1861, they found themselves in a new nation—a breakaway republic. Georgia had seceded from the United States on January 19 and along with other Southern states had formed the Confederate States of America on February 4. T. J. and Lurana discovered that their new president was Jefferson Davis, elected February 18, and that their new congress had adopted the Confederate Constitution on March 11. Though the Civil War did not officially begin until April 12 when the Confederates opened fire on Fort Sumter, the Bowens felt immediate repercussions from its prelude. Escalating tensions caused their baggage from Brazil to be detained in Baltimore. That luggage consisted of twenty-five trunks containing almost all their clothing and essential household items. Since T. J. was too weak to work, they felt this loss keenly. The trunks did not arrive in Greensboro until years later. As trying as they were, the hardships of the Civil War and subsequent Reconstruction were eclipsed by the difficulties the couple faced as a result of T. J.'s physical and mental struggles.

Africa had devastated Thomas J. Bowen physically. Writing in 1868, he observed, "Since 1849 I have suffered more than 20 attacks of fever." At the age of forty-five, he reflected:

> I have not been well nor felt well a day since
> I lay forty days at Awaye in 1852 without
> medicines and with no bed but two blankets...
> The [subsequent] violent inflammatory attack...
> did not kill me as I had all along suspected,
> but it left me a wreck, and I am still a wreck.
> For more than four years, I have had attacks
> of ague monthly, and often more frequently. I
> believe I am never quite free from fever a week
> at a time.

T. J. did have seasons when he felt better. Later that same year he wrote, "Since May I have had no agues, and for several weeks past my health has improved so rapidly that I am now as well as I have been in fifteen years." Yet invariably his health would decline again. Of this same period, he noted, "Since the first of Nov. and contrary to expectations, I have suffered much with my spleen and liver."

T. J. experienced a wide variety of symptoms. Most frequently he suffered the fever and chills of agues which are commonly associated with malaria. The accompanying severe headaches tortured him. His medical report from the mental hospital where he was treated stated: "When in Africa his health became very bad. Had disease of the liver, and awfully violent headaches occurring at intervals of two weeks, under which he could not sleep, and would beg for a hammer to knock his brains. Yet has those headaches, but not so violently or frequently. T. J. also repeatedly complained of a swollen and painful liver and spleen. He remarked, "I am sorry to be always complaining, but my liver and my spleen lead me a wretched life." He admitted, "I am sometimes afraid that my liver which protruded from under my ribs will never be restored to soundness." In addition, at times T. J. experienced frequent pain related to his heart. He told Taylor, "My own symptoms are much the same except more distress about the heart." At times he described this pain as "a most alarming congestion and cramp about the heart." Occasionally, his skin erupted. In 1852 he noted, "After my last fever I was afflicted with many boils." Later he mentioned, "I had a red eruption on the face and body." Additionally, T. J. faced other symptoms such as failing memory, sleeplessness, erysipelas, impetigo, edema, dysentery, rheumatism, neuralgia, and convulsions.

Extraordinary attacks of severe pain and even paralysis also plagued T. J. From Brazil in August 1860 he wrote to Taylor, "I have had another of those terrible attacks of excruciating pain in the limbs, joints, and head, which reduce me for the time to a state little short of insanity. For three days and two nights in succession I was scarcely able to fall into a doze for a few minutes." Two similar episodes had occurred that year, and this one left him unable to use his right foot and ankle for several days afterward. Such paroxysms of pain caused T. J. to roll on the bed or the floor "in a most extravagant manner, because it was impossible to be still." At other times T. J.'s illness seemed to immobilize him. Soon after his return from Brazil he reported, "On two occasions I have fallen into a stupor of lethargy from which I could not be aroused for three or four hours, and once a similar attack extended only from the hips downward. I was standing on the floor when I suddenly found myself incapable of moving another foot."

What specific diseases could T. J. have been dealing with? Two modern-day physicians who read every primary-source description of his physical and mental health have offered some possible answers. Dr. William Lunders attributed T. J.'s symptoms to three probably primary diseases—malaria, sleeping sickness, and schistosomiasis. Regarding malaria he observed, "Since it didn't kill him, he probably became a long-term carrier. This is characterized by fever, headaches, muscle pains, splenomegaly, and anemia. Malaria is caused by protozoa and these parasites settle in the liver. The relapses come from these liver parasites and can occur for years." In regard to sleeping sickness, Lunders explained:

> I suspect that the worst of his mental problems came from Gambian variety sleeping sickness. This is also a protozoan illness. In West Africa the symptoms are not generally as severe, but can become chronic and last for years. The main symptoms are fever, headaches (ague), insomnia, and inability to concentrate. You may also have convulsions (apoplectic episodes). As

the protozoa go through their life cycles, you
get the relapses with new onset of symptoms.

Lunders also suspected that with T. J.'s constant mention of liver tenderness, there seems a good chance he suffered with schistosomiasis. He clarified, "This is caused
by worms that can penetrate our skin or oral cavity...[T]
he schistosomiasis worms in chronic form tend to congre-
gate in the liver. This would have caused hepatomegaly
(enlarged liver) and been very painful."

To these three major infections, Dr. Alan Hardwicke
suggested two more possibilities—typhoid fever and
strep. He notes, "One of the chief symptoms of Bowen
was recurrent diarrhea. Several times he mentions a slow
pulse with the fever. Typhoid fever is a cause of diarrhea which can cause a fairly severe febrile illness, and
is known for causing a fever that is associated with a relatively low heart rate." Hardwicke further observed that
typhoid could possibly account for T. J.'s nervousness,
headaches, delirium, stupor, joint pains, and red-colored
skin eruptions. Moreover, Hardwicke suspected that a
strep infection may have induced rheumatic fever, which
could explain his fever and arthritis. Strep could also
account for his boils, erysipelas, and impetigo. Whatever
the precise combination of the above suspected illnesses,
the primary-source descriptions from letters, journals,
and medical reports leave no doubt that from T. J.'s first
expedition to Africa until his death twenty-five years
later he suffered from recurrent cycles of debilitating
chronic disease.

Similarly, T. J. also suffered recurrent cycles of debilitating mental illness. He tended to have a quiet, more serious personality. His friend D. T. Everett once commented about him, "He was always taciturn and uncommunicative in reference to himself & I presume I know as much about him as anybody." But T. J. was widely admired and loved and no obvious symptom of mental illness appeared in the historical record until his first expedition to Africa. After repeated attacks of fever, he began to comment about nervousness. For example, in November 1851 he mentioned, "Besides I am sometimes so nervous that confinement to study is almost intolerable." After he returned to Africa the second time, he admitted that even on his furlough home he was struggling emotionally. He wrote, "My nervous system was so completely shattered that I was always unhappy and I fear often rendered myself disagreeable by appearing fretful and ill tempered."

His depression deepened in the spring and summer of 1854. Subsequently, during a severe bout of fever that fall, he experienced a lingering break with reality when he found himself stuck in a hallucination in which he saw his disease as a monster he was fighting with a sword. Years later he admitted, "For a long time in Africa I was apprehensive that I should go crazy, and had only too much reason for this fear. I sometimes flogged myself severely, and even compelled my servant to flog me on the bare back as the only known means of producing sufficient nervous reaction to save me from absolute mania." It is a heart-rending tragedy that a hundred years before psychotropic medicines, isolated in Africa, and determined to continue his missionary work, T. J. found painful self-flagellation his only temporary relief from insanity. He traced his worst mental problems to that acute illness in the fall of 1854. He observed, "I have been almost half-crazy at times ever since my severe sickness in 1854."

Those "half-crazy" times and other mental symptoms did not abate much after T. J.'s return to America in 1856. Depression haunted him. He frequently made comments like, "I am clean out of heart and distressed in mind." He spoke of being "low spirited," "troubled with the blues," being "more unhappy than ever before in my life, and more than I thought I could be," facing, "the dark abyss of despair," having "sadness of heart," being "in dumps," and experiencing a "gloomy fit."

In addition to depression, anxiety also stalked the wounded missionary. The looming probability that his health would not permit him to return to Africa caused him much angst. He often described this anxiety as nervousness, and said it frequently kept him from sleeping. During the time he was speaking and testifying in Washington, D. C., he confessed, "[W]hile my nervous system is so much shattered, I have not slept much for two or three nights, and last night I lay awake the whole night long." The anxiety during that time reached such heights that T. J. admitted to Taylor, "I am often so nervous that I cannot sleep till late at night, and sometimes till the break of day. From this cause I have several times been driven to the very borders of frenzy."

T. J. acknowledged that he was often in danger of passing beyond the borders of frenzy. Speaking of returning to Africa, he admitted, "I should probably go crazy or die or both before a great while in that country." In 1858 he noted in his diary, "Whether sane or insane, my conduct for the last eight years has often been very erroneous." The next year, he confessed to Taylor, "When I wrote yesterday I was still crazy from the effects of a terrible headache." Writing from Brazil in October 1860, he confided, "Many a time within a few years I have appeared to be on the borders of a total wreck of body and mind." T. J. suffered much. To Poindexter, he declared that he had been "looking back with an indefinable horror upon the bodily and mental woes through which I have passed."

After his return from Brazil, T. J.'s mental symptoms apparently took new forms. He hatched numerous money-making schemes which his friends saw as impractical and a sign of instability. For example, at the beginning of the Civil War, he proposed to launch a news periodical and enlisted a number of subscribers. Taylor wrote to discourage him from the scheme, and on the same day wrote to his brother-in-law, Judge Thomas Stocks, sending him money for the Bowens because he did not trust T. J. with it. Taylor confided, "I fear that Bro. Bowen will sink all his money into his new enterprises. He must lose by it. Please inform me confidentially, what is his state of mind?" Taylor's fears proved well-founded. A few weeks later, Lurana wrote:

He was in a very bad state of mind all last week. I did all in my power to pacify and console him and kept a close watch over him, lest he should go away, for he said continually, that he would not stay here. On Sabbath he grew worse. I followed him all day everywhere he went, trying to soothe his mind, but at last, he escaped my vigilance, and ran off to the 7 o'clock train, after the whistle sounded, without baggage or money.

Such irrational behavior became a frequent occurrence in T. J.'s life. Somehow trying to start his life over, he once burned his clothes. He told Lurana, "I have carried renunciation so far that I have thrown away or burned all my papers and all my clothing except what was lost before. I came here with one suit only, and that I wore."

Lurana was feeling immense stress. Besides being the caretaker for her blind father, frail mother, and three-year-old daughter, she had to single-handedly deal with a physically and mentally ill husband. Hundreds of Greensboro men had already left to fight in the War, and the tension and anxiety in the town was palpable. Besides that, because their trunks were detained in Baltimore, she had very few clothes and personal items. Her husband could not work and earn a living, the FMB's finances were decimated and they could hardly send them any money, and because of the War, inflation had skyrocketed in Greensboro. So in addition to everything else she was trying to do, she began teaching in a private school.

T. J.'s mental illness seems to have been connected to his physical illness. For example, in October 1860 he rejoiced, "My improved health has brought with it a buoyancy of mind to which I have long been a stranger." Conversely, his severe attacks of physical pain would bring accompanying irrationality. Similarly, in 1874 T. J. observed, "Some three weeks ago, I was taken sick suddenly...My brain has been greatly affected, so that I have been half-crazy, unable to write or to think I feel discouraged, and will not try to preach anymore, till I get so that I quit talking to myself, and getting up in my sleep." From Milledgeville the next year, he wrote Lurana, "I have been in a bad way at times—gloomy, half-frenzied, full of pains, sleepless, and the impetigo on my lip, which always grows better or worse with my mind, has given me much trouble." Thus the historical record indicates that T. J.'s mental illness stemmed from or at least was severely aggravated by the diseases which infected him in Africa.

---

T. J.'s irrationality eventually brought him to the Lunatic Asylum of the State of Georgia. Established by an act of the Georgia legislature on December 18, 1841, the Asylum was located on forty acres of land on a hill two miles south of the state capital of Milledgeville near the village of Midway. When T. J. came to the Asylum it consisted of two resident buildings, "130 by 40 feet, four stories high." Peter Cranfield reports, "There were twenty rooms in the basement and twenty-three rooms on each of the other three floors. All doors opened into an airy passage running the length of the floor." Thus each room would have been about ten by fifteen feet in size. Men resided on the first and second floors, women on the third and fourth, supervised by a resident matron.

The Asylum's resident physician and superintendent during T. J.'s stays, Dr. Thomas A. Green, carried a reputation for integrity, humility, compassion, innovation, and excellence. Becoming superintendent in 1845, and serving until 1879 when he had a stroke while ministering to a patient, Green was widely recognized as being the primary founder of the Asylum. The chief personality of the institution, Green was described by his assistant and successor as "full of life, cheerful, merry, courteous, considerate. He was a sincere Christian...one of the most benevolent and unselfish of men...He was a delightful companion, a true and sympathetic friend, a man whom all loved."

Green developed strikingly innovative ways of dealing with the insane. He despised restraints. Cranfield remarked, "It was Green's spectacular custom to personally release the manacled patients when they arrived at the hospital, and of the almost two hundred insane, only twelve had to be secluded for any length of time." Further, Green did not separate himself or his family from the patients. Cranfield commented, "One of the most stimulating conditions of the atmosphere of the hospital was that the status of patient and staff were not socially exclusive. Dr. Green, it will be recalled, fed many at his personal table and, when the hospital became crowded, had an addition built to his residence in order to take care of them." One of the results of this policy is that Green's daughter married one of the patients, a young man apparently recovering from alcoholism, in 1869. Their marriage lasted 42 years until his death in 1911.

Green also instituted chapel services for the spiritual welfare of the patients and staff. Moreover, he encouraged patients to get outside and work with their hands in the Asylum's large garden and farm. At one point, T. J. enjoyed working in that garden three hours a day. Green's understanding of insanity and his treatments were ahead of his time. Not surprisingly, during his tenure the Asylum became "the noblest and almost the largest of its kind in America." Since Green was T. J.'s personal physician during at least the last sixteen years of his life, he received expert diagnosis and care.

When did T. J. first seek Dr. Green's help? The Asylum's official medical report indicates that he went to Green years before he was officially admitted. That medical report began, "Rev. T. J. Bowen of Greensboro, Geo. Native of Georgia. Age 45." T. J. turned 45 in 1859, two years before he was admitted to the Asylum. Further, the report continued, "The first indication was observed in 1858. Has not seemed to be entirely free from mental disorder since. Is said to have had an attack continuing for some months." Thus the report seems to imply that Green had first observed T. J.'s insanity the previous year. It also revealed that he was struggling with severe mental illness while he was serving as the pastor of two churches, writing, speaking, and testifying before Congress. In addition, it seems significant that in 1859, the year he was appointed as a missionary to Brazil, he was experiencing an attack of insanity that had continued for some months.

According to his official medical report, T. J. was first admitted to the Lunatic Asylum on November 11, 1861. Evidently, Lurana visited him there in March 1862, because Taylor sent her a letter addressed to Milledgeville in which he responded to her news that T. J. appeared to be improving. The medical report noted that he was discharged June 7, 1862, but returned to the Asylum less than a month later on July 2. In a letter written from the Asylum on March 2, 1863, T. J. indicated that he had recently returned to the Asylum, so he must have left for a while and then been admitted a third time. Another letter revealed that he left the Asylum at the close of 1863.

At the beginning of 1864, T. J. moved back to Greensboro and joined his family on a farm owned by Lurana's brother George. She told Taylor, "Mr. Bowen & my little girl are with me at my brother's...Mr. Bowen is better, <u>mentally</u>, than I have seen him in a long time. He had improved so much, and seemed so desirous of living on a farm, that I thought it best to indulge him, and remove him from the Asylum for a while, at least." Three months later she had good news:

> Mr. Bowen has improved wonderfully since
> we have settled in this quiet place. He is the
> busiest man you ever saw—digging, planting,
> cutting, sawing, doing a little of everything

which comes to hand. I think the experiment
will succeed beyond my expectations...he feels
so much better than when at the Asylum. He
frequently expresses himself as being "happy
as a king."

T. J. appears to have stayed home with Lurana for at least
eighteen months because their third child, Mayme, was
conceived around September 1865.

Their happy and peaceful time together on the farm
in 1864 was threatened by the terrible storm of war. In
May the Union Army invaded Georgia fighting to take
its flagship city, Atlanta, only 75 miles from Greensboro.
That summer every store and church in Greensboro was
turned into a make-shift hospital to care for the flood
of wounded soldiers coming from Atlanta. Though they
lived on the farm, the Bowens socialized, shopped, and
worshipped in Greensboro, and they could not escape the
horror. T. J.'s medical experience and their compassion
probably compelled them to join many other citizens and
help tend the wounded. Jonathan Bryant describes a typical scene:

This was grim work, as Ella Thomas discovered
in late July 1864, when the threat of a raid
on Greensboro forced the removal of many
casualties to Augusta. Thomas went to the
Catholic church to help and "found a state
of destitution I had never imagined before."
Wounded men filled the church, straw spread

on the floor serving as their beds. Shocked, Thomas saw every type of wound: "some with arms and legs cut off, others with flesh wounds, two men dying." The next morning she returned to the church and found one man she had tried to comfort the day before dead and "swarming with flies." Ella Thomas never again tried to aid the wounded and asked later, "Oh God, will this war never cease?"

After his army had captured and burned Atlanta, on November 15, 1864, General William Tecumseh Sherman and his massive army began their march across Georgia to the sea. The left wing of his army, under General Henry Slocum marched east along the Georgia Railroad toward Greensboro. On Sunday, November 20, General John Geary's Division routed the Confederate cavalry protecting Greensboro, and captured the town for several hours before moving on. This devastating and demoralizing event affected the Bowens personally. After years of waiting, their trunks with their possessions had finally arrived in Greensboro. Lurana said they came "just in time for Sherman's stragglers to wreak their vengeance by jabbing their bayonets through my best dresses, and what they did not destroy, they gave to the Negroes, who begged for them."

T. J.'s medical report noted that he was admitted to the Asylum again on February 23, 1868, from Greene County. This would have been the fourth time he entered the hospital. Though the medical report did not list his dismissal, diary entries and letters indicate that he was home in Greensboro during October and November 1868. Nonetheless, in February 1869 T. J. was arrested in Atlanta. Family friend J. J. Toon told Lurana, "To be plain, let me say that Bro. B. was suffering from an attack incident to his state of mind on his arrival in the city or soon after, and was taken by policemen and confined. It was necessary, so I am informed." From Atlanta, T. J. was transported back to the Asylum at Milledgeville. He did not stay long. His medical report showed that he escaped from the institution on April 4, 1869. From Florida that September he explained to Lurana, "If you have not yet written to Dr. Green, give him my compliments, and tell him that I am ashamed of running away, but I was growing worse there, and now I am better than ever before." Over the next several years T. J. roamed the South, but between August and October 1873 he involuntarily spent two additional weeks at the Asylum before he escaped again. He told his wife, "At Brunswick they arrested me to send me to Midway. I stayed 2 weeks and was worse when I escaped than at first."

T. J. entered the Asylum for the seventh and final time on November 5, 1874. Weak and sick, he no longer tried to escape, but settled down under the kind care of Dr. Green. He told Lurana, "I have every liberty here; a key to go in and out at pleasure...when I cannot sleep, I come down to Dr. Green's office, where I have fire and gas." T. J. expressed his resignation, "I shall remain here till I get well or die, painful as it is, for I have tried hard and often to do something." T. J. kept his word. He never left the Asylum again.

T. J. Bowen's achievements are all the more remarkable because he accomplished most of them while fighting mental illness. Anxiety and depression hounded him before his second expedition to Africa. He began to be psychotic in 1854, suicidal in 1855, and was diagnosed by his physician as insane for months in 1859. Yet it was after 1854 that T. J. saw his greatest success in Ijaye, established a mission station in Ogbomosho and attempted one in Ilorin, authored *Central Africa,* completed his *Grammar and Dictionary of the Yoruba Language,* testified before Congress, lectured and preached throughout the Eastern United States, served as the honored pastor of two churches, and pioneered Baptist mission work in Brazil. Even after his symptoms worsened in 1861 and he was institutionalized several times, he continued to preach with noticeable usefulness. Considering that in the United States, almost half (46.4%) of adults will experience some form of mental illness during their lifetime, T. J.'s life is an encouragement to persevere in following God's call, while at the same time, getting all the medical help available.

"I was a stricken deer that left the herd
Long since; with many an arrow deep infixt
My panting side was charged, when I withdrew
To seek a tranquil death in distant shades.
There I was found by one who had himself
Been hurt by the archers. In his side he bore,
And in his hands and feet, the cruel scars."
—William Cowper, who also fought mental illness

"You know my reproach and my shame and
my dishonor...For they have persecuted him
whom You Yourself have smitten, and they tell
of the pain of those You have wounded."
—Psalm 69: 19, 26

## CHAPTER 14
# Facing Rejection

F ew things are so painful as experiencing those who
once pursued you, pushing away from you, those
who once praised you, criticizing you. Compounding
T. J. Bowen's severe chronic physical and mental illness
was something he'd not experienced before—widespread

rejection. Part of that was the stigma of mental illness, but coupled to that was his use of alcohol and laudanum. During his sane years, T. J. appears to have used alcohol only medicinally. He testified that even in his "wildest days" before his conversion, he did not abuse alcohol. Moreover, the Baptist churches in the American South that he attended and served held to strict standards, especially in regard to the use of alcohol. In Africa, his convictions reflected the same standards. Speaking of the young African men, he wrote, "They love a dram, which they never get from me, and I tell them plainly why I bring no rum to treat them." For health in Africa, he prescribed, "[D]rink no stimulating liquors." In fact, later he said that during these years he had "hated" drinking. Nevertheless, T. J. and other missionaries did commonly use alcohol to mix medicines and preserve fruit.

However, beginning about 1860, T. J. began to occasionally abuse alcohol and to drink to the point of drunkenness. Writing to an acquaintance who also had a problem with alcohol in 1868, he admitted, "It was then that I began to drink and kept it up at intervals for eight years. Many times I was absolutely incapable of self-control." He wrote that letter to share his own victory at the time over alcohol and to encourage his friend to find similar help from Christ. T. J.'s first episode of drunkenness seems to have occurred in early 1860 shortly before he left as a missionary for Brazil. Months later he confessed in vague terms to Taylor:

When I was taken sick again in the winter, I was greatly dejected. I cannot enter into details now as I would if we could be together, but the final result was that I awoke as it were from a dream and found myself thoroughly wretched. I felt utterly unworthy to live, and much more so to preach. No words can describe what I suffered for two or three weeks. It was then that I wrote to you wishing to delay my departure to Brazil.

T. J.'s "self-abhorrence" continued for weeks, but by focusing on the love of Christ, he found that "toward the end of Feb. my troubles departed and it seems to me that I have gradually grown stronger ever since."

T. J. vigorously denied one accusation of drunkenness in 1861. Nevertheless, after that time, though his letters evidence extended times of soberness or medicinal, moderate use of alcohol, they also reveal bouts of drunkenness. The times he used alcohol moderately, he did so to help control his mental symptoms. In 1874 he told Lurana, "For some time I have been in the habit of drinking one dram, rarely two—daily. It helps me and I keep a bottle on hand. I never drink enough to excite me or to feel it in the head." Similarly, his hospital medical report noted that to help him mentally, he took "brandy occasionally, very little of which affects him."

T. J. Bowen's spells of drunkenness found their source in his mental illness. They did not begin until after he was diagnosed by Dr. Green as having periods of insanity. The patient himself recognized his insanity as the font of his alcohol abuse. He observed, "There was something the matter which at times completely demented me, and led me far from duty. It was then that I began to drink." Speaking of his drunkenness, he asked Lurana, "Can you believe me when I affirm that I never did when I was able to reflect [on] what I was doing?" Later, he gave an instance, "I arose one morning soon after day, and without the least reflection or consideration went to town and drank too much liquor. It never occurred to me that I was acting in any way improperly."

Others also recognized that T. J.'s drinking sprang from his diseased mind. From Bainbridge, Georgia, he wrote, "The brethren in these regions know all my sins, but they attribute them to diseases and they do not believe that I have willfully and wickedly departed from God. I do trust and believe that they are correct; and their cordial love and confidence is unspeakable consolation to a broken and desolate heart." From his extensive observation of mental patients, T. J.'s physician, Thomas Green, concluded that alcohol abuse often sprang from mental illness. He commented, "Insanity often comes on slowly and imperceptibly; the workings of disease are hidden from our view and the real cause, in many cases, lies beneath the apparent one. In this way, intemperance, religious feeling, the solitary vice...are the supposed causes, when in fact, they are only the effect of the first impulses of the disease." T. J.'s medical report gave no indication that Green felt otherwise in T. J.'s case.

T. J.'s recognition that his occasional drunkenness had its basis in his mental disease did not lead him to excuse his behavior long. He humbly admitted to Lurana, "I <u>have</u> repented...I <u>do</u> understand that there is no excuse for sin...The weakness which produces sin, is itself sin." He made similar comments two days later to a Bro. Gaulden, admitting, "Satan has tried to make me excuse my sins, on the ground that I could not appreciate what I was doing. But the weakness which produces sin is itself sin and needs pardon. The follies of youth, the sins of riper years, even the errors of insanity are inexcusable. The Lord looks at the fact of sin, and not the cause."

The consequences of his alcohol abuse felt like a crushing weight. Recognizing the sinfulness of his actions brought him a deep sense of wretchedness and self-loathing. It made him question at times whether he should ever attempt to preach again. He grieved, "My race is run and my doom is sealed. I am in great doubt whether I should ever preach again in this country." As the word of his alcohol problems became widespread, it brought increasing shame to Lurana. After hearing one such report, she pleaded, "I beg you never to <u>touch any stimulants again</u>. For by their use you bring disgrace upon <u>yourself</u>, <u>your family</u>, and <u>the cause of Christ</u>. Think of these things, and in your manhood and Christian strength rise superior to the depraved appetite and every temptation and be <u>yourself</u> again."

T. J. also felt the displeasure of Lurana's family, particularly her influential brother-in-law, Judge Thomas Stocks. Stocks served with distinction as a Southern Baptist leader, not only in the Greensboro church, but on the state and national level. In his later years, most of the time T. J. stayed away from his family in Greensboro, in large measure because he believed Stocks disapproved of him on account of his drunkenness. In one letter to Lurana, after mentioning a list of friends, T. J. added:

> "My heart would add Thos. Stocks, but he has cast me off. Like many others, he thinks he understands my case. He thinks I could have done better, and does not know how often I struggled and prayed, how utterly helpless I was, and how I could not reflect or see what I was doing sometimes, even when I had a dim perception of my state, actions, etc. If he knew my present state, feelings and actions, he would say that I have at last repented."

In part, the perception of Stock's disapproval may have come from the Greensboro church's denial of his request for a letter to another church stating that he was in good standing. Stocks led the appointed committee to investigate his case. The church's minutes reveal that he and the committee were actually kind and considerate in dealing with the matter. Two years later when he was home in Greensboro, T. J. wrote a poem of repentance which he read before the church. Three stanzas read:

> Dear brethren, unto you and God
> My sins and follies I confess;
> Dark are the paths which I have trod
> And full of pain and wretchedness...

Tis not my purpose to excuse
The conduct, which I should lament;
God grant that I may ne'er refuse
To see my errors and repent.

Yet oh! How often I have been
Stung by disease till half insane
I sought by means, which led to sin,
To lull the agony of pain.

The drama of their former pastor now disgraced and standing before them reading this poem would have been tearful and memorable for the church and excruciating for T. J.

---

Besides alcohol, T. J. sometimes used another questionable substance—laudanum, a form of opium. Burks explained, "In its more common medical form, tincture of laudanum, opium powder was first softened with water and then mixed with wine or alcohol. Laudanum was routinely prescribed at the time to treat pain, diarrhea, and dysentery." Known to be addictive, it should have been taken under the supervision of a physician. Nonetheless, like T. J., many people in his day often read medical texts and treated themselves. Speaking of Dr. Gunn's *New Family Physician, or Home Book of Health,* T. B. Rice observed, "The mere fact that this publication reached its one hundredth edition in 1870, gives some idea of how universal home diagnosis and treatment was practiced... His praise of opium and its derivatives were termed as 'Divine Medicine' and caused its use to be resorted to all too freely." T. J. knew to be cautious in his use of laudanum. He knew of an Anglican missionary in Africa who had died of an overdose.

FMB Corresponding Secretary James Taylor heard second-hand that a physician suspected that T. J. was addicted to laudanum. Writing to him in Brazil, Taylor mentioned the rumor—"that you are in the habit of using opium...Now my dear brother, if this be so, I ask, if every dictate of providence and of deity, does not require the abandonment of such a habit? It may require a severe conflict, and cost serious self-denial, but it seems to me, that you ought at any & every sacrifice of feeling to give up the indulgence." T. J. responded graciously and non-defensively. He recalled that Dr. O'Keefe saw him in "one of those paroxysms of pain, or rather agony, which no one else has witnessed except my own family." He then explained:

> I remember his coming, but not his leaving. He was told as I learn that nothing but laudanum would relieve me. Then he went to Penfield and told Dr. Crawford that in his opinion these paroxysms were caused by taking opium. Now the truth is I had suffered in this way for several years before I took any opium at all. At the time of the attack in which he saw me I had taken none for some weeks, it may have

been two or three months. [He then explained about his self-flagellation in Africa to attempt to stay sane.]...Sometime after my return home I learned that laudanum would give me relief. I then began to carry it with me when I left home...Being very unwilling to have an attack among strangers, I used to take it to keep them off. At home, however, I did not take it even in my attacks unless they became severe. Sometimes I would take none for three or four months together. T. J.'s revelations of the depth of his physical and mental agony shocked the FMB leadership. Writing on behalf of Taylor, Poindexter admitted, "The reference which you made to your sufferings caused me...horror. I knew that you had been a great sufferer, but I had not imagined your suffering is so great." T. J.'s answer seemed to satisfy them that he was not addicted to laudanum. They never mentioned it again.

Broken in mind and body, feeling rejected by extended family and friends in Greensboro, and desperate to try to make a living for himself and his family, T. J. spent much of the last fourteen years of his life traveling. He seemed to revert to the familiar pattern of his life before Africa as an itinerant worker in the American South. He found his life full of contradictions. Though married, he lived alone. Though once acclaimed as a national hero, he experienced ridicule and rejection. Though he had many plans to make a decent living, none ever worked out. Though at times he received hospitality from kind Christians, at other times he lived like a tramp—hopping trains and sleeping in the woods.

T. J.'s mental illness fueled his wanderings in two ways. First, he felt better mentally when traveling. Speaking of "rest and mental quiet," in May 1858 he told Taylor, "[M]y disposition is such that I cannot enjoy either in <u>idleness</u>. I might remain at home and neither work nor read, but the weariness of doing nothing would do me more injury than reading and preaching. For this reason I will...start on a <u>wander</u>, without any very definite object or destination." He made a similar statement to Lurana in 1873, writing, "If I stop to teach, my health soon gives way, and I suffer far more mentally than when traveling." Second, T. J. suffered from "flighty impulses," seeking rest for his troubled soul. In 1873, he wrote Lurana from Texas, "Where shall I go? I have impulses to return west, to go east, north, south, etc. But I well know that there is not rest anywhere."

Though he returned to Greensboro, Georgia, from Brazil seriously ill in early April 1861, by May 7 T. J. had traveled to Pensacola, Florida, and arrived home by May 20. He stayed there until mid-August when in a state of mania he ran away from home and jumped on a train. The next day he wrote Lurana from Atlanta asking her to send clothes and money, saying he was going "out West."

However, a few days later he sent a letter saying he was planning to buy a house and a small farm near Atlanta. From there, T. J. wrote Taylor on October 1 telling him about his farm, remarking, "My wife has been with me more than a week, but returns tomorrow to prepare for coming up permanently." Shortly after, T. J. told Taylor that the sale of the farm had fallen through, complaining, "Prostrated in health, without home, money, or friends, with nearly all our clothing & all my books lost in Baltimore, I can truly say that I am in distressed circumstances." It seems no surprise that from such a situation, T. J. was admitted to the Asylum shortly after on November 11, 1861.

T. J. began wandering again in 1866. After being released from the hospital and subsequently living on a farm with his family for at least eighteen months, the *African Repository* published a letter from him written September 1, 1866, from Ringgold, in the northwest corner of Georgia. He must have spent some time there. The 1867 Minutes of the Georgia Baptist Convention list him as a minister in the Coosa Association with a residence in Ringgold. Being listed as a resident minister did not mean he was serving as a pastor at the time. However, T. J. moved on. In a letter dated May 1867, he revealed that he was teaching school near Atlanta, trying to get a farm so his family could join him. He also mentioned six spiritual exercises he was practicing to try to stay sane. He recognized the impropriety of living apart from Lurana, acknowledging, "To live apart in this way would be sinful, shameful, and intolerably painful. I must have my place ready by the first of October." Sometime after this T. J. must have returned home to Lurana because on February 23, 1868, he was admitted to the Asylum from Greene County.

When T. J. escaped from the Asylum on April 4, 1869, he headed for Florida. The first surviving letter from him was written five months later. He told Lurana he had been deeply depressed, but now was considering touring Florida. Evidently, he took the tour. He wrote Lurana from Jacksonville in January 1870, from Sand Point, Indian River, in April, and from Fort Myers in October. At Sand Point he was cultivating three acres of rented ground and sleeping in a hammock on a bear skin, two and a half miles from where he took his meals. Not surprisingly, he was suffering with pain and sickness. The farming project failed. Financially, he took a "3 month clear loss there." At Fort Myers, he was dreaming of establishing a lumber mill.

By March 1871, T. J. was in Cedar Bayou, Texas, near Houston. He had been chopping wood and had offers to teach. That August, his friend, D. T. Everett, who was serving as a pastor in Texas at the time, was delighted to see him again. Everett informed Lurana that he had "his same old notions of various enterprises, and [was] determined as ever to make money on which to settle comfortably and have the chance to preach." Everett told him to go home to his family as soon as he finished his three-month teaching assignment. Instead, T. J. was determined to make some money and bring his family to join him in Texas.

Evidently, he stayed in Texas throughout 1872. However, Lurana apparently waited almost two years before she heard from him again. T. J. seemed surprised, writing, "Yesterday I saw Bro. E. A. Vandivere...who informed me that you had not heard from me in a long time. I was in very bad health last summer and fall, but I thought, and still think, that I wrote to you repeatedly... [I]f my mind has been seriously affected, I did not know it...I was grieved and shocked when I heard that you had not heard from me." T. J. explained that until August 1872 he was in Atascosa County in South Central Texas at the home of a Brother Rutledge. He then moved to Wilson County southeast of San Antonio where a Methodist preacher took him in. From October to December he was cared for by a Brother Currie, then by W. J. Blewett, whom he had known in Georgia. At the time of his writing, he resided in the city of Cameron in Milam County about sixty-five miles south of Waco.

T. J. missed his family. In January 1873, he told Lurana, "It is likely that I shall teach school here for at least three months. Then if you cannot come to Texas, I must come to Georgia. Truly, I am weary of wandering, and I fully intend to settle down, permanently and finally, somewhere." He then began to write more than once a month saying things like, "Oh, how often and vividly I see you and the children at home, passing to & fro and quietly seated in the house. This comes upon me especially when I stop a week or two and see other people at home and happy. I envy no one, but the contrast is almost unbearable." Tragically, T. J.'s longing to be with his family seemed to be overridden by his mental illness. Although his friend, D. T. Everett, borrowed money to buy him some clothes and a ticket to return him to his family, T. J. never came home again.

The symptoms of his physical and mental illness appeared to worsen during his wanderings in 1873. When he wrote Lurana from New Orleans in late March, he confessed, "I have reached a crisis, and what next? Perhaps the grave. Oh! I am weary, weary." A week later he mentioned a couple of ideas he had for making money and admitted that he had "started to Arizona, but I retraced my steps." Although in his third letter from New Orleans, he claimed, "My nervous system is much improved—no frenzies or states of oblivion," the letter itself reveals a confused and troubled mind. T. J. reached Atlanta on April 30, and for a while seemed in better spirits, though struggling physically. Still in Atlanta in late May, he told Lurana he would try to find a home for their family by Christmas. Yet in less than a month he told her he was going to cut loose from the past and to not "be surprised if I disappear." However, by the next month he was talking again about buying a farm so they could settle down together. Nevertheless, by the end of the letter he had changed his mind and decided to go back full-time into the ministry. By August, he had traveled to Brunswick on the Georgia coast, seventy miles north of Jacksonville, Florida. He told Lurana that he had been having dreams that were predicting his future.

T. J.'s erratic behavior caused Lurana much suffering. He had not been supporting her and the children financially. His drunkenness, arrests, and repeated visits to the Lunatic Asylum humiliated her. Though she had patiently stood by him, by the fall of 1873, he had abandoned his family for five years; nearly two years of which he had failed even to write her. As a result, for a time she seriously considered a legal separation. In the end, however, she decided against it. D. T. Everett told her, "I am glad you acted as you did. It was of the Lord and your wisest course. A legal separation I would never advise until a <u>scriptural cause</u> occurs. Do <u>right</u> and the God of righteousness will care for you." In T. J.'s next letter, he sent her the addresses where she could write for several hundred dollars that was due him for teaching school. He wanted her to have it.

Nonetheless, in that same letter T. J. tells how the authorities at Brunswick had arrested him and sent him back to the Asylum, and how after only two weeks, he escaped. He told Lurana how his insanity brought the attention of the authorities in city after city: "At Savannah the police called me that crazy man, but they treated me very kindly and did not arrest me. So for two weeks at Jacksonville they gave me a sofa to sleep on in the mayor's office, and I went where I pleased night and day." Despite this severe mental illness, T. J. managed to teach school near King's Ferry, Florida, between mid-November and late January, 1874. But not surprisingly, when he wrote Lurana from Colerain, Georgia, on January 26, he commented, "I have been sick. Also half-crazy." By February he was working as a night watchman at a sawmill, feeling cold and pain. Abandoning the mill, he bought two rafts of timber, but could not get teams of horses to haul them. He gave up and determined to head west and "see after my salt boilers." Since people commonly boiled sea water to make salt as a business in that day, it seems that this was yet another one of his schemes to make money.

T. J. typically fared better in the spring, and true to form, the spring of 1874 proved to be a better season for T. J. mentally. He observed, "My mind is restored, and I often feel happy." He had looked in vain throughout five counties for a teaching opportunity, but was preaching frequently. He determined to walk "all the way to Texas" to check on the possibility of a pension for his earlier military service there and to try to find a place to teach. It eventually turned out that he was not eligible for a pension. By late April his writing reflected a growing rationality and peace. By June he was preaching and teaching around Bainbridge, Georgia, and writing a commentary on the book of Revelation. Yet at times he found himself, "sad, lonely, and weak."

The autumn of 1874 found T. J. getting worse again. In early September he told Lurana, "I was taken sick suddenly and unable to fill my appointment in Thomasville. My brain has been greatly affected, so that I have been half-crazy." When he became ill like this, Christian families often took him into their homes and cared for him. He mentioned one such family: "When I have wandered about, desolate and heart-hungry, I always met with love and sympathy from Newton Thurmon and others here." T. J. must have deteriorated mentally after this point. He entered the Asylum in Milledgeville two months later on

November 5. His wanderings ended; he never left the Asylum again.

---

Despite all his physical and mental challenges between 1861 and 1875, T. J. Bowen never completely gave up trying to minister to others. That determination can only be appreciated in light of all the difficulties he was experiencing. During these years the recurring cycles of his physical illness were intensifying to the point where he was totally incapacitated for months at a time. Likewise, the cycles of his mental illness deepened to the place where he was confined to a mental institution for years at a time. Even when he was out of the institution, he appeared to be rarely, if ever, completely free of the symptoms of his mental illness. His resulting misuse of alcohol erected further barriers to his ministry. It brought widespread reproach upon him as a minister, especially in Georgia. His subsequent shame and humiliation tended to deepen his depression and caused him, at times, to give up trying to preach. His years of wandering the American South in dire poverty—unable to keep a steady job, depending often on the kindness of friends and acquaintances, and at times living like a tramp without proper clothing—further impeded his ability to find and seize opportunities to minister. However, in spite of these tremendous obstacles, T. J. did find ways to minister, beginning during the American Civil War.

Southern Baptists zealously supported the South in the Civil War. In 1861 the Georgia Baptist Convention resolved to "express the confident belief that, whatever the conflict the madness of Mr. Lincoln and his government may force upon us, the Baptists of Georgia will not be behind any class of our fellow citizens in maintaining the independence of the South by any sacrifice of treasure or blood." Part of that sacrifice was sending chaplains to minister to Confederate troops. To do so, Southern Baptists redirected almost all their domestic mission efforts toward support and supplies for these chaplains. Orr explained, "The Southern Baptists withdrew 150 missionaries from domestic mission work and employed as many as seventy-eight military missionaries to accompany the troops on long marches, to live along with them in the camps, to converse with them about their need of salvation, to distribute tracts and papers, and to conduct meetings for prayer and exhortation." By 1863, through their chaplains, Southern Baptists had "distributed... thousands of Testaments and millions of pages of religious reading matter in tracts and religious papers."

Though he was struggling with broken health after his return from Brazil, this war-charged atmosphere motivated Captain Bowen to volunteer to be one of those Confederate chaplains. In early May 1861 he was preaching to "large congregations" in Pensacola, Florida, as "an independent volunteer" who "came so far to the fight that almost everybody knew me." His historian son-in-law recorded, "After the Bowens reached home from Brazil, Mr. Bowen went to Montgomery, Alabama, and offered his services as chaplain of the Confederate Army. He wrote a letter to Mrs. Bowen from Montgomery, Alabama, that bears the postmark of the date that Virginia joined the Confederate States." That date was May 23, 1861. Less than a week later T. J. wrote Taylor:

> I have been out on horseback to the extreme parts of the county collecting money to pay for the tests &c of "the Green Rifles." The Bows are unanimous in wishing me to go with them as their chaplain. It is uncertain whether I can get an appointment; but my friends in Richmond might do me a favor by speaking to President Davis, who is now there. The case is simply this: I am going...whether I am appointed or not, but if not appointed I shall get no pay, and no remuneration of expenses.

However, after another bout of sickness, T. J. changed his mind. He told Taylor, "I have been presumptuous and self-willed, refusing to submit when my strength was gone. I had no business at Pensacola; no business to volunteer for the war in Virginia...I am ashamed of myself for acting so unreasonably." Still the pull of the war on T. J. continued. Relating the news of the death of a nephew at the battle of Manassas, he confessed, "My continual desire to be in this war almost alarms me. I forbid the feeling to arise, but it will return." Evidently, T. J. did not serve as an officially-appointed chaplain. In fact, T. J.'s obituary in *The Christian Index* stated, "During the late war, he served in Florida as a voluntary chaplain." That two weeks in Florida in May 1861 is the only documented period of his service as a chaplain.

---

Preaching and teaching is another way a broken T. J. Bowen attempted to minister during these years. But after his early years of insanity and drunkenness, it took years for him to gain confidence about returning to preaching. By late summer 1866, he had wandered to Ringgold, Georgia. He preached often that summer. The following year he admitted, "It is true that I preached repeatedly and with great pleasure last summer, but I am not sure that I did right." T. J. was concerned that his episodes of drunkenness may have disqualified him from the ministry. Though still struggling mentally, by October 1870 he had more confidence about preaching. He told Lurana that when asked, "I durst not refuse. If I must be condemned now or hereafter, I prefer it should be for doing all I can in God's service. And so I preach and grow clearer, stronger, and happier."

When in Texas in 1871, his friend, D. T. Everett, invited him to preach at the annual meeting of his association of churches. It must have been a remarkable sermon. Everett told Lurana:

> I clip from the Editorial Report in the *Texas Baptist Herald* what one of the first preachers in the state, Bro. Zealy, thought of Bro. Bowen's

sermon. Everybody said he went into too deep water for them. Bro. Zealy said to me privately that, listening to Bro. B.s thoughts and comments, he felt like a great mountain was falling upon him—for my own self, I couldn't have even <u>exhorted</u> afterwards and couldn't <u>get</u> this sermon out of my mind, sufficiently to enjoy any other at all.

After that sermon, T. J. found a number of opportunities to preach in Texas. Though fighting serious illness, in 1872 he preached widely in the central part of the state, as well as taught school. A. E. Vandivere confirmed to Lurana, "I saw Brother Bowen last week. I think his health has greatly improved...he is now teaching school near Cameron, Milam Co., and is boarding in a good family and is preaching some." D. T. Everett also corroborated T. J.'s Texas preaching opportunities that year, writing, "He preached twice for me." T. J. may have been asked to preach so often, in part, because there were relatively few Baptist preachers in Texas. Roy Fish observed that just a few years before 1858, "Texas was regarded as 'missionary ground' and as needy as any home or foreign mission field. There were many large towns with no Baptist preacher in them. San Antonio, a town of some 10,000 people, was without Baptist preaching. Many counties were completely destitute of Baptist preachers."

Returning to Georgia in the spring of 1873, T. J. continued his preaching and teaching. In early April he wrote, "I preach frequently, in poor destitute places." However, because of his reputation as an occasional drunkard in Georgia, he found it more of a struggle. He confessed to Lurana, "I refused to preach Sunday before last. But last Sunday I tried and gave satisfaction. Shall never refuse again if well enough to stand. Thank God I feel at peace with him, and am independent of any and all men who malignantly, carelessly, or even innocently misunderstand & misrepresent my case."

T. J. felt that in his brokenness, God used his preaching. He acknowledged, "I preach when urged, but I feel very unworthy. For some reason, my words which are poor and sad like myself, have a powerful effect, & it is said to have caused strong men to weep and pray, who were never known to feel before. Then, I am willing to bear my burden & reproach, and to preach on." He affirmed this sentiment to Bro. Gaulden, "Hence, I have preached about 7 times of late, and must go to preach at Concord next Sunday. I am also encouraged by the fact that the Lord blesses my labors, beyond a doubt. Although I work in sadness, I shall do all I can and leave the event to God." Thus, the testimony of the historical documents is remarkable. Despite overwhelming physical and mental illness, as well as pervasive reproach for his failings, T. J. Bowen continued to minister with surprising effectiveness during these difficult years.

---

One final letter came from T. J. to Lurana, written thirty-seven days before his death. Lurana had written to ask what information he wanted H. A. Tupper to write about him. T. J. gave her two brief lines, then commented, "To say much about me in my present state, alone, broken-hearted, diseased, and in want, would be worse than cruel mockery." He said he was "gloomy, half-frenzied, full of pains, sleepless." His suffering would not last much longer. His official medical report contained this stark notation: "Died, November 24, 1875, Maniacal Exhaustion." Shortly after, the Asylum buried his body in its cemetery in an unmarked grave.

Although there is no historical record that Lurana had seen T. J. during the last eight years of his life, she grieved all the more because she was not with him at his death. Writing the FMB Corresponding Secretary, she lamented:

> Oh, Brother Tupper, this blow has fallen hard upon my heart! To think, I was spared to come from Africa to soothe the dying pillows of both my parents, and was denied the privilege of attending my dear, suffering, heart-broken husband in his last moments! But all is right with him now. I am left to toil on, and battle with life awhile longer. Pray for me, that I may have grace and strength for every duty, until the Lord shall call me to join the loved ones in the "Beautiful City."

Lurana lived another thirty-three years, and those who knew her testified that she did indeed continue to serve others with grace and strength.

Very few official bodies or periodicals gave notice of T. J.'s death. *The Christian Index* provided a short obituary, remarking in part, "The Rev. T. J. Bowen died recently in Milledgeville. He was, at one time, a prominent minister of our denomination, and a missionary to Africa. He was in his sixty-second year." It took two years for the Bowen Association to honor him with this short statement:

> Whereas our Allwise Father in Heaven has called away from this earth our beloved missionary, T. J. Bowen, therefore, RESOLVED: That in the long, sad affliction and death of our brother, we feel that God has stricken not only us, but all who loved the missionary cause. RESOLVED: That we are thankful that our Association was honored at its formation with the name of the deceased, and we deem this providential name as a call to us to be true to the Foreign Mission cause which the lamented Mr. Bowen so conspicuously represented.

From that point forward, Southern Baptists, and, consequently, the world demonstrated what seemed to be a purposeful hush about T. J. Bowen. Thus, his widespread rejection continued after his death.

It appears that Southern Baptists overlooked T. J. for two reasons—his insanity and, more importantly, his drunkenness. His insanity embarrassed them. They did not want to celebrate the life of a man who spent the last fourteen years of his life in and out of a mental institution. They did not want to teach their children to honor a man who spent years roaming the country like a tramp, separated from his wife. However, if T. J.'s insanity mortified Southern Baptists, his drunkenness horrified them. The Bible they revered taught that drunkenness was a serious sin, serious enough to bring exclusion from church membership. That T. J. was a minister and a missionary made this sin all the more shameful.

Two lines of evidence support those conclusions. First, the knowledge of T. J.'s insanity and drunkenness had spread by word of mouth and private letter throughout the Southern Baptist Convention (SBC). His church in Greensboro, which Lurana attended, knew the situation intimately. Her brother-in-law, Thomas Stocks, had influence throughout the SBC and communicated with leaders about T. J.'s condition. For example, the FMB Minutes of January 6, 1862, note, "A letter was received...from Judge Thomas Stocks of Georgia with reference to the health of Brother Bowen." From those leaders and others, T. J.'s stays in the Asylum became common knowledge. In fact, when a man with T. J's same last name died at the Asylum, T. J. had to write to a friend, "Permit me to inform the brethren of Southwest Georgia that I did not die at Midway last September, as some of them were informed at that late meeting of the Bowen Association." It came to a point where people took T. J.'s mental illness as an established fact. He commented, "The fact is people take it for granted that I am too crazy to engage in anything." Of course, the public arrests and sometimes imprisonment in several cities in Georgia and Florida due to his "craziness" contributed to the widespread knowledge of his condition.

Reports of his drunkenness also spread quickly. Thomas Stocks received a letter from a Mr. Holman in Pensacola claiming that T. J. had been drunk on his visit there in May 1861 when he came to preach to the Confederate troops. This and other reports led Lurana's family and many in Greensboro to find fault with him. Lurana must have confided their feelings to D. T. Everett. In response, Everett replied, "I had no idea of the feeling at home towards Bro. B. or I would have by no means got him to go back." Stories of his drunkenness kept coming to Lurana. In November 1873 she wrote him, "[V]isiting brethren from that part of the state to the Georgia Association in Oct. brought some sad accounts of you. I was grieved and mortified to hear of your condition." T. J. felt the sting of many critics. He bemoaned, "You know that I have met harsh treatment and cold contemptuous neglect from some who ought to have been my friends in the day of my great calamity."

As a result of their embarrassment about T. J.'s later years, Southern Baptist writers deliberately smoothed over or covered up the facts about his insanity and drunkenness. His son-in-law, T. B. Rice compiled a mistake-filled statement about T. J.'s later years that appeared to cover up his insanity. In his writing about him, H. A. Tupper simply said, "After Mr. Bowen's return from Brazil...such was his nervous state, that at times he lost all self-control. This part of his history is too painful to recall." This cover-up continued for nearly a century. As late as 1953, Nigerian missionary I. N. Patterson, in a private letter to the editor of *The Commission* about the article he had submitted on T. J, confessed:

> Now, as to the closing part of the article, I am entirely willing to accept your abbreviated version, if you, Dr. Means, and Dr. Sadler think it better to draw a veil over the tragedy of Bowen's later years. This veil has been so well drawn that I, though a fairly close student of his life and work, had never heard of it nor suspected it till during this last leave... Apparently, this was well known to an earlier generation... To me, the above knowledge emphasizes the extent to which Bowen gave himself to Africa.

Because Southern Baptists neglected to publish much of anything about T. J. Bowen's life, secular historians did the same. As a result, for over a century he was overlooked. It wasn't until the Bowen Papers were compiled in 1960 that historians had access to the fuller picture of his life. Even that access was very limited with only a handful of copies of the Bowen Papers available and some of them are difficult to read. Thus, the man who was once hailed as his denomination's greatest missionary and as a national hero was forgotten.

"If I should only live long enough to plant the Redeemer's standard on those bulwarks of heathenism as an ensign for others I trust that my labor would not be in vain."
—T. J. Bowen

"I sent you to reap that for which you have not labored; others have labored and you have entered into their labor."—John 4:38

## CHAPTER 15

# Leaving a Legacy

T he true worth of a person's lifework often only becomes evident years after they are gone. The seeds which T. J. Bowen sacrificed so much to plant produced a harvest so bountiful that it would have surprised even a man with big dreams like him. First, he inspired others to colonize Africa. In 1859 two African-Americans, Martin R. Delany and Robert Campbell, headed an expedition to explore the Niger Valley. Sent out by a "Convention of Colored Persons," they were commissioned to "select a location for the establishment of an Industrial Colony."

A circular published in England about this undertaking stated, '[S]uch an enterprise is of importance in the evangelization and civilization of Africa, and in affording an asylum in which the oppressed descendants of that country may find the means of developing their mental and moral facilities unimpeded by unjust restrictions." In the exploring party's Official Report, Delany noted, "During this time (the spring of 1858), 'Bowen's Central Africa' was published, giving an interesting and intelligent account of that extensive portion of Africa known on the large missionary map of that country as Yoruba." As a result, he said he was "more encouraged to carry out my scheme at this juncture." Delany and Campbell expressed sympathy with the missionary cause in Yoruba, staying for a time in the Baptist mission house in Abeokuta at the hospitality of T. J.'s associates.

Evidently, they had adopted T. J.'s colonization philosophy wholeheartedly. Delany observed, "Christianity certainly is the most advanced civilization that man every attained to, and wherever propagated in its purity, to be effective, law and government must be brought into harmony with it." Delany and Campbell were able to secure a treaty in December 1859 with the people of Abeokuta which granted "the right and privilege of settling in common with the Egba people." However, likely due to the American Civil War and subsequent emancipation of slaves there, the colony never materialized. It seems that at least one other colonization plan was inspired by T. J. After Delany and Campbell had left for Africa, T. J. wrote to Poindexter, "I have just received an offer to conduct a colony to the banks of the Niger. Would that I could go! But I can—I dare not."

Eventually, the British did colonize Nigeria. In 1866, Sir George Goldie organized the Royal Niger Company which launched English rule in the Niger area and developed Nigeria into an orderly and prosperous British colony, established in 1900 as the Protectorate of South Nigeria. With the founding of the colony and the stabilization of the country, most of T. J.'s dreams for commerce, civilization, and Christianity came to fulfillment. In 1914 the trans-country railroad he had envisioned was completed and it helped to develop the country immensely. In 1928, missionary Louis Duvall noted that along that railroad were "many Baptist churches." As T. J. suspected, the Niger River and some of its tributaries proved navigable, opening up significant commercial trade. Just as he predicted, palm nut oil became the primary export of the region. In addition, as he prayed, such commerce opened up the whole region for missionary expansion. Eighty years after T. J. left Africa, FMB missionary to Nigeria C. Sylvester Green remarked about this commercial expansion, "[T]hese natural assets may also be utilized for taking the Christian message to those isolated sections as soon as reserves are available to expand the work."

Such missionary expansion engulfed the cities which T. J. Bowen had toiled so hard to reach. Although the station that he established in Ijaye in 1853 was destroyed in 1862 by intertribal war, the first three African Baptist pastors in Nigeria came from among the boys who were evacuated from Ijaye and completed their education in

Abeokuta. Later, the Ijaye station was reestablished. The work T. J. founded in Ogbomosho has since flourished. Orville Taylor comments, "[T]oday Ogbomosho is a great Baptist center with a theological seminary, a hospital, a leprosy and public health center, a children's home, and dozens of churches." The city of Igboho in the Saki district became T. J.'s first target. The 1925 Annual Report of the FMB noted that more than seventy years after his attempt, a church had been formed there and "a promising work is springing up." The attempt T. J. made to establish Baptist work in Ilorin also came to fruition more than seventy years later, when Baptist laymen from Ogbomosho planted a church there. In 1947, FMB missionaries moved into the northern region of Nigeria that T. J. had so longed to reach. His vision of reaching the Muslims of Central Africa also began to be realized. Travis Collins observed, "The Baptist Mission has expanded even beyond Bowen's dreams. Our earliest missionary would even be excited to hear many Baptist missionaries speaking Fulfulde (Fulani), for he himself wanted to learn that language and minister to the Fulbe people."

The small seeds T. J. planted have produced a significant harvest. The home web page of the Nigerian Baptist Convention states: "The Nigerian Baptist Convention, which Thomas Jefferson Bowen started in 1850, has grown into over 10,000 churches with about 3,000,000 baptized members and up to 6.5 million non-baptized members spread across the nation." Another place on the same web page lists the current number of member churches in July 2020 as 18,135. Those approximately ten million participants in Nigerian Baptist Convention churches account for ninety-seven percent of all Baptists in Nigeria. Moreover, as T. J. envisioned, Nigerian Baptists have taken the gospel and established churches in other countries. In 1918, Baptist Yoruba traders moved to Benin, settled in seven towns and villages, and established churches in each. At their request, the first FMB missionaries were brought to Benin from the work in Nigeria. Other Yoruba traders established the Baptist work in Ghana in 1947, Togo in 1964, and Cote D'Ivoire in 1966. Thus, T. J. correctly anticipated that commerce would carry the gospel from Yoruba to other lands. The website of the Nigerian Baptist Convention lists mission work in seven additional nations: Burkina Faso, Chad, Sierra Leone, Mali, Mozambique, Niger, and South Sudan. It also notes missionary influence in the United States and the United Kingdom. T. J. Bowen envisioned that Christianity would spread from Central Africa like "a river of light and life upon the African continent." In large measure, that vision has been fulfilled.

T. J. and Lurana's dream of Baptist Christian education in Nigeria has also been realized. Travis Collins commented, "Mrs. Lurana Bowen would almost certainly be pleased with the descendants of her Sunday School and Day School classes—the Adult Education Department of the Nigerian Baptist Convention, the Convention's Sunday School and Church Training ministries, and institutions of learning like Baptist High School, Jos." T. J. had a goal to plant a Baptist High School in Awyaw (Oyeo). That goal has been achieved. In fact, thousands of Baptist primary and secondary schools exist in Nigeria today. A Nigerian Baptist educational institution notes, "[B]y 1960, there was a Baptist school almost everywhere that was found a Baptist congregation."

Although largely forgotten in America, Baptists in Nigeria revere T. J. Bowen and have demonstrated that in several ways. Not far from the site of his original mission, a school bears the name, "Bowen Memorial Baptist Secondary Modern School." Near the main entrance of the school a memorial called "Bowen's Tomb" was erected by the Sunday School Department of the Nigerian Baptist Convention to honor his work.

J. T. Okedara and S. Ademola Ajayi claim, "In the Nigerian Baptist Convention circle, Bowen has become a household name among the young and old...His name is immortalized in numerous ways. At the Baptist Boy's High School (BBHS) Abeokuta, a students' hostel is christened Bowen House, while an association in the Oyo West Baptist Conference is named Bowen Association." Nigerian Baptists bestowed on T. J. their highest honor by naming their first university after him. Established in 2002, Bowen University is the first and only Baptist university in Africa. In addition, a 400-bed hospital was connected with the University in 2007 and re-named Bowen University Teaching Hospital.

T. J.'s missionary strategies have also produced a significant legacy. Evidently, the FMB adopted his emphasis on self-support in Africa. In 1861, their *Home and Foreign Journal* stated that the matter of self-support had been "frequently urged upon the attention of our missionaries there" since 1854. David Carson Davis added, "The guide-lines he suggested for terms of service, salaries, medical examinations, and outfits for missionaries were followed for many years by the Foreign Mission Board." Regarding terms of service, Peter Gilliland clarified, "Bowen's sug-gestions about sending missionaries home every four years became FMB policy for West African missionaries since that time." Isaac Ayranrinola noted that T. J.'s book, *Central Africa,* "clearly presents his vision of education as a network of schools established in strategic centers as training schools for pastors, teachers, and industrial workers. On completion of their training, Bowen expected that these workers would dramatically impact the evan-gelization of Nigeria." Southern Baptists subsequently implemented T. J.'s plan for such training schools in Nigeria. For example, by 1940 they had established the MacLean Training College and Industrial Institute. T. J.'s legacy also includes missionary fundraising strategies. Both the Southern Baptist Convention and the Nigerian Baptist Convention have adopted a plan similar to T. J.'s for an annual foreign missions offering. In addition, both conventions have implemented an arrangement similar to his for churches to set aside a certain percentage of their budgets to be sent to the convention for distribution to various missions causes.

In an indirect way, T. J. also left a significant legacy on another continent in the nation of Brazil. In 1847 when he was sixteen years old, Richard Ratcliff heard Florida Baptist Associational Missionary T. J. Bowen preach in Walton County, Florida, near Pensacola. As a result, he committed his life to Christ and was baptized. Alverson De Souza noted that Ratcliff wanted "to follow in the same steps as Bowen." Thus, while he was a student at Mount Lebanon University in Louisiana, Ratcliff wrote the FMB requesting to be appointed to the Central African Mission. The FMB Minutes of July 10, 1860, read, "Brother Richard Ratcliff of Louisiana was present in accordance with the request of the Board and having been examined was accepted as a missionary to Central Africa."

However, when the Civil War decimated the FMB's treasury and they were not able to send him to Africa, Ratcliff resigned to serve as a pastor in Louisiana. At the end of the war, a group of Confederate supporters, including Ratcliff, immigrated to Brazil. On September 10, 1871, in the district of Santa Barbara, some of them formed the First North American Baptist Missionary Church of Brazil and called Ratcliff as their pastor. The church consisted entirely of transplanted Americans, but desired to be a catalyst to reach Brazilians. For years they pleaded with the FMB to send missionaries to Brazil, and to use their church as a base of operations. During this time, Ratcliff indicated that he was familiar with T. J.'s work in Brazil. Writing the FMB, he said, "If the Board wish, I can give some of the causes why Brother T. J. Bowen in 1860 did not recommend Brazil as a favorable mission field."

After his wife's death, Ratcliff returned to the States and spoke at the Southern Baptist Convention in Atlanta in 1879. A. R. Crabtree recounted, "He spoke with such enthusiasm in favor of sending missionaries to Brazil that the Convention voted to adopt the Santa Barbara Church, but with no obligation of financial support." The next year, a church that broke away from the Santa Barbara Church, the Station Baptist Church, baptized the first Brazilian—former Roman Catholic priest, Antonio Teixeira de Albuquerque. Because of its connection with the church, when the FMB dispatched missionary William Buck Bagby and his wife to Brazil in 1881, they sent them to Santa Barbara. Within a month after his arrival, Bagby became the acting pastor of the church, reunited it with the Station Church, and helped bring spiritual renewal to the work. Shortly after, Bagby and a missionary associate recruited de Albuquerque, and launched the first Baptist Church in Brazil for Brazilians.

From that point on, Southern Baptist missionary work in Brazil blossomed. Today the Brazilian Baptist Convention has some 1.8 million members in more than 8,000 congregations. It supports some 600 missionaries in fifty-eight countries of the world. Although T. J.'s initial attempt in Brazil might be looked upon by some as a failure, his inspiration and influence, especially upon Richard Ratcliff, was instrumental in establishing one of Southern Baptists' greatest missionary successes.

Thus, while experiencing immeasurable suffering from physical and mental illness, T. J. Bowen courageously pioneered Southern Baptist mission work in dangerous and difficult places on two continents. Between 1845 and 1863 the FMB had pioneered work in only four countries—China, Liberia, Yoruba, and Brazil. Thus by 1860 T. J. had pioneered the work in half of them. Today, the legacy of that combined work includes nearly eleven million believers congregating in 21,000 churches and missions which support hundreds of missionaries in scores of nations. In addition, because Yoruban believers began Baptist work in other West Africans nations, there are over 1,800 related churches in Ghana, more than 400 churches in Togo, some 300 churches in Benin, and 100 churches in Cote d'Ivoire that directly sprang from the work T. J. Bowen established. Since this stunning legacy and T. J.'s heroic achievements have been largely over-looked for over 150 years, it is time to once again celebrate them and be inspired by them.

## Chronology of T. J. Bowen's Life

| | |
|---|---|
| January 2, 1814 | He was born. |
| Spring 1836 | He began fighting in the Creek Indian War. |
| February 14, 1837 | He enlisted in the Texas Army. |
| November 1839 | He returned to Georgia. |
| October 1840 | He converted to Christianity. |
| September 1841 | He began preaching. |
| Fall 1842 | He was ordained and began missionary work in Alabama, Georgia, and Florida. |
| October 1845 | He was employed as a missionary by the Florida Baptist Association. |

| | |
|---|---|
| 1847 | He served as the pastor of the Hebron Baptist Church. |
| 1848 | He served as the pastor of Hebron, Liberty, Providence, and Lake Jackson churches in the West Florida Baptist Association. |
| February 22, 1849 | He was appointed as a missionary by the Southern Baptist Foreign Mission Board, the first resident of Florida to be appointed. |
| December 17, 1849 | He sailed from Providence, Rhode Island, to Africa. |
| February 8, 1850 | He arrived in Monrovia, Liberia. |
| April 13, 1850 | His missionary associate, Hervey Goodale, died. |
| August 4, 1850 | He arrived alone at Badagry on the African coast. |
| August 15, 1850 | He set out as the only white man on a 65-mile journey into the interior. |
| August 19, 1850 | He arrived at Abeokuta. |
| September 9, 1850 | He set out on a 65-mile journey to Iketu, but had to return to Abeokuta. |
| March 3, 1851 | The army of Dahomey attacked Abeokuta. |

| | |
|---|---|
| April 28, 1851 | He set out again for Iketu, stayed one month, then returned to Abeokuta. |
| October 11, 1851 | He received his first letters from America. |
| January 5, 1852 | He helped develop and witnessed a treaty between the British government and the Egba of Abeokuta. |
| February 1, 1852 | He arrived in Biolorunpellu in the mountains and stayed six weeks. |
| May 1852 | He arrived in Ijaye. |
| August 8, 1852 | He sailed for America by way of London. |
| January 1853 | He arrived in New York. |
| May 31, 1853 | He married Lurana Davis in Greensboro, Georgia. |
| June 1853 | He preached at the Southern Baptist Convention in Baltimore. |
| July 6, 1853 | He sailed with his wife and companions from Boston to Africa. |
| August 28, 1853 | They arrived in Lagos. |
| October 31, 1853 | The Bowens traveled to Ijaye to begin the first station of the Central African Mission. |
| December 6, 1853 | His associate, J. H. Lacy, and his wife left Africa. |

| | |
|---|---|
| January 1854 | The wife of his associate, J. L. Dennard, died. |
| January 22, 1854 | Lurana Bowen began the first Baptist school and Sunday School in what would become Nigeria. |
| February 25, 1854 | Lurana Bowen gave birth to Mary Yoruba Bowen. |
| May 28, 1854 | Mary Yoruba Bowen died. |
| June 17, 1854 | His associate, J. L. Dennard, died. |
| July 23, 1854 | He baptized his first African convert, Tella. |
| September 29, 1854 | His associate, William H. Clarke, arrived in Ijaye. |
| April 11, 1855 | He set out on an investigative trip to Ogbomosho and Illorin. |
| September 20, 1855 | The Bowens moved to Ogbomosho to establish a new station. |
| February 27, 1856 | The Bowens received word that three new missionaries had arrived in Ijaye—Rev. and Mrs. A. D. Phillips and John Beaumont. |
| March 14, 1856 | The wife of A. D. Phillips died. |
| April 13, 1856 | The Bowens left Ogbomosho to return to the States. |
| July 15, 1856 | The Bowens arrived in New York. |

| | |
|---|---|
| Late 1856 | The Bowen Baptist Association in Southwest Georgia formed and honored Bowen by taking his name. |
| February 1857 | His *Central Africa* was published. |
| February 1857 | He preached at the Capitol in Washington, D. C. |
| February 1857 | He testified before Congress. |
| 1858 | His *Grammar and Dictionary of the Yoruba Language* was published. |
| April 10, 1858 | He accepted the pastorate of Greensboro Baptist Church in Georgia. |
| May 12, 1858 | Lurana gave birth to Lurana Bowen whom they called "Lulu." |
| 1858 | He accepted the pastorate of Beech Island Baptist Church in South Carolina. |
| 1858 | He received an honorary master's degree from Mercer University. |
| November 9, 1859 | He was appointed as a Southern Baptist missionary to Brazil. |
| March 30, 1860 | The Bowens sailed from Richmond, Virginia, to Brazil. |
| May 12, 1860 | The Bowens arrived in Rio de Janeiro. |
| February 1861 | The Bowens left Brazil to return to the States. |

| April 1861 | The Bowens arrived in the States. |
| May 1861 | He served briefly as a Confederate chaplain in Florida. |
| November 11, 1861 | He was admitted to the Lunatic Asylum of the State of Georgia. |
| July 2, 1862 | He was admitted a second time to the Asylum. |
| February 1863 | He was admitted a third time to the Asylum. |
| January 1864 | He moved to a farm with his family near Greensboro, Georgia. |
| June 8, 1866 | Lurana gave birth to Maymie Gant Bowen. |
| 1866-1867 | He spent time in Ringgold, Georgia. |
| February 23, 1868 | He was admitted a fourth time to the Asylum. |
| October-November 1868 | He was home with his family in Greensboro. |
| February 1869 | He was arrested in Atlanta and admitted a fifth time to the Asylum. |
| April 4, 1869 | He escaped from the Asylum and began wandering in Florida. |
| Spring 1871-spring 1873 | He wandered around Texas. |
| Spring 1873 | He returned to Georgia to wander there and in Florida. |

| | |
|---|---|
| Fall 1873 | He was admitted a sixth time to the Asylum. |
| November 5, 1874 | He was admitted a seventh time to the Asylum. |
| November 24, 1875 | He died at the Asylum in Milledgeville, Georgia. |

# Author's Note

*U* *nthinkable: The Triumph and Endurance of a Forgotten American Hero* is an adaptation of my 2010 Ph.D. dissertation, "An Examination of the Life and Work of Forgotten Missionary Pioneer T. J. Bowen." To the material involved in that work, I have added a significant amount of additional research, detail, and story development in this volume. *Unthinkable* is primarily based on 1,091 primary sources discovered in several years of research.

It is astounding to realize that T. J. Bowen was one of the most famous people in nineteenth-century America and yet he is basically unknown today. I wrote this book to tell his remarkable story that generations to come might be challenged and inspired by it.

# Notes

Abbreviation: BP        Bowen Papers

The first number indicates the section of the Bowen Papers.

The second number indicates the page number of the Bowen Papers.

## Preface

1 Abeokuta background: T. J. Bowen, *Central Africa: Adventures and Missionary Labors in Several Countries in the Interior of Africa, from 1849 to 1856,* (Charleston: Southern Baptist Publication Society, 1857), 108-9, 120-1; Fragment of Diary of T. J. Bowen found in his notebook, Bowen Papers, 2:77 (The Bowen Papers consist of a 614-page collection of personal and official correspondence, diaries, journal articles, and other documents related to T. J. and Lurana Bowen); J. E. Ade Ajayi, *Christian Missions in Nigeria 1841-1891: The Making of a New Elite, Ibadan History Series* (ed. by K. O. Dike; London: Longmans, 1965), *19.*

2 Army of Dahomey: Bowen, *Central Africa*, 115-119; Mike Dash, "Dahomey's Women Warriors," Smithsonian. com, Sept. 23, 2011.

3 Amazons: Dash, "Dahomey's Women Warriors"; A. Moore, "Ten Fearless Female Warriors throughout History," AtlantaStar.com, Oct. 29, 2013; Ajayi Kolawole Ajisafe, *History of Abeokuta,* (Abeokuta, Nigeria: M. A. Ola, Fola Bookshops, 1964), 97-98; Wikipedia.org, "Gbalefa Peninsula."

4 The desperation of the Abeokutans:*"African Proverbial Philosophy," Putnam's Monthly,* Vol. 4, (October, 1854): 362-371; Bowen, *Central Africa,* 110, 115-116, 120.

5 Bowen's role: Bowen, *Central Africa,* 120.

6. Bowen as a hero: *The Christian Index* (September 16, 1857): 145, Bowen Papers, 1:45; R. L. Robinson, *History of the Georgia Baptist Association,* n.p., 1928; James B. Hardwicke, "An Examination of the Life and Work of Forgotten Missionary Pioneer T. J. Bowen," (PhD diss., Southeastern Baptist Theological Seminary, 2010), 12, 20.

## Chapter 1—Charging Forward

1 Frontier Georgia: Cecil Roberson, Bowen or an Evidence of Grace, International Mission Board Archives, 1969, 2. This is an unpublished book. Samuel Dale would later fight in Texas with Davy Crockett, Sam Houston, and T. J. Bowen.; Thaddeus Brockett Rice, *History of Greene County Georgia, 1786-1886,* ed. Carolyn White Williams; (Macon, Ga.: J. W. Burke, 1961), 178-9, xvii.

2 Life in early Jackson County: Edgar H. Burks, *Planting the Redeemer's Standard: A Life of Thomas J. Bowen, First Baptist Missionary to Nigeria* (Columbus, Ga.: Brentwood Christian, 1994), 9; T. J. Bowen to James Taylor, October 1, 1861, BP 5: 548; George Gilman Smith, *The Story of Georgia and the Georgia People, 1732 to 1860* (Macon, Ga.: George G. Smith, 1900), Kindle Loc. 3904, 3929; Rebecca Latimer Felton, *Country Life in Georgia in the Days of My Youth* (Laconia Publishers, 1919; CreateSpace Independent Publishing Platform, 2016), 30-4, 46-7.

3 Bowen's family: T. J. Bowen to James Taylor, January 25, 1860, BP 5: 501; John F. Bowen to T. J. Bowen, October 6, 1859, BP 3: 154; Extracts from a letter by T. B. Rice to "Otis," April 12, 1943, BP: 1: 32. Rice states that many of those who practiced medicine in those days did not have medical degrees, but referenced popular medical books such as *Dr. Gunn's Practice of Medicine.*

3 Bowen's struggles for direction: T. J. Bowen to James Taylor, July 12, 1858, BP 5: 468; H. A. Tupper, *The Foreign Missions of the Southern Baptist Convention* (Richmond: Foreign Mission Board, 1880), 373-4.

4 Fighting Indians: George B. Taylor, *Life and Times of James B. Taylor* (Philadelphia: The Bible and Publication Society, 1872), 166; I. N. Patterson, "Thomas Jefferson Bowen: Heroic Pioneer," Bowen Correspondence Box 9. Hereafter, items labeled as "Bowen Correspondence Box 9" are from Bowen's

Missionary Correspondence file at the Southern Baptist Historical Library and Archives in Nashville.; Tupper, *Foreign Missions,* 374; Record of Bowen's election as captain of volunteer army, 1836, BP 1: 29-30.

5 Southern sympathy for Texas: Gorton Carruth, *What Happened When: A Chronology of Life and Events across America* (New York: Signet, 1989), *256;* Claude Elliot, "Georgia and the Texas Revolution," *Georgia Historical Quarterly* 28, no. 4 (December 1944): 4, 7-8; 11, 17-18.

6 Bowen as a Texas Ranger: Joseph Milton Nance, *After San Jacinto: The Texas-Mexican Frontier, 1836-1841* (Austin: University of Texas Press, 1963), 33; Thomas Lloyd Miller, *Bounty and Donation Land Grant of Texas, 1835-1888* (Austin: University of Texas Press, 1967), 120; Tupper, *Foreign Missions,* 374; T. J. Bowen to Lurana Bowen, March 22, 1871, BP 3: 174.

7 Bowen and Comanches: Orville W. Taylor, "Thomas J. Bowen: A Man for All Seasons," *Viewpoints: Georgia Baptist History 8* (1982): 52. Only two poems were actually about the Comanches.; Miller, *Bounty and Donation Land Grants,* 120; Copy of the Texas Land Grant to Bowen and transfer to Tho. T. Gosley, 1838, BP 1: 32.

### Chapter 2—Surrendering Everything

1 Bowen's conversion: Tupper, *Foreign Missions,* 374-75; T. J. Bowen to James Taylor, May 16, 1851, BP 5: 300.

2 Bowen as itinerant minister: Bowen to Lippincott and Co., November 21, 1868, BP 3: 167; J. Edwin Orr, *The Event of the Century: The 1857-1858 Awakening* (Wheaton, Ill.: International Awakening, 1989), 4-5; Extracts from a paper by T. B. Rice containing extracts from Mrs. Bowen's diary, BP 1: 70; Taylor, "A Man for All Seasons," 52; Minutes of the Georgia Baptist Convention, Macon, May 16, 18-19, 1846, microfilm; Minutes of the Georgia Baptist Convention, Savannah, May 15-17, 1847, microfilm; Minutes of the Georgia Baptist Convention, Griffin, May 1-6, 8, 1848, microfilm; Elba Wilson Carswell, *Holmes Valley: A West Florida Cradle of Christianity* (Bonifay, Fla.: Central, 1969), 71-2; Minutes of First Baptist Church of Valdosta, Georgia, November 1847 and December 1847.

3 Financial support: Gordon Crawford Reeves, "A History of Florida Baptists" (MA thesis, John B. Stetson University, 1938), 3; W. T. Cash, "Social Life in Florida in 1845," foreword to *Florida Becomes a State,* ed. by Dorothy Dodd (Tallahassee: Florida Centennial Commission, 1945), 8; Bowen's later letters reveal this pattern; Rice, *History of Greene County,* 178-9.

4 Florida missionary work: Roy Fish, *When Heaven Touched Earth: The Awakening of 1858 and Its Effects on Baptists,* 1996, 253, 255, 259; Cash, "Social Life in Florida in 1845," 5; Minutes of Florida Baptist Association of Florida, Madison County, October 18-21, 1845, microfilm; Minutes of the Florida Baptist Association, Montecello, October 10-13, 1846,

microfilm; Minutes of the Florida Baptist Association, Indian Springs Church, October 9-11, 1847, microfilm; Circular letters generally consisted of a doctrinal study which was published with the annual minutes and sent to the churches.; Minutes of the Florida Baptist Association of Florida, Lowndes County, Georgia, October 7-9, 1848, microfilm; Minutes of the West Florida Baptist Association of Florida, Bethlehem Church, Jackson County, commencing October 27, 1849, microfilm.

5 Frontier church life: Edward Earl Joiner, *A History of Florida Baptists* (Jacksonville, Fla.: Convention, 1972), 28-9; Cash, "Social Life in Florida in 1845," in *Florida Becomes a State,* 21-22; Carswell, *Holmes Valley,* 70-77.

6 Renaissance man: Hardwicke, "An Examination," 12-13.

### Chapter 3—Risking Everything

1 Danger of West Africa: Philip D. Curtin, *The Image of Africa: British Ideas and Action, 1780-1850,* vol. 1, (Madison, Wis.: University of Wisconsin Press, 1964), 177; J. Du Plessis, *The Evangelization of Pagan Africa: A History of Christian Missions to the Pagan Tribes of Central Africa* (Cape Town: J. C. Juta, 1929), 134-5.

2 Creation of the Southern Baptist Convention: William R. Estep, *Whole Gospel Whole World: The Foreign Mission Board of the Southern Baptist Convention 1845-1995* (Nashville: Broadman & Holman, 1994),

76; Minutes of Florida Baptist Association of Florida, Madison Co., October 18-21, 1845, microfilm, 2.

3 Creation of the Foreign Mission Board: Estep, *Whole World,* 58, 61-62, 64; At the Board's first meeting on May 20, 1845, they "styled" themselves as "The Board of Foreign Missions of the Southern Baptist Convention." See FMB Minutes, May 20, 1845, accession no. 437. (The original is located at the Archives, International Mission Board (IMB) of the Southern Baptist Convention (SBC), Solomon Database, available online at http:archives.imb.org. Hereafter, all minutes, periodicals, or annual reports of the SBC, unless otherwise noted, are from the IMB Archives' online database, 283 of which relate to the life and work of T. J. Bowen.) However, the shortened designation, "Foreign Mission Board," appeared in SBC publications within three years and became commonly accepted. To avoid confusion, this work uses the term "Foreign Mission Board" throughout its early history, including the period of Bowen's relationship with the Board.

4 First correspondence with the FMB: Bowen's first letter to James Taylor has been lost. Taylor's reply provides the only record of its existence; James Taylor to T. J. Bowen, October 4, 1848, FMB Copy Books. (Almost every letter that the early corresponding secretaries wrote regarding Foreign Mission Board work was copied by hand in the various volumes of its Copy Books which were arranged by date. The author has

190 transcribed documents of every legible letter that relates to the life and work of T. J. Bowen. The originals are located in the Archives of the International Mission Board in Richmond, Virginia.); T. J. Bowen, "Central Africa," *Southern Baptist Missionary Journal* 3, no. 6 (November 1848): 126-8. The IMB's Solomon database does not contain this issue. An article written by Bowen the next June reveals that he was well-acquainted with the writings of other West African explorers such as Mungo Park and the Landers. See T. J. Bowen, "Central Africa," *Southern Baptist Missionary Journal* 4, no. 1 (June 1849): 14, accession no. 489.

5 Earlier missionaries: Isaac DurosinJesu Ayranrinola, "The Mission Program of the Nigerian Baptist Convention: Analysis and Recommendations 1850-1997" DMiss diss., Southern Baptist Theological Seminary, 1999), 17-21; "The Present Aspect of the Missionary Field," *Southern Baptist Missionary Journal* 2, no. 8 (January 1848): 185-7, accession no. 462; "Third Annual Meeting of the Board of Foreign Missions," *Southern Baptist Missionary Journal* 3, no. 1 (June 1848): 4, accession no. 488; Travis Collins, *The Baptist Mission of Nigeria 1850-1993: A History of the Southern Baptist Convention Missionary Work in Nigeria* (Ibadan, Nigeria: Y-Books, 1993), 2-3.

6 Bowen willing to die: Annual Report of FMB to the SBC, Nashville, May 2, 1849, accession no. 2617; T. J. Bowen to James Taylor, October 23, 1848, BP 5: 264;

T. J. Bowen to James Taylor, December 28, 1848, BP 5: 265.

7 Bowen appointed: FMB Minutes, February 22, 1849, accession no. 519; Annual Report of FMB to SBC, Nashville, May 2, .

8 Fund raising: "Appointments," *The Christian Index* (April 19, 1849): 127, BP 1: 36; James Taylor to T. J. Bowen, April 2, 1849, FMB Copy Books; "Contributions of Colored People," *The Commission* 1, no. 7 (July 1849): 14, accession no. 489.

9 Robert Hill's appointment: Minutes of the FMB, October 1, 1849, accession no. 705; "Rev. Robert F. Hill," *African Repository* 46 (September 1868): 278.

10 Hervey Goodale: Tupper, *Foreign Missions,* 377; Hervey Goodale to James Taylor, December 13, 1847, FMB Missionary Correspondence, Box 23; "Departure of Bro. Hervey Goodale," *Southern Baptist Missionary Journal* 3, no. 12 (May 1849): 274, accession no. 483; "Death of Mrs. Goodale," *Southern Baptist Missionary Journal* 4, no. 1 (June 1849): 14, accession no. 489; Hervey Goodale to James Taylor, July 11, 1849, FMB Missionary Correspondence, Box 23; FMB Minutes, October 18, 1849, accession no. 706.

11 Bowen's commissioning service: "Designation," *The Commission* 1, no. 11 (November 1849): 42, accession no. 587.

12 Arriving in Africa: Annual Report of the FMB to the SBC, Hampton, Va.: June 3, 1850, accession no. 2618; Bowen, *Central Africa,* 21, 28.

13 Bowen's initial illness: Bowen, *Central Africa,* 27-8; T. J. Bowen to James Taylor, February 14, 1850 in "Central African Mission," *Southern Baptist Missionary Journal* 5, no. 1 (June 1850): 11-12, accession no. 490.

14 Vonzwaw: H. Teague to James Taylor, March 14, 1850, in "Central African Mission," *Southern Baptist Missionary Journal* 5, no. 1 (June 1850): 12-13, accession no. 490; Bowen, *Central Africa,* 73.

15 Goodale's death: Bowen, *Central Africa,* 80-82; Robert Hill to James Taylor, March 20, 1850, FMB Missionary Correspondence, Box 28; T. J. Bowen to James Taylor, March 31, 1850, BP, 5: 279; T. J. Bowen to James Taylor, May 9, 1850, BP 5: 282.

16 Back to the coast: Annual Report of the FMB, May 9, 1851, Nashville, accession no. 2650.

17 Robert Hill: T. J. Bowen to James Taylor, March 31, 1850, BP 5: 279; T. J. Bowen to James Taylor, June 18, 1850, BP 5: 288; FMB Minutes, December 4, 1850, accession no. 686; Robert F. Hill to James Taylor, July 2, 1850, FMB Missionary Correspondence, Box 28; Annual Reports of the FMB from 1850-1862; Taylor's letters to Hill in the FMB Copy Books; Hill's letters to Taylor in FMB Missionary Correspondence, Box 28.

18 Journey alone into the interior: Fragment of Diary of T. J. Bowen found in his notebook containing original notes for his Yoruba Grammar, BP 2: 76; T. J. Bowen to James Taylor, June 18, 1850, BP 5: 288; Bowen, *Central Africa,* 102; David Carson Davis, "Thomas Jefferson Bowen and His Plans for the Redemption of Africa" (MA thesis, Baylor University, 1878), 19; Bowen and others often spelled the name of the city as "Abbeokuta."

## Chapter 4—Enjoying Adventure

1 Arriving at Abeokuta: Bowen, *Central Africa,* 104; Fragment of Diary of T. J. Bowen found in his notebook, BP 2: 76; Bowen, *Central Africa,* 107; Taylor to Bowen, June 24, 1852, FMB Copy Books.

2 Always the adventurer: Bowen, *Central Africa,* 109; Burks, *Planting the Redeemer's Standard,* 29; "Appointments," *Christian Index* (A[ril 19, 1849): 127, BP 1: 36; Bowen, *Central Africa,* 128, 131, 133.

3 Writing to Taylor: T. J. Bowen to James Taylor, October 1, 1850, BP 5: 289; Bowen, *Central Africa,* 135-9.

4 Use of interpreters: T. J. Bowen to James Taylor, October 1, 1850, BP 5: 292; T. J. Bowen to James Taylor, November 21, 1851, BP 5: 313; Bowen, *Central Africa,* 187.

5 Diligent study: Bowen, *Central Africa,* 136; T. J. Bowen to James Taylor, November 21, 1854, BP 5: 356; T. J.

Bowen to Unknown, December 21, 1854, BP 5: 356; T. J. Bowen to N. M. Crawford, February 13, 1856, BP 5: 390; T. J. Bowen to James Taylor, December 31, 1851, BP 5: 315.

6 Immerse in culture: Bowen, *Central Africa,* 139; T. J. Bowen to James Taylor, November 21, 1851, BP 5: 314.

7 Appreciated Yoruba culture: E. A. Ayandele, introduction to *Adventures and Labours in Several Countries in the Interior of Africa from 1849 to 1856,* by T. J. Bowen, 2n ed. (London: Frank Cass, 1968), xix, xvi-xvii; Bowen, *Central Africa,* 290, 289; Fragments of a diary of Thomas J. Bowen, BP 2: 102, 100; Bowen, *Central Africa,* 286.

8 Increasingly lonely: T. J. Bowen to James Taylor, October 1, 1850; BP 5: 289; T. J. Bowen to Unknown, P. S. to a letter not included, outside postal mark of February 12, 1851, BP 5: 292; T. J. Bowen to Bro. Thomas, September 20, 1851, BP 5: 310.

9 Something dramatic: Bowen, *Central Africa,* 120-1; Fragment of Diary of T. J. Bowen found in his notebook, BP 2: 77; Bowen, *Central Africa,* 118.

10 In preparation: Bowen, *Central Africa,* 119-120; T. J. Bowen to James Taylor, July 1, 1851, BP 5: 306; Ajayi Kolawole Ajisafe, *History of Abeokuta* (Abeokuta, Nigeria: M. A. Ola, Fola Bookshops, 1964), 96.

11 Early on the morning: Bowen, *Central Africa,* 120-1.

12 The ferocious battle: Bowen, *Central Africa,* 121-22.

13 Historian Biobaku: Biobaku, *The Egba and Their Neighbors,* 44-5.

14 Changed history: Ajayi, J. E. Ade, *Christian Missions in Nigeria 1841-1891: The Making of a New Elite, Ibadan History Series,* edited by K. O. Dike (London: Longmans, 1965), 71-73; Bowen, *Central Africa,* 123.

15 Days later: T. J. Bowen to James Taylor, November 21, 1851, BP, 5: 314; Fragment of Diary of T. J. Bowen found in his notebook, BP 2: 77; Bowen Journal, January 5-25, 1852, BP 2: 96; Ajayi, *Christian Missions in Nigeria,* 76-7; The Abeokuta Treaty of 1852, BP 1: 37-9.

16 New doors had opened: Bowen, *Central Africa,* 145; Ayanrinola, "The Mission Program of the Nigerian Baptist Convention," 31; T. J. Bowen to James Taylor, May 16, 1851, BP 5: 299.

17 Filled with danger: T. J. Bowen to James Taylor, May 16, 1851, BP 5: 301; Bowen, *Central Africa,* 150.

18 Despite these dangers: T. J. Bowen to James Taylor, May 16, 1851, BP 5: 303.

## Chapter 5—Enduring Hardship

1 Bowen's miserable living conditions: Bowen to Taylor, May 16, 1851, BP 5: 303, 304.

2 Beyond bodily afflictions: Bowen to Taylor, May 16, 1851, BP 5: 310.

3 When Bowen began to preach openly: Bowen, *Central Africa,* 150, 152-3.

4 Back in the Anglican compound: T. J. Bowen to Bro. Thomas, September 20, 1851, BP 5: 310; Fragment of Diary of T. J. Bowen found in his notebook, BP 2: 77.

5 Burden for missionary associates: Bowen to Taylor, May 16, 1851, BP 5: 303; T. J. Bowen to Bro. Thomas, September 20, 1851, BP 5: 310.

6 New doors open: Bowen Journal, January 5-25, 1852, BP 2: 96-8; Bowen to Taylor, February 3, 1852, BP 5: 318; Fragment of Diary of T. J. Bowen found in his notebook, BP 2: 77; Bowen, *Central Africa,* 160; Bowen to Taylor, February 28, 1852, BP 5:320.

7 Converts in Biolorunpellu: Bowen to Taylor, February 28, 1852, BP 5: 321; Bowen, *Central Africa,* 162-3.

8 Moved deeply: Bowen to Taylor, February 28, 1852, BP 5: 320; William H. Clarke to James Taylor, March 8, 1853, FMB Missionary Correspondence, Box 13.

9 Leaving Biolorunpellu: Bowen, *Central Africa,* 170-1; Bowen to Taylor, June 1852, BP 5: 322; Diary Fragment , Ijaye, 1855, BP 2: 108.

10 After recovering: Fragment of Diary of T. J. Bowen found in his notebook, BP 2: 77; Bowen, *Central Africa,* 178-9; Bowen to Taylor, June 1852, BP 5: 322.

11 Back in the American South: James Taylor to T. J. Bowen, June 24, 1852, FMB Copy Books; Bowen to

Taylor, June 1852, BP 5: 322; Bowen, *Central Africa,* 179; Bowen to Taylor, November 10, 1852, BP 5: 327.

12 Left most of his luggage: Bowen, *Central Africa,* 179-81; Bowen to Taylor, November 10, 1852, BP 5: 328; Fragment of Diary of T. J. Bowen found in his notebook, BP 2: 78; Davis, "Thomas Jefferson Bowen and His Plans," 35.

13 He survived and succeeded: "Central African Mission, *Home and Foreign Journal* 3, no. 2 (August 1853): 6, accession no. 364; Bowen to Taylor, May 16, 1851, BP 5: 303.

## Chapter 6—Inspiring Others

1 A flurry of traveling: Bowen to Taylor, November 19, 1853, BP 5: 341; Bowen to Taylor, June 1852, BP 5: 322.

2 With the FMB: FMB Minutes, February 7, 1853, accession no. 868; FMB Minutes, February 15, 1853, accession no. 872; Taylor to Bowen, August 16, 1852, FMB Copy Books.

3 James Taylor to J. H. Lacy, February 8, 1853, FMB Copy Books; Bowen to Taylor, March 14, 1853, FMB Missionary Correspondence, Box 9. This is the only letter available in the United States in Bowen's own handwriting.; Bowen to Taylor, August 14, 1855, BP 5: 375.

4 Special attention to one candidate: Proceedings of the SBC, Baltimore, June 1853, 12 (That brother-in-law

was Thomas Stocks.); Bowen to Taylor, March 23, 1853, BP 5: 329; Lurana had turned 21 on March 6 that year. See Family Record of Rev. and Mrs. T. J. Bowen, BP 1: 1; T. J. Bowen to Lurana, March 31, 1873, BP 3: 179; Lurana H. Davis to T. J. Bowen, May 14, 1853, BP 4: 212.

5 Lurana's upbringing: "Family History," by T. B. Rice, BP 1:21-23; Cliff Lewis, "Woman of Duty: Lurana Davis Bowen and the Missionary Spirit," *Georgia Historical Quarterly* 64, no. 3 (Fall 2000): 472-501; Jonathan M. Bryant, *How Curious a Land: Conflict and Change in Greene County, Georgia, 185-1885* (Chapel Hill, N. C.: University of North Carolina Press, 1996), 27, 30. Smith, *The Story of Georgia,* Kindle Locations 5274-5284.

6 Her family's wealth and influence: Bryant, *How Curious a Land,* 18; Freda Reid Turner, *Greene County, Georgia Wills 1786-1877* (Fernando Beach, Fla.: Wolfe, 1998), 316; Bryant, *How Curious a Land,* 22, 60; Robert G. Gardner, Charles O. Walker, J. R. Huddleston, and Waldo P. Harris III, *A History of the Georgia Baptist Association 1784-1984* (Atlanta: Georgia Baptist Historical Society, 1988), 251.

7 Lurana's education: Lewis, "Woman of Duty," 473-4;

8 Lurana's missionary calling: Lewis, "Woman of Duty," 473-4; Lurana to T. J. Bowen, May 14, 1853, BP 4:212.

9 Her family's sacrifice: Tupper, *Foreign Missions,* 383; "Family History," by T. B. Rice, BP 1:23.

10 Commissioning and marriage: "Religious services in Greensboro, Georgia, Baptist Church," BP 1:40.

11 Bowen's letters: Hardwicke, "An Examination," 16; Cal Guy, "T. J. Bowen—Southern Baptist Innovator on the African Scene," *Baptist History and Heritage,* 2, no. 2: 67; "Africa," *Alabama Baptist* 6, no. 13 (July 27, 1854): 1, microfilm.

12 Bowen's speaking and recruiting: "Interior Africa— Progress of Discoveries," *African Repository* 29, no. 11 (November 1853): n.p. [cited 24 June 2008], APS Online: http://proquest.com; Taylor to Bowen, May 24, 1853, FMB Copy Books. Penfield, Georgia, was the original location of Mercer University.

13 Dennard: Roberson, Bowen or an Evidence of Grace, 27; H. A. Tupper, *The Foreign Missions of the Southern Baptist Convention* (Richmond: Foreign Mission Board of the Southern Baptist Convention, 1880), 390-1; Dennard to Taylor, March 8, 1852, FMB Copy Books.

14 Georgia Baptist Convention: Minutes of Georgia Baptist Convention, April 22-23, 25, 1853, Microfilm; "African Colonization," *New York Observer and Chronicle* 31, no. 18 (May 5, 1853), no pages, Cited 24 June 2008; APS Online, 142; Online: http://proquest.com; R. R. Gurley, "Rev. R. R. Gurley's Report, of His Labors in Georgia and New York," *African Repository* 29, no. 9 (September 1853), no pages, Cited 24 June 2008, APS Online, 274, Online: http://proquest.com.

15 Lacy: Tupper, *Foreign Missions,* 391; Lacy to Taylor, January 11, 1853, FMB Copy Books; Lacy to Taylor, January 24, 1853, FMB Copy Books.

16. Southern Baptist Convention: "Southern Baptist Missions," *The Missionary Herald* 49, no. 8 (August 1853), n.p., cited 24 June 2008, APS Online, 245, Online: http://proquest.com.

17 Missionary marriages: Taylor to Lacy, March 29, 1853, FMB Copy Books; Tupper, *Foreign Missions,* 391, 383.

## Chapter 7—Overcoming Tragedy

1 Fire on the ship: T. J. Bowen to Unknown, August 2, 1853, BP 5: 333.

2 Stops off Africa: Fragment of Diary of T. J. Bowen found in his notebook, BP 2: 78; T. J. Bowen to *New York Tribune,* October 4, 1853, BP 3: 137.

3 Medical supplies and ministry: Extracts from a paper by T. B. Rice containing extracts from Mrs. Bowen's diary, BP 1: 72; Fragments of Diary of Thomas J. Bowen, BP 2: 103.

4 Immediate sickness: Bowen, *Central Africa,* 182-3; Copy of a diary of Mrs. T. J. Bowen, BP 2: 81; This was Bowen's own opinion. See T. J. Bowen to James Taylor, November 19, 1853; BP 5: 341; Lurana Bowen to Mrs. Thomas Stocks, October 24, 1853, BP 4: 215.

5 Pleasantness of Abeokuta: Lurana Bowen to Mrs. Stocks, October 24, 1853, BP 4: 215.

6 Ready to press on: Bowen to Thomas, October 17, 1853, BP 5: 336; Lurana Bowen to Mrs. Thomas Stocks, October 24, 1853, BP 4: 215; Bowen to Taylor, October 27, 1853; BP 5: 339; Lurana to Taylor, October 25, 1853, BP 4: 337.

7 Journey to Ijaye: Extracts from a paper by T. B. Rice, BP 1:72.

8 Warmly received: Extracts, BP 1:72; Burks, *Planting the Redeemer's Standard,* 52.

9 Tiny rented house: Robertson, Bowen, 29; Bowen, *Central Africa,* 358.

10 Sickness: Bowen to Taylor, November 19, 1853, BP 5: 341; Bowen's Diary, December 3, 1853, BP 1: 99; Lurana to her sister, Mrs. Jackson, December 14, 1853, BP 4: 213.

11 Building a house: Bowen, *Central Africa,* 183-5.

12 Evangelizing: Lurana to Mrs. Jackson, December 14, 1853, BP 4: 214; Fragments of Diary of Thomas J. Bowen, BP 2: 100-101.

13 Lacy's eyesight: T. J. Bowen to James Taylor, December 17, 1853, BP 5: 342; J. H. Lacy to James Taylor, June 13, 1854, FMB Missionary Correspondence, Box 32; J. H. Lacy to James Taylor, September 7, 1855, FMB Missionary Correspondence, Box 32.

14 Deserted by Lacy: Lurana to Mrs. Jackson, December 14, 1853, BP 4:213; T. J. Bowen to James Taylor, December 17, 1853, BP 5: 342; James Taylor to J. H. Lacy, May 26, 1854, FMB Copy Books.

15 Deserted by Dennard: Dennard to Taylor, November 23, 1853, "Executive Committee & Mission Minutes & Reports MM #50" from Lagos.

16 Death of Dennard's wife: Dennard to Taylor, January 10, 1854, transcribed letter.

17 Lurana's schools: Copy of a diary of Mrs. T. J. Bowen, BP 2: 83.

18 School growth: Copy of a diary of Mrs. T. J. Bowen, BP 2: 84; Fragments of Diary of Thomas J. Bowen, BP 2: 105.

19 People adored Lurana: C. E. W. Priest to A. M. Poindexter, December 26, 1857, FMB Correspondence, Box 46.

20 Lurana's health and baby: Copy of a diary of Mrs. T. J. Bowen, BP 2: 83; Bowen, *Central Africa,* 185; Fragments of a diary, BP 2: 105; Ague is the fever and chills associated with malaria.

21 Discouragement: Copy of a diary of Mrs. T. J. Bowen, BP 2: 84; T. J. Bowen to James Taylor, March 19, 1854, BP 5: 343.

22 Deteriorating health: T. J. Bowen to James Taylor, April 1, 1854, BP 5: 344.

23 Their suffering child: Copy of a diary of Mrs. T. J. Bowen, BP 2: 84.

24 Carrying on: Copy of a diary of Mrs. T. J. Bowen, BP 2: 84; T. J. Bowen to Unknown, June 2, 1854, BP 5: 346.

25 Dennard's death: Annual Report of the FMB to the SBS, Washington, Ga., April 22, 1854, accession no. 2611; T. J. Bowen to James Taylor, June 24, 1854, BP 5: 348; Dennard to Taylor, January 10, 1854, transcribed letter.

## Chapter 8—Dreaming Big

1 Response to his preaching: Lurana Bowen to Mrs. Mallory, June 10, 1854, BP 4: 220; T. J. Bowen to James Taylor, July 15, 1854, BP 5: 350.

2 Efforts bore fruit: Copy of a diary of Mrs. T. J. Bowen, 2: 86; T. J. Bowen, "African Missions—No. 2, " *Christian Index* (November 2, 1859): 2, BP 6: 597.

3 Despondent: Copy of a diary of Mrs. T. J. Bowen, BP 2: 85.

4 Arrival of Clarke: Fragment of a Diary of T. J. Bowen found in his notebook, BP 2: 78; Copy of a diary of Mrs. T. J. Bowen, BP 2: 87; Bowen, *Central Africa,* 185; T. J. Bowen to James Taylor, October 2, 1856, BP 5: 417; T. J. Bowen to A. M. Poindexter, October 13, 1856, BP 5: 420.

5 October illness: Copy of a diary of Mrs. T. J. Bowen, BP
2: 87; Bowen, *Central Africa,* 185.

6 Hallucinations: T. J. Bowen to Unknown, December 21,
1854, BP 5: 355-6.

7 Dreams of expansion: T. J. Bowen to James Taylor,
January 18, 1855, BP 5: 362; T. J. Bowen to James
Taylor, February 16, 1855, BP 5: 366; "Glorious
Openings in Yoruba," *Home and Foreign Journal* 5,
No. 2 (August 1855): 7, accession no. 366.

8 Pressing for new missionaries: T. J. Bowen to James
Taylor, February 21, 1855, BP 5: 367.

9 Clarke sick and the ants: Copy of a diary of Mrs. T. J.
Bowen, BP, 2: 89; Diary Fragment, Ijaye, 1855, BP
2: 107-8; T. J. Bowen to A. M. Poindexter, March 17,
1855, BP 5: 368; Bowen, *Central Africa,* 265; T. J.
Bowen to James Taylor, April 11, 1855, BP 5: 369.

10 Professing faith: Diary Fragment, Ijaye, BP 2: 108-9;
T. J. Bowen to James Taylor, April 11, 1855, BP 5: 369;
Copy of a diary of Mrs. T. J. Bowen, BP 2: 90; Lurana
Bowen to her mother, June 18, 1855, BP 4: 227.

11 Felt the spiritual needs: Lurana Bowen to her parents,
July 16, 1855, BP 4: 227.

12 Focusing on Muslims: T. J. Bowen, "Central Africa,"
*The Southern Baptist Missionary Journal,* 3, no. 6
(November 1848): 127; Bowen, *Central Africa,* 68-9;
The author examined all the publications on the IMB's
Solomon Database for those years, as well as all the

correspondence files of FMB missionaries during those years. See Hardwicke, "An Examination," 87.

13 Positive responses from Muslims: T. J. Bowen to James Taylor, February 28, 1852, BP 5: 320; T. J. Bowen to James Taylor, November 10, 1852, BP 5: 326; Copy of a diary of Mrs. T. J. Bowen, BP 2: 86; T. J. Bowen to James Taylor, February 16, 1855, BP 5: 36; Diary Fragment, Ijaye, 1855, BP 2: 107; Bowen Journal in *Home and Foreign Mission Journal,* December 1855, BP 2: 117; Lurana Bowen to Mrs. Judge Thomas Stocks, published in *The Christian Index,* January 18, 1855, BP 4: 224.

14 Passion unstoppable: T. J. Bowen to James Taylor, April 11, 1855, BP 5: 369; Copy of a diary of Mrs. T. J. Bowen, 2: 89; William H Clarke, *Travels and Explorations in Yorubaland, 1854-1858* (ed. J. A. Atanda; Ibadan, Nigeria: Ibadan University Press, 1972), 92.

15 Investigative trip: Copy of a diary of Mrs. T. J. Bowen, BP 2: 89; Bowen, *Central Africa,* 192.

16 His reception: T. J. Bowen to James Taylor, October 1, 1855, BP 5: 379-80.

17 Self-supporting work challenge: T. J. Bowen to James Taylor, October 1, 1855, BP 5: 380.

18 On to Ilorin: Bowen, *Central Africa,* 194; Bowen Journal in *Home and Foreign Journal,* December 1855, BP 2: 114.

19 Delighted with Ilorin: Bowen Journal in *Home and Foreign Journal,* December 1855, BP 2: 114-5; Bowen, *Central Africa,* 221, 198.

20 Enthusiasm about the interior: T. J. Bowen to James Taylor, May 12, 1855, BP 5: 372; Lurana Bowen (fragment), May 16, 1855, BP 4: 225; Lurana Bowen to her parents, July 16, 1855, BP 4: 227.

21 Ministry in Ijaye and results: Copy of a diary of Mrs. T. J. Bowen, BP 1: 91; Diary of Rev. T. J. Bowen, Ijaye, September 1855, "Systematic Labors," BP 2: 118-9.

22 Adaptation of culture: Bowen, *Central Africa,* 327-8; Ayandele, introduction to *Adventures,* xxxix.

23 Like Hudson Taylor: Bowen Journal from *Home and Foreign Mission Journal,* December 1855, BP 2: 117; T. J. Bowen to James Taylor, April 11, 1855, BP 5: 369.

24 Western housing: T. J. Bowen to James Taylor, March 31, 1850, BP 5: 280.

25 So why did he?: T. J. Bowen to James Taylor, April 11, 1855, BP 5: 369.

26 Leaving Ijaye: T. J. Bowen to A. M. Poindexter, September 28, 1855, BP 5: 378; Copy of a diary of Mrs. T. J. Bowen, BP 2: 91; Lurana Bowen to her parents, October 2, 1855, BP 4: 230

27 Journey and arrival in Ogbomosho: T. J. Bowen to James Taylor, October 1, 1855, BP 5: 379-80; Lurana Bowen to her parents, October 2, 185, BP 4: 22; Copy

of a diary of Mrs. T. J. Bowen, BP 2: 91; Lisa A. Lindsay, *Atlantic Bonds: A Nineteenth-Century Odyssey from America to Africa* (Chapel Hill: The University of North Caroline Press, 2017), Kindle Location 2418.

28 Preaching to chiefs: T. J. Bowen to James Taylor, October 1, 1855, BP 5: 380.

29 Encouragement and tipping point: T. J. Bowen to James Taylor, October 1, 1855, BP 5: 381.

30 Something wrong in Ilorin: Copy of a diary of Mrs. T. J. Bowen, BP 2: 92, Bowen, *Central Africa*, 205-7.

31 Lurana on T. J.'s health: Copy of a diary of Mrs. T. J. Bowen, BP 2: 92; Lurana to her parents, December 18, 1855, BP 4: 233.

32 T. J. on his health: T. J. Bowen to A. Thomas, January 1, 1856, BP 5: 383; T. J. Bowen to A. M. Poindexter, January 3, 1856, BP 5: 384.

33 New home and new missionaries: Copy of a diary of Mrs. T. J. Bowen, BP 2: 93; T. J. Bowen to A. M. Poindexter, January 3, 1856, BP 5: 384; Besides his preaching and other missionary work this month, T. J. used scientific instruments three times a day (8 a.m., 12 noon, and 8 p.m.) to measure the weather conditions in Ogbomosho. He recorded detailed measurements of the temperature, humidity, barometric pressure, rain, cloud conditions, and wind. See Weather Recordings by T. J. Bowen in Africa, February 1856, BP 1: 41-2;

Tupper, *Foreign Missions,* 405-8; T. J. Bowen to James Taylor, March 21, 1856, BP 5: 397.

34 Concern for Lurana and Beaumont: T. J. Bowen to wife, March 18, 1856, BP 3: 140; Tupper, *Foreign Missions,* 405; James Taylor to T. J. Bowen, August 28, 1855, FMB Copy Books; T. J. Bowen to Unknown, undated, published in *The Commission,* BP 5: 402.

35 Discord between Beaumont and Phillips: A. M. Poindexter to T. J. Bowen, October 9, 1856, FMB Copy Books; T. J. Bowen to A. M. Poindexter, October 13, 1856, BP 5: 420; T. J. Bowen to James Taylor, October 2, 1856, BP 5: 417; Unknown to All the Missions, April 23, 1857, FMB Copy Books.

36 Mission Meeting: Copy of a diary of Mrs. T. J. Bowen, BP 2: 93; T. J. Bowen to A. M. Poindexter, October 13, 1856, BP 5: 420; T. J. Bowen, W. H. Clarke, and A. D. Phillips to James Taylor, March 20, 1856, BP 5: 394-5.

37 Plans to return home: T. J. Bowen to James Taylor, March 21, 1856, BP 5: 397; T. J. Bowen to James Taylor, April 13, 1856, BP 5: 400.

38 Explanation of sickness: T. J. Bowen to A. M. Poindexter, October 11, 1859, BP 5: 493; T. J. Bowen to Unknown, undated, but evidently from April 1856, published in *The Commission,* BP 5: 402.

39 Travel to Freetown: Copy of a diary of Mrs. T. J. Bowen, BP 2: 93-4; Bowen, *Central Africa,* 209-11;

T. J. Bowen to A. Thomas, June 10, 1856, BP 5: 405; Lindsay, *Atlantic Bonds,* Kindle Locations 2174, 2366.

40 Freetown and journey home: T. J. Bowen to A. Thomas, June 10, 1855, BP 5: 405; Bowen, *Central Africa,* 213-4; Copy of a diary of Mrs. T. J. Bowen, BP 2: 94; T. J. Bowen to James Taylor, July 16, 1856, BP 5: 406; T. J. Bowen to James Taylor, July 22, 1856, BP 5: 407; James Taylor to T. J. Bowen, July 23, 1856, FMB Copy Books; T. J. Bowen to James Taylor, July 28, 1856, BP 5: 410; James Taylor to T. J. Bowen, July 29, 1856, FMB Copy Books; James Taylor to T. J. Bowen, July 29, FMB Copy Books (a second letter). There was one-day mail service between New York and Richmond, although T. J. did send an additional tele-graph; Bowen to Taylor, August 8, 1856, BP 5: 412-13.

## Chapter 9—Capturing the Imagination of a Nation

1 Celebrated by his denomination: James Taylor to T. J. Bowen, late April or early May, 1854, FMB Copy Books.

2 Poindexter: A. M. Poindexter to T. J. Bowen, October 25, 1855, FMB Copy Books; Quoted from an editorial in *The Christian Index,* September 1856, BP 1: 44; Minutes Georgia Baptist Convention, Washington, Wilkes County, Georgia, April 1854, 9.

3 *The Commission:* "Bowen's Central Africa," *The Commission* 1, no. 12 (June 1857): 361-5, accession no. 520.

4 Compared to missionary heroes: "Encouraging Aspects of Central African Missions," *The Commission* 1, no. 6 (December 1856): 164-5, accession no. 550; R. L. Robinson, *History of the Georgia Baptist Association*, n. p., 1928; Cal Guy, "T. J. Bowen—Southern Baptist Innovator on the African Scene," *Baptist History and Heritage* 2, no. 2: 67; "Africa," *Alabama Baptist* 6, no. 13 (July 27, 1854): 1, microfilm; "Bowen's Work on Africa" and "Researches in Central Africa," *The Commission* 1, no. 8 (February 1857): 249-50, accession no. 500; Minutes of the Georgia Baptist Convention, Augusta, April 24-2, 27, 1857, microfilm.

5 Greensboro: Bryant, *How Curious a Land,* 13, 22-23; "Samuel Davis and Related Families" by T. B. Rice, BP 1: 23; Rice, *History of Greene Country Georgia,* 342.

6 Restoring their health: Bowen to Taylor, August 26, 1856 (from Montvale Springs, Tenn.), BP 5: 415; Bowen to Taylor, August 27, 1856, BP 5: 416; Bowen to Taylor, October 2, 1856, BP 5: 417; "Montvale Springs," Wikipedia.com.

7 Writing *Central Africa:* T. J. Bowen, *The Rise and Progress of the Baptists* (Tallahassee: Office of the Florida Sentinel, 1850); James Taylor to T. J. Bowen, October 24, 1853, FMB Copy Books; T. J. Bowen to James Taylor, December 11, 1856, BP 5: 424; A. M. Poindexter to William Clarke, February 26, 1857, FMB Copy Books; Davis, "Thomas Jefferson Bowen and His Plans," 61; "Bowen's Africa," *Alabama Baptist* 9,

no. 20 (September 24, 1857): 1, microfilm (This article quoted the *New York Observer* of August 20, 1857).

8 Praise for *Central Africa:* T. J. Bowen to James Taylor, December 11, 1856, BP 5: 424; "Central Africa," *The Commission* 1, no. 9 (March 1857): 281, accession no. 505; Comments on Bowen's *Central Africa* by various newspapers and magazines, BP 1: 47; "Proposal for Colonizing Central Africa," *Daily National Intelligencer* (October 30, 1858): 428 [cited 25 June 2008], Nineteeth-Century U. S. Newspapers. Online: http://www.columbia.edu/cquibin/cul/resolve?clio6003232.

9 Southern Baptists liked it: Bowen, *Central Africa,* 218; "Bowen's Central Africa," *The Commission* 1, no. 12 (June 1857): 361, accession no. 520; Burks, *Planting the Redeemer's Standard,* 66.

10 *Grammar and Dictionary:* T. J. Bowen to James Taylor, September 29, 1857, BP 5: 441; T. J. Bowen to James Taylor, November 9, 1857, BP 5: 443; T. J. Bowen to James Taylor, January 28, 1848, BP 5: 450; T. J. Bowen to A. M. Poindexter, January 25, 1859, BP 5: 482; T. J. Bowen to A. M. Poindexter, March 15, 1858, BP 5: 457.

11 Toil not in vain: S. G. Pinnock, *The Romance of Missions in Nigeria* (Richmond: Jenkins, 1917), 99; C. Sylvester Green, *New Nigeria: Southern Baptists at Work in Africa* (Richmond: Foreign Mission Board, 1936), 69; T. B. Rice, "Equatorial Africa as Seen by a

Greensboro Lady in Oc. 1853," *The Herald-Journal,* Greensboro, Georgia, September 27, 1940, FMB Missionary Correspondence, Box 9.

12 Other writing: "Review 1→No Title, *New York Evangelist* 29, no. 43 (December 16, 1858): n. p. [cited 25 June 2008] APS Online, 8. Online: http// proquest.com; T. J. Bowen, "The Church," *Christian Index* (May 13, 1857), BP 6: 562-3; T. J. Bowen, "The Church, concluded," *Christian Index* (May 13, 1857), BP 6: 564-5; T. J. Bowen, "The Unorganized Church Again," *Christian Index* (June 10, 1857), BP 6: 580-1; T. J. Bowen, "Theodosia, Vol. 2," a book review in *Christian Index* (August 1856): 41, reprinted from *The Commission,* BP 6: 561; T. J. Bowen, Book Review of *The Living Epistle; or the Moral Power of a Religious Life, Christian Index* (April 6, 1859): 2, BP 6: 575; T. J. Bowen, Book Reviews of *Emily Gray: or Light behind the Cloud and the Pastor's Household; or Lessons on the Eleventh Commandment, Christian Index* (April 6, 1859): 2, BP 6: 576; T. J. Bowen, "African Missions—No. 1," *Christian Index* (October 19, 1859): 2, BP 6: 594-5; T. J. Bowen, "African Missions—No. 2," *Christian Index* (November 2, 1859): 2, BP 6:596-7; T. J. wrote other similar articles.

13 Written thoughts on missions: T. J. Bowen to James Taylor, June 11, 1859, BP 5: 486; William R. Estep, *Whole Gospel Whole Word: The Foreign Mission Board of the Southern Baptist Convention 1845-1995* (Nashville: Broadman & Holman, 1994), 123-3, 208;

T. J. Bowen, "Preambles and Resolutions," *Christian Index* (July 20, 1859): 1 BP 6: 592; Leon H. McBeth, *The Baptist Heritage* (Nashville: Broadman, 1987), 418; T. J. Bowen, "A Missionary Agency," *Christian Index* (June 29, 1859): 1, BP 6: 585; T. J. Bowen to James Taylor, June 29, 1859.

14 Proclaimed a hero: Quotations from an editorial in *The Christian Index* (September 16, 1857): 145, BP 1: 45.

15 Requests to speak: T. J. Bowen to James Taylor, June 21, 1858, BP 5: 446; "Lecture on Central Africa," *Southwest Baptist* 10, no. 30 (December 2, 1858): 2 microfilm; T. J. Bowen to Unknown (FMB), August 8, 1859 (never mailed), BP 5: 490.

16 Speaking at large gatherings: T. J. Bowen to James Taylor, October 2, 1856, BP 5: 417-8; T. J. Bowen to James Taylor, September 29, 1857, BP 5: 441; Gardner, *A History of the Georgia Baptist Association,* 187, 195, 538; T. J. Bowen to A. M. Poindexter, August 29, 1859, BP 5: 492; T. J. Bowen to James Taylor, October 12, 1857, BP 5: 442; T. J. Bowen to Lurana Bowen, May 3, 1873, BP 3: 185; T. J. Bowen to Lurana Bowen, June 16, 1873, BP 3: 187; T. J. Bowen to Lurana Bowen, July 5, 1873, BP 3: 189.

17 Speaking in nontraditional settings: T. J. Bowen to James Taylor, February 8, 1858, BP 5: 453; T. J. Bowen, "Africa Opening to Civilization and Christianity: Central Africa," *African Repository* 33, no. 4 (April 1857): n.p. [cited 24 June 2008], APS Online, 97.

Online: http://proquest.com; "The American
Livingstone—T. J. Bowen," *North American and
United States Gazette* (January 10, 1859): 28 [cited
25 June 2008], Nineteeth-Century U. S. Newspapers.
Online: http://www.columbia.edu/cqu-bin/cul-re-
solve?clio6003232; "Advertisement 2—No Title,"
*The New York Evangelist* 29, no. 39 (September
30, 1858): n. p. [citied 24 June 2008] APS Online, 5,
Online: http://proquest.com; "Summary of News,"
*Christian Inquirer* 13, no. 1 (October 2, 1858): n.p.
[cited 25 June 2008], APS Online, 4, Online: http://
proquest.com; "Miscellany," *Christian Inquirer* 13, no.
7 (November 13, 1858): n.p. [cited 25 June 2008], APS
Online, 4, Online: http://proquest.com; "A Preacher
to the Slaves," *New York Observer and Chronicle*
36, no. 39 (September 30, 1858): n.p. [cited 25 June
2008], APS Online, 310. Online: http://proquest.com;
"Brother Bowen's Lecture," *Southwest Baptist* 10, no.
35 (January 13, 1859): 1, microfilm.

18 Inspiring Congress: Chairman Com. On Congress,
House of Rep. to T. J. Bowen, February 3, 1857; "The
Navigation of the Niger," *The Commission* 1, no. 9
(March 1857): 284-5, accession no. 505; T. J. Bowen
to Lippincott and Co., November 21, 1868, BP 3: 167.

## Chapter 10—Mixing Politics and Ministry

1 The American Colonization Society: Ayandele, introduction to *Adventures,* xiii; Amos Jones Beyan, *The
American Colonization Society and the Formation
of Political, Economic, and Religious Institutions*

*in Liberia, 182-1900* (Ann Arbor, Mich.: University Microfilms, 1985), 2; "African Colonization," *New York Observer and Chronicle,* 31, no. 18 (May 5, 1853): n.p. [cited 24 June 2008], APS Online, 142. Online: http://proquest.com; Early Lee Fox, *The American Colonization Society 1817-1840* (John Hopkins University Studies in Historical and Political Science under the Direction of the Departments of History, Political Economy, and Political Science, Series XXXVII, no. 3, 1919, repr., New York: AMS, 1971, 46-52.

2 ACS's Christian Foundation: Earle E. Cairns, *An Endless Line of Splendor: Revivals and Their Leaders from the Great Awakening to the Present* (Wheaton, Ill.: Tyndale House, 1986), 278-9, 286; Werner Theodor Wickstrom, "The American Colonization Society and Liberia (An Historical Study in Religious Motivation and Achievement) 1817-1867" (PhD diss., Harford Seminary Foundation, 1958), 37, 25. This sentiment was included in the preamble to the ACS constitution (40-1); Elgin S. Moyer, *The Wycliffe Biographical Dictionary of the Church* (rev. and enl. Earle E. Cairns, Chicago: Moody, 1982), 276-7.

3 ACS and churches: Wickstrom, "The American Colonization Society," 179-86; Fox, *The American Colonization Society,* 73; "African Colonization," *New York Observer and Chronicle;* Ayandele, introduction to *Adventures,* xiii; Hardwicke, "An Examination," bibliography.

4 Speaking for colonization: "Mr. Bowen and the Colored People," *New York Observer and Chronicle* 36, no. 7 (February 18, 1858): n.p. [cited June 2008], APS Online, 50. Online: proquest.com; A. A. Constantine to T. J. Bowen, October 1, 1859, BP 3: 153; James Taylor to T. J. Bowen, November 19, 1856, FMB Copy Books; James Taylor to T. J. Bowen, December 16, FMB Copy Books; "The Navigation of the Niger, *The Commission* 1, no. 9 (March 1857): 285, accession no. 505.

5 Thinking big: Bowen, *Central Africa,* 58, 330.

6 Distinctly Christian colony: "Letter from Rev. T. J. Bowen, on the Commerce, Civilization, and Colonization of Yoruba," *African Repository* 33, no. 9 (September 1857): n.p. [cited 24 June 2008], APS conline, 279. Online: proquest.com; "Africo-American Nationality," *African Repository* 34, no. 10 (October 1858): n.p. [cited 24 June2008], APS Online 306. Online: http:// proquest.com; David, "Thomas Jefferson Bowen and His Plans," 87; Bowen, *Central Africa,* 62.

7 Liberia as a Christian state: R. R. Gurley, *Mission to England in Behalf of the American Colonization Society* (Washington: Wm. W. Morrison, 1841), 153, 157; Beyan, *The American Colonization Society,* 75-6;

8 Not Christian devotion alone: Beyan, *The American Colonization Society, 77-8; Gurley, Mission to England,* 163.

9 Bowen's vision for Yoruba: "Letter from Rev. T. J. Bowen, on Commerce," *African Repository* (September

1857): n.p.; "Proposed Colony in Yoruba," *African Repository* 34, no. 5 (May 1858); n.p [cited 24 June 2008], APS Online, 150, Online: http://proquest.com; T. J. Bowen to Gen. Duff Green, February 18 (?), 1858, BP 3: 149; Ayandele, introduction to *Adventures,* xlviii; T. J. Bowen to James Taylor, January 28, 1858, BP 5: 450; In a letter to Taylor in February 1858, he wrote, "My business here is to aid in getting a charter to *colonize Yoruba.*"; T. J. Bowen to James Taylor, February 23, 1858, BP 5: 455; T. J. Bowen to James Taylor, December 3, 1858, BP 5: 478.

10 Never materialized: T. J. Bowen to Lippincott and Co., November 21, 1868, BP 3: 167; Bowen, *Central Africa,* 58.

11 Convinced about civilization: "Proposal for Colonizing Africa," *Daily National Intelligencer* (October 30, 1858): 428 [cited 25 June 2008]. Online: http://infotrac.galegroup.com/itw/info-mark/208/522/33805328w16/puri=rc1_NCNP_0_GT30178...html; Bowen, *Central Africa,* 327, 321-2.

12 Importance of commerce: "Proposal for Colonizing Africa," *Daily National Intelligencer,* 428; "African Civilization—Letter from the Rev. T. J. Bowen, the African Explorer," *Charleston Courier Tri-Weekly* (March 17, 1859): n.p. [cited 25 June 2008]. Online: http://infotrac.galegroup.com/itw/info-mark/208/522/33805328w16/puri=rc1_NCNP_0_GT30047...html; Bowen, *Central Africa,* 329-30.

13 Inspired by Muslim traders: Bowen, *Central Africa,* 82, 338; "Letter from Rev. T. J. Bowen," *African Repository* 29, no. 11 (November 183): 335, microfilm; "Yoruba—Rev. T. J. Bowen," *African Repository* 34, no. 1 (January 1858): n.p. [cited 24 June 2008], APS Online, 28. Online: http://proquest.com.

14 Practical steps: "Letter from Rev. T. J. Bowen, on the Commerce," *African Repository* (September 1857): n.p.; Bowen, *Central Africa,* 351-2.

15 Civilization without colonization?: Bowen, *Central Africa,* 84-5.

16 Tribal wars: Bowen, *Central Africa,* 109; "Letter from T. J. Bowen," *African Repository* 30, no. 10 (October 1854): n.p. [cited 24 June 2008], APS Online, 290. Online: http://proquest.com.

17 Other missionaries agreed: Ayandele, introduction to *Adventures,* xxxiv, xxxv; "From Bro. Newton," *Foreign Mission Journal* 23, no. 12 (July 1892): 369-70, accession no. 90.

18 His appreciation for education: T. J. Bowen to Unknown, January 8, 1859, BP 5: 479; Bowen, *Central Africa,* 322-3.

19 Civilize others: G. Winfrey Hervey, *The Story of Baptist Missions in Foreign Lands: From the Time of Carey to the Present Date* (St. Louis: Barns, 1886), 599; Unsigned to Unknown, Undated, published in *Home*

*and Foreign Mission Journal,* November 1854, BP 5: 347; Bowen, *Central Africa,* 112-3.

20 Experience with more civilized tribes: T. J. Bowen to James Taylor, November 10, 1853, BP 5: 327, 326; Bowen Journal in *Home and Foreign Mission Journal,* December 1855, BP 2: 115, 114; "Letter from Rev. T. J. Bowen, on the Commerce," *African Repository* (September 1857): n.p.

21 Plan to stop polygamy: Bowen, *Central Africa,* 342.

22 Assumption of force: Andrew F. Walls, "Imperial Invasion," *Christian History* 21, no. 2 (2002): 42; Wickstrom, "The American Colonization Society," 123-6; "letter from Rev. T. J. Bowen, on the Commerce," *African Repository* (September 1857): n.p.

23 Barriers to the gospel: Ravi Zacharias, "An Ancient Message, through Modern Means, to a Postmodern Mind," in *Telling the Truth: Evangelizing Postmoderns* (ed. D. A. Carson: Grand Rapids, Mich.: Zondervan, 2000), 21.

24 Ill effects lingered long: "Justice and Peace: A Conversation with J. Dudley Woodberry," *Christian History,* 21, no. 2 (2002): 44; Zacharias, "An Ancient Message," 22; Ajith Fernando, "The Uniqueness of Jesus Christ," in *Telling the Truth: Evangelizing Postmoderns,* 128.

## Chapter 11—Struggling with Racial Bias

1 T. J. hated the slave trade: Diary Fragment, Ijaye, 1855, BP 2: 109.

2 Area near Abeokuta: Bowen, *Central Africa,* 109-10; T. J. Bowen, "The African Apprentice System," *African Repository*34, no. 6 (June 1858): n.p. [cited 24 June 2008], APS Online, 189. Online: http://proquest.com.

3 In the same letter: T. J. Bowen, "The African Apprentice System," *African Repository;* Bowen, "Africo-American Nationalitiy," *African Repository* (October 1858): n.p.

4 Colonization and racism: G. B. Stebbins, *Facts and Opinions Touching the Real Origin, Character, and Influence of the American Colonization Society: Views of Wilberforce, Clarkson, and Others, and Opinions of the Free People of Color of the United States* (1853; repr., New York: Negro Universities, 1969), 190; Albert G. Oliver, *The Protest and Attitudes of Blacks towards the American Colonization Society and the Concepts of Emigration and Colonization in Africa, 1817-1865* (Ann Arbor, Mich.: University Microfilms, 1987), 21.

5 T. J.'s racist beliefs: Ayandele, introduction to *Adventures,* xiv, xxxiii; "Letter from T. J. Bowen," *African Repository* (October 1854), n.p.; Bowen, *Central Africa,* 62, 280-1.

6 Colonization the natural duty of white man to the black: "Rev. T. J. Bowen's Lecture: Ethnology of the Negro Races," *Christian Index* (February 9, 1859): 2, BP 6: 573-4.

7 Racism became accepted science: Samuel George Morton, et. al., *Types of Mankind: or Ethnological Researches, based upon the Ancient Monuments, Paintings, Sculptures, and Crania of Races, and upon their Natural, Geographical, Philological, and Biblical History* (London: Trubner & Co., 1854), 458-9; Philip D. Curtin, *The Image of Africa: British Ideas and Action, 1780-1850* (vol. 1, Madison, Wis.: University of Wisconsin Press, 1964), 364, 372.

8 T. J. denied more extreme racist views: Ayandele, introduction to *Adventures*, xxxiii-iv.

9 T. J. spoke against the racist belief that Africans could not be civilized: "Letters from Rev. T. J. Bowen," *African Repository* 28, no. 10 (October 1852): n.p. [cited 24 June 2008], APS Online, 303. Online: http://proquest.com; Bowen, *Central Africa*, 62-4.

10 Saw blacks as the best missionaries: Bowen to Taylor, April 13, 1856, BP 5: 400; Bowen to Taylor, May 4, 1858, BP 5: 461-2;

11 Surrounded by slavery in Georgia: "History of Slavery in Georgia (U.S. state)" Wikipedia [cited 2 July 2020], Wikipedia.com; "Indian Slave Trade in the American Southeast," Wikipedia [cited 2 July 2020], Wikipedia.

com; John T. Ellisor, *The Second Creek Indian War,*
Kindle Locations 454, 460.

12 Surrounded by slavery in Africa: Lisa A. Lindsay,
*Atlantic Bonds,* Kindle Location 2384.

13 Loved by African-background people: "Proposal for
Colonizing Africa," *Daily National Intelligencer*
(October 30, 1858): 428 [cited 25 June 2008],
Nineteeth-Century U.S. Newspapers. Online:
http://www.columbia.edu/cqui-bin/cul-resolve?-
clio6003232; "Contributions of Colored Members,"
*Home and Foreign Journal* 1, no. 3 (September 1851):
10, accession no. 373.

14 Lurana's love for African-background people: Lurana to
My Dear Friends, Presumably July 16, 1855, BP 4: 229-
30; Lurana Bowen to her parents, October 2, 1855, BP
4: 230; C. E. W. Priest to A. M. Poindexter, December
26, 1857, FMB Missionary Correspondence, Box 46.

15 Essence of missionary spirit: "Africa," *Home and
Foreign Journal,* (February 1853), 32.

### Chapter 12—Accepting Change

1 Struggle to get back to Africa: James Taylor to T. J.
Bowen, September 19, 1856, FMB Copy Books; T. J.
Bowen to James Taylor, July 20, 1857, BP 5: 434; T. J.
Bowen to James Taylor, August 3, 1857, BP 5: 436.

2 Financial crisis: J. Edwin Orr, *The Event of the Century:
The 1857-1858 Awakening* (ed. Richard Owen

Roberts; Wheaton, Ill.: International Awakening, 18=989), 14-16.

3 Pursuing him as pastor: T. J. Bowen to James Taylor, November 9, 1857, BP 5: 443; Minutes of Greensboro Baptist Church, April 10, 1858.

4 Financial pressure pushed him: Bowen to Thomas, March 27, 1858, BP 5: 459; Bowen to Poindexter, March 27, 1858, BP 5: 458; Bowen to Taylor, May 4, 1858, BP 5: 462; Minutes of Greensboro Baptist Church, September 11, 1858 and December 10, 1859; T. J. to James Taylor, November 13, 1859, BP 5: 496; T. J. Bowen to James Taylor, December 2, 1859, BP 5: 497; "South Carolina Canal and Railroad Company," Wikipedia [cited 4 July 2020], Wikipedia.com.

5 Lurana was pregnant: T. J. Bowen to James Taylor, February 8, 1858, BP 5: 451-3, [Part of the letter was torn.]; Family Record of Rev. and Mrs. T. J. Bowen, Bowen Papers 1: 1.

6 Lurana's family dominated: Minutes of Greensboro Baptist Church, January 9, 1858, September 11, 1858, September 22, 1858.

7 Spiritual awakening began among blacks: Orr, *The Event of the Century*, 23, 39-42.

8 The awakening in Georgia: Orr, *The Event of the Century*, 168-9; Roy Fish, *When Heaven Touched Earth: The Awakening of 1858 and Its Effects on Baptists* (Azel, Tex.: Need of the Times, 1996), 123, 253-4.

9 The awakening in T. J.'s church: Minutes of Greensboro Baptist Church, September 11, 22, December 12, 1858; T. J. Bowen to James Taylor, October 23, 1858, BP 5: 476; T. J. Bowen to James Taylor, December 3, 1858, BP 5: 478.

10 Bowen's efforts: T. J. Bowen to A. M. Poindexter, August 29, 1859, BP 492; Minutes of Greensboro Baptist Church, January 8, 1859, November 12, 1859; Rice, *History of Greene County, Georgia,* 353; T. J. Bowen to James Taylor, December 2, 1859, BP 5: 497.

11 The process of applying for Brazil: T. J. Bowen to A. M. Poindexter, August 20, 1858, BP 5: 472; T. J. Bowen to James Taylor, January 8, 1859, BP 5: 480; A. M. Poindexter to T. J. Bowen, January 13, 1859, FMB Copy Books; Minutes of the FMB, December 21, 1872, accession no. 1071; T. J. Bowen to A. M. Poindexter, January 20, 1859, BP 5: 481; T. J. Bowen to A. M. Poindexter, January 25, 1859, BP 5: 482; James Taylor to T. J. Bowen, June 24, 1859, FMB Copy Books; T. J. Bowen to A. M. Poindexter, August 29, 1859, BP 5: 492; T. J. Bowen to James Taylor, October 11, 1859, BP 5: 494.

12 The FMB's favorable response: James Taylor to T. J. Bowen, October 18, 1859, FMB Copy Books; FMB Minutes, November 9, 1859, accession no. 759; T. J. Bowen to James Taylor, November 13, 1859, BP 5: 496.

13 Pioneering a new field: Estep, *Whole World,* 419; H. A. Tupper, *The Foreign Missions of the Southern Baptist*

*Convention* (Richmond: Foreign Mission Board of the Southern Baptist Convention, 1880), 8-9.

14 FMB knew of his precarious health: T. J. Bowen to James Taylor, February 2, 1860, BP 5: 507; T. J. Bowen to A. M. Poindexter, August 20, 1858, BP 5: 471; James Taylor to Brother & Sister Stone, February 27, 1860, FMB Copy Books; Annual Report of the FMB to the SBC, Richmond, Va., April 2, 1860, accession no. 2622.

15 Preparing for his new assignment: T. J. Bowen to James Taylor, March 27, 1860, BP 5: 510; T. J. Bowen to James Taylor, December 22, 1859, BP 5: 498; T. J. Bowen to James Taylor, February 11, 1860, BP 5: 504; Estep, *Whole World,* 113.

16 Voyage to Rio: "Extracts from Mrs. Bowen's Diary of the Trip to and Stay in Brazil," BP 1:67; T. J. Bowen to James Taylor, May 25, 1860, BP 5: 512; James Taylor to T. J. Bowen, January 12, 1860, FMB Copy Books; T. J. Bowen to James Taylor, June 10, 1860, BP 5: 515.

17 Ever the evangelist: T. J. Bowen to James Taylor, May 25, 1860, BP 5: 512; T. J. Bowen to James Taylor, December 19, 1860, BP 5: 536; Alverson De Souza, "A Black Heart: The Work of Thomas Jefferson Bowen among Blacks in Africa and Brazil between 1840 and 1875" (MTh diss., University of KwaZula-Natal, 1998), Section 5.2 [cited 25 June 2009]. Online: http://nos-reveal.om/hompage4a. Raised and educated in Brazil,

De Souza had access to Portuguese documents and literature unavailable or difficult to find elsewhere.

18 Dramatic reaction: T. J. Bowen to James Taylor, December 19, 1860, BP 5: 536; T. J. Bowen to James Taylor, June 10, 1860, BP 5: 516; "Biographical Sketches of T. J. Bowen by T. B. Rice," BP 1: 8.

19 Mission work limited: T. J. Bowen to James Taylor, June 10, 1860, BP 5: 515-6.

20 Preaching to Brazilians illegal: T. J. Bowen to James Taylor, October 3, 1860, BP 5: 525.

21 Frustrated: T. J. Bowen to James Taylor, August 31, 1860, BP 5; 522-3; T. J. Bowen to James Taylor, October 10, 1860, BP 5: 528.

22 Discouraged: T. J. Bowen to James Taylor, December 11, 1860, BP 5: 532.

23 Packing up to move: T. J. Bowen to James Taylor, December 11, 1860, BP 5: 533-6.

24 Southern Baptist doubts about Brazil: James Taylor to T. J. Bowen, December 6, 1860, FMB Copy Books; FMB Minutes, December 13, 1860, accession no. 858; "Extracts of a letter from T. J. Bowen dated October 17, 1860, with editorial comments published in *The Christian Index,* January 30, 1861, Bowen Papers 3: 157.

25 Sources of financial pressure: James Taylor to T. J. Bowen, July 4, 1860, FMB Copy Books. This philosophy,

called "Landmarkism," held that the work of mission boards was unscriptural because the sending of missionaries belonged exclusively to individual churches. After a full day of debate at the 1859 Convention, the SBC affirmed the work of the FMB. See H. Leon McBeth, *The Baptist Heritage: Four Centuries of Baptist Witness* (Nashville: Broadman, 1987), 452-3; Minutes of the Georiga Baptist Convention, Athens, April 26-27, 29, 1861, microfilm; "1860s Overview," [cited 24 Jul 2020], imb.org.

26 Approaching Civil War: James Taylor to T. J. Bowen, December 6, 1860, FMB Copy Books [This portion of the letter was damaged.]; James Taylor to T. J. Bowen, December 24, 1860, FMB Copy Books; A. M. Poindexter to T. J. Bowen, February 19, 1861, FMB Copy Books.

27 Lurana's parents needed help: Samuel Davis of Greensboro, Georgia, and Related Families by T. B. Rice, BP 1: 22; Mrs. Samuel David to T. J. and Lurana Bowen (while they were in Brazil), January 24, BP 4: 236. Mrs. Bowen's grammar was not corrected.

28 One further pressure: Lurana Bowen to James Taylor, February 6 (?), 1861, BP 5: 538; Annual Report of the FMB to the SBC, Savannah, Ga., May 10, 1861, accession no. 2623.

## Chapter 13—Fighting
## Physical and Mental Illness

1 Shattered soldier/shattered nation: Bryant, *How Curious a Land,* 60-1.

2 New nation: Gorton Carruth, *What Happened When: A Chronology of Life and Events in America* (New York: Signet, 1989), 406-7; T. J. Bowen to James Taylor, May 7, 1861, BP 5: 540; T. J. Bowen to James Taylor, May 2, 1861, BP 5: 541.

3 Devastated physically: T. J. Bowen to Lippincott and Co., November 21, 1868, BP 3: 167; T. J. Bowen to James Taylor, February 8, 1858, BP 5: 451; T. J. Bowen to James Taylor, October 15, 1858, BP 5: 474; T. J. Bowen to James Taylor, January 8, 1858, BP 5: 480.

4 Wide variety of symptoms: T. J. Bowen to James Taylor, February 8, 1858, BP 5: 451; Copied presumed original report from the Georgia State Hospital for the mentally ill at Milledgeville, BP 1: 57; T. J. Bowen to James Taylor, August 14, 1856, BP 5: 376; T. J. Bowen to James Taylor, May 24, 1856, BP 5: 404; T. J. Bowen to James Taylor, May 3, 1856, BP 5: 403; T. J. Bowen to James Taylor, December 11, 1860, BP 5: 534; T. J. Bowen to James Taylor, June 1852, BP 5: 322; T. J. Bowen to James Taylor, August 1, 1856, BP 5: 411; Bowen Diary fragment in *Home and Foreign Mission Journal,* October 1855, BP 2: 111; T. J. Bowen to A. Thomas, March 27, 1858, BP 5: 459; T. J. Bowen to Lurana Bowen, October 17, 1875, BP 3: 207; T. J.

Bowen to Lurana Bowen, April 24, 1870, BP 3: 171; T. J. Bowen to Lurana Bowen, July 5, 1873, BP 3: 188; T. J. Bowen to Lurana Bowen, December 12, 1873, BP 3: 192; T. J. Bowen to Lurana Bowen, April 3, 1874, BP 3: 195; Copy of a diary of Mrs. T. J. Bowen, BP 2: 92. Erysipelas is a deep-red rash of the skin and mucous membranes accompanied by fever and pain.

5 Extraordinary attacks: T. J. Bowen to James Taylor, August 30, 1860, BP 5: 520; T. J. Bowen to James Taylor, December 11, 1860, BP 5: 533; T. J. Bowen to James Taylor, May 20, 1861, BP 5: 541.

6 Specific diseases: Hardwicke, "An Examination," 158-9.

7 Hardwicke suggested: Hardwicke, "An Examination," 159.

8 Cycles of mental illness: T. J. Bowen to Lurana Bowen, May 3, 1873, BP 3: 185; D. T. E. (D. T. Everett) to Unknown, (fragment), BP 3: 208; James Taylor to T. J. Bowen, August 16, 1852, FMB Copy Books; T. J. Bowen to Unknown, November 7, 1851, BP 5: 308; T. J. Bowen to James Taylor, November 18, 1853, BP 5: 341.

9 Depression deepened: T. J. Bowen to James Taylor, December 11, 1860, BP 5: 534; Psychotropic drugs were not freely available until 1955-6. See Gaius Davies, *Genius, Grief, and Grace: A Doctor Looks at Suffering and Success* (London: Christian Focus, 2001), 361; T. J. Bowen to James Taylor, August 30, 1860, BP 5: 423.

10 Other mental symptoms—depression: T. J. Bowen to
James Taylor, November 28, 1856, BP 5: 423; T. J.
Bowen to James Taylor, November 23, 1857, BP 5:
444; T. J. Bowen to James Taylor, July 12, 1858, BP 5:
467; T. J. Bowen to James Taylor, June 11, 1859, BP 5:
485; T. J. Bowen to James Taylor, May 26, 1860, BP
5: 513; Diary Notes, Abstracts, etc. 1868, BP 2: 126;
T. J. Bowen to Lurana Bowen, September 13, 1869, BP
3: 168; T. J. Bowen to Lurana Bowen, April 16, 1873,
BP 3: 182.

11 Anxiety: T. J. Bowen to James Taylor, October 12, 1857,
BP 5: 442; T. J. Bowen to James Taylor, November
23, 1857, BP 5: 444; T. J. Bowen to Lurana Bowen,
February 3, 1858, BP 3: 147; T. J. Bowen to James
Taylor, February 8, 1858, BP 5: 451.

12 Beyond the borders of frenzy: T. J. Bowen to Lurana
Bowen, February 3, 1858, BP 3: 147; Bowen diary
found in his notebook containing his notes on the
Portuguese language, BP 2: 122; T. J. Bowen to James
Taylor, June 30, 1859, BP 5: 489; T. J. Bowen to James
Taylor, October 3, 1860, BP 5: 525; T. J. Bowen to A.
M. Poindexter, August 20, 1858, BP 5: 472.

13 New forms: "News from the War: A Documentary
History of the Confederate States," A Circular adver-
tising a proposed monthly magazine published by T. J.
Bowen with nearly three pages of subscribers' hand-
written names), BP 6: 605; James Taylor to Judge
Thomas Stocks, July 17, 1861, FMB Copy Books;
Lurana Bowen to Jeames Taylor, August 21, 1861, BP

4: 237; T. J. Bowen to Lurana Bowen, November 16, 1873, BP 4: 191.

14 Lurana's stress: Bryant, *How Curious a Land,* 72, 83-5; "Entry in Mrs. Bowen diary," BP 1: 68.

15 The Lunatic Asylum: Peter G. Cranfield, *But for the Grace of God: Milledgeville!* (Augusta, Ga.: Great Pyramid, 1981; repr., Atlanta: Georgia Consumer Council, 198), 4-6. Thus when T. J. spoke of going to Midway, he was speaking of entering the Asylum.

16 Dr. Thomas Green: James C. Bonner, *Milledgeville: Georgia's Antebellum Capital* (Athens, Ga.: University of Georgia Press, 1989), 82; Cranfield, *But for the Grace of God,* 39; Anna Maria Green Cook, *History of Baldwin County, Georgia* (Anderson S. C.: Keys-Hearn, 1925), 85. Cook was the daughter of Dr. Green.

17 Innovative ways: Cranfield, *But for the Grace of God,* 26, 43; James C. Bonner, introduction to *The Journal of a Milledgeville Girl,* ed. by James C. Bonner (Athens, Ga.: University of Georgia Press, 1964), 4-5). The journal is that of Dr. Green's daughter, Anna Maria Green Cook.

18 Chapel services, etc.: Cranfield, *But for the Grace of God,* 27; T. J. Bowen to Lurana Bowen, January 27, 1875, BP 3: 206; "Georgia's Insane Asylum," n.p. [cited 23 July 2009]. Online: http://mgagnon.myweb.ugaedu/students/Aldrich.htm; Cook, *History of Baldwin County, Georgia,* 80.

19 When did T. J. first seek help?: Copied presumed original report, BP 1: 57.

20 His first admissions to the Asylum: Copied presumed original report, BP 1: 57. For a chronology of T. J. Bowen's life, including admissions to the Asylum, see the Timeline in Appendix A.; James Taylor to Lurana Bowen, March 13, 1862, FMB Copy Books; T. J. Bowen to Lurana Bowen, March 2, 1863, BP 3: 159; T. J. Bowen to Lippincott and Co., November 21, 1868, BP 3: 167.

21 On a farm with his family: Lurana Bowen to James Taylor, January 12, 1864, BP 5: 550; Lurana Bowen to James Taylor, April 8, 1864, BP 4: 239; Mayme Gant Bowen was born June 8, 1866. See Family Record of Rev. and Mrs. T. J. Bowen, BP 1: 1. The scarcity of records make it possible that T. J. may have left the farm at times.

22 War wounded in Greensboro: Bryant, *How Curious a Land,* 82.

23 Invasion of Greensboro: Bryant, *How Curious a Land,* 90-1; "Extracts from a paper by T. B. Rice containing extracts from Mrs. Bowen's diary," BP 1:68.

24 Further admissions to the Asylum: Copied presumed original report, BP 1: 57; Diary Notes, Abstracts, etc. 1868, BP 2: 12508; T. J. Bowen to Prof. Brumley, October 13, 1868, BP 3: 164-6; T. J. Bowen to Lippincott and Co., November 21, 1868, BP 4: 167; J. J. Toon to Lurana Bowen, February 15, 1869, BP 4:

237; J. J. Toon to Lurana Bowen, February 21, 1869, BP 4: 246; T. J. Bowen to Lurana Bowen, September 13, 1869, BP 3: 168; T. J. Bowen to Lurana Bowen, November 16, 1873, BP 3: 191.

25 Final admission to Asylum: Copied presumed original report, BP 1: 57; T. J. Bowen to Lurana Bowen, January 2, 1875, BP 3: 206. This letter was evidently written in Green's office, because it used his official letterhead as did his letter dated October 18, 1875.

26 T. J.'s achievements: "Five Surprising Mental Health Statistics," Mental Health First Aid, News, mentalhealthfirstaid.org [cited 8 July 2020].

## Chapter 14—Facing Rejection

1 Early use of alcohol: T. J. Bowen to James Taylor, June 26, 1861, BP 5: 544; Carswell, *Holmes Valley,* 73; Diary Fragment, Ijaye, 1855, BP 2: 108; Diary of Rev. T. J. Bowen, Ijaye, September 1855, "Systematic Labors," BP 2: 120; D. T. Everett to Lurana Bowen, October 10, 1871, BP 4: 253; Lurana Bowen to Mrs. Stocks, October 24, 1853, BP 3: 217.

2 Drunkenness: T. J. Bowen to Prof. Brumley, October 13, 1869, BP 3: 166; T. J. Bowen to James Taylor, August 30, 1860, BP 5: 520.

3 Continued use of alcohol: T. J. Bowen to James Taylor, June 6, 1861, BP 5: 544; T. J. Bowen to Lurana Bowen, September 13, 1869, BP 3: 168; D. T. Everett to Lurana

Bowen, October 10, 1871, BP 4: 253; T. J. Bowen to Lurana Bowen, June 16, 1873, BP 3: 187; T. J. Bowen to Lurana Bowen, February 2, 1874, BP 4: 193; T. J. Bowen to Lurana Bowen, February 11, 1874, BP 4: 193; T. J. Bowen to Lurana Bowen, September 9, 1874, BP 4: 205; T. J. Bowen to Lurana Bowen, May 1 (no year), BP 4: 193; Copied presumed original report, BP 1: 57.

4 Sourced in his mental illness: Copied presumed original report, BP 1: 57; T. J. Bowen to Prof. Brumley, October 13, 1869, BP 3: 166; T. J. Bowen to Lurana Bowen, February 11, 1874, BP 4: 193; T. J. Bowen to Lurana Bowen, Ma 1 (no year), BP 3: 210.

5 Others also recognized this: T. J. Bowen to Lurana Bowen, April 22, 1874, BP 3: 197; Cranford, *But for the Grace of God,* 25; Copied presumed original report, BP 1: 57.

6 Crushing weight: T. J. Bowen to James Taylor, August 30, 1860, BP 5: 521; T. J. Bowen to James Taylor, May 12, 1867, BP 5: 551; Lurana Bowen to T. J. Bowen, November 20, 1873, BP 4: 258.

7 Displeasure from Thomas Stocks: Robert G. Gardner, et. al., *A History of the Georgia Baptist Association, 1784-1984* (Atlanta: Georgia Baptist Historical Society, 1988), 251; "Donations," *Southern Baptist Missionary Journal* 2, no. 2 (July 1847): 48, accession no. 492; Virginia Reed to Lurana Bowen, May 8, 1868, BP 4: 243; T. J. Bowen to Lurana Bowen, June 20, 1874, BP 3: 202.

8 Feeling of the Greensboro church: Minutes of Greensboro Baptist Church, Greensboro, Georgia, August 4, 1866, possession of First Baptist Church of Greensboro, Georgia; Poem by T. J. Bowen read to the Greensboro Baptist Church (with an additional poem), BP 6: 606-7. This poem has nine additional stanzas.

9 Use of laudanum: Edgar H. Burks, *Planting the Redeemer's Standard: A Life of Thomas J. Bowen, First Baptist Missionary to Nigeria* (Columbus, Ga.: Brentwood Christian, 194), 83-4; Rice, *History of Greene County, Georgia,* 166, 168.

10 FMB's concern: James Taylor to T. J. Bowen, July 4, 1860, FMB Copy Books; T. J. Bowen to James Taylor, December 11, 1860, BP 5: 533-4; A. M. Poindexter to T. J. Bowen, February 19, 1861, FMB Copy Books.

11 Mental illness fueled wandering: T.J. Bowen to James Taylor, May 26, 1858, BP 5: 464; T. J. Bowen to Lurana Bowen, February 12, 1873, BP 4: 177; T. J. Bowen to James Taylor, May 12, 1867, BP 5: 551; T. J. Bowen to Lurana Bowen, February 12, 1873, BP 3: 177.

12 Travels to Florida, Atlanta: T. J. Bowen to James Taylor, May 7, 1861, BP 5: 540; T. J. Bowen to James Taylor, May 20, 1861, BP 5: 541; Lurana Bowen to James Taylor, August 21, 1861, BP 4: 237-8; T. J. Bowen to James Taylor, October 1, 1861, BP 5: 548; T. J. Bowen to James Taylor, Undated, BP 5: 549; Copy of presumed official report, BP 1: 57.

13 Travels to Ringgold, Atlanta, home: "Letter from Rev. T. J. Bowen," *African Repository* 42, no. 11 (November 1866): n.p. [cited 25 June 2008], APS Online, 344. Online: http://proquest.com; Minutes of the Georgia Baptist Convention, Columbus, April 25-26, 28, 1867, microfilm; T. J. Bowen to Lurana Bowen, June 21, 1867, BP 3: 162; Copied presumed official report, BP 1: 57.

14 Travels around Florida: Copied presumed official report, BP 1: 57; T. J. Bowen to Lurana Bowen, September 13, 1869, BP 3: 168; T. J. Bowen to Lurana Bowen, January 1870, BP 3: 170; T. J. Bowen to Lurana Bowen, April 24, 1870, BP 3: 171-2; T. J. Bowen to Lurana Bowen, October 31, 1870, BP 3: 173; T. J. Bowen to Lurana Bowen, April 24, 1870, BP 3: 171; T. J. Bowen to Lurana Bowen, October 31, 1870, BP 3: 173.

15 In Texas with Everett: T. J. Bowen to Lurana Bowen, March 22, 1871, BP 3: 174; D. T. Everett to Lurana Bowen, August 24, 1871, BP 4: 252; D. T. Everett to Lurana Bowen, October 10, 1871, BP 4: 253.

16 Various places in Texas: The Bowen Papers date T. J.'s letter from Brunswick, Georgia, on page 175 as August 29, 1872. The date should read August 29, 1873 for two reasons: 1) T. J. wrote Lurana a letter from Brunswick ten days earlier. See T. J. Bowen to Lurana Bowen August 19, 1873, BP 3: 190. 2) T. J. told Lurana that he had been in South Central Texas in August 1872. See T. J. Bowen to Lurana Bowen, January 17, 1873, BP 3: 176; T. J. Bowen to Lurana Bowen, January 17,

1873, BP 3: 176. No extant letter exists between T. J. to Lurana between March 22, 1871 and January 17, 1873.

17 Missed his family: T. J. Bowen to Lurana Bowen, January 17, 1873, BP 3: 176; T. J. Bowen to Lurana Bowen, February 12, 1873, BP 3: 177. For the frequency of his writing, see the Bowen Papers.; D. T. Everett to Lurana Bowen, April 8, 1873, BP 4: 255. The historical records give no instance of T. J. returning to Greensboro.

18 Physical and mental symptoms worse: T. J. Bowen to Lurana Bowen, March 31, 1873, BP 3: 179; T. J. Bowen to Lurana Bowen, April 8, 1873, BP 3: 180; T. J. Bowen to Lurana Bowen, April 14, 1873, BP 3: 181; T. J. Bowen to Lurana Bowen, April 16, 1873, BP 3: 182; T. J. Bowen to Lurana Bowen, April 21, 1873, BP 3: 183-4; T. J. Bowen to Lurana Bowen, May 3, 1873, BP 3: 185; T. J. Bowen to Lurana Bowen, May 20, 1873, BP 3: 186; T. J. Bowen to Lurana Bowen, June 16, 1873, BP 3: 187; T. J. Bowen to Lurana Bowen July 5, 1873, BP 3: 187; T. J. Bowen to Lurana Bowen, August 19, 1873, BP 3: 190; T. J. Bowen to Lurana Bowen, August 29, 1873, BP 3: 175. The Bowen Papers incorrectly dates this letter 1872.

19 Caused Lurana much suffering: D. T. Everett to Lurana Bowen, October 29, 1873, BP 4: 257; T. J. Bowen to Lurana Bowen, November 16, 1873, BP 3: 191.

20 Brunswick and other places: T. J. Bowen to Lurana Bowen, November 16, 1873, BP 3: 191; T. J. Bowen

to Lurana Bowen, January 26, 1874, BP 3: 193; T. J. Bowen to Lurana Bowen, February 11, 1874, BP 3: 193; T. J. Bowen to Lurana Bowen, February 2 and 3, 1874, BP 3: 194; "A History of Salt," [cited 23 May 2008], Online: http://saltworks.us/salt_info?si_HistoryOfSalt.asp.

21 Better in the spring: T. J. Bowen to James Taylor, May 12, 1867, BP 5: 551; T. J. Bowen to Lurana Bowen, April 3, 1874, BP 3: 195; T. J. Bowen to Lurana Bowen, Undated, BP 3: 196. Though undated, the references indicate that this letter was probably written in mid-April 1874.; D. T. Everett to Lurana Bowen, March 21, 1875, BP 4: 260; T. J. Bowen to Lurana Bowen, April 22, 1874, BP 3: 197-9; T. J. Bowen to Lurana Bowen, June 20, 1874, BP 3: 202-3; T. J. Bowen to Bro. Gaulden, June 22, 1874, BP 3: 204.

22 Worse again in the fall of 1874: T. J. Bowen to Lurana Bowen, September 9, 1874, BP 3: 205; Copied presumed official report, BP 1: 57.

23 Southern Baptists supported the South: Minutes of Georgia Baptist Convention, Athens, April 26-27, 29, 1861, microfilm; Orr, *Event of the Century,* 229-30; Minutes of Georgia Baptist Convention, Griffen, April 24-25, 27, 1863, microfilm.

24 Captain Bowen volunteered: T. J. Bowen to James Taylor, June 16, 1861, BP 5: 544; T. J. Bowen to James Taylor, May 7, 1861, BP 5: 540; T. J. Bowen to James Taylor, May 20, 1861, BP 5: 541; Biographical Sketches

of T. J. Bowen by T. B. Rice, BP 1: 11; Gorton Carruth, *What Happened When,* 407; T. J. Bowen to James Taylor, May 29, 1861, BP 5: 542.

25 After sickness, changed his mind: T. J. Bowen to James Taylor, Undated, BP 5: 553. From the references, this letter was probably written in late June or early July 1861.; T. J. Bowen to James Taylor, July 26, 1861, BP 5: 546; Extensive research revealed no record of T. J. serving as an official chaplain with the Confederate Army.; "Georgia Baptist News," *The Christian Index,* December 9, 1875, BP 1: 58.

26 Preaching and teaching: "Letter from Rev. T. J. Bowen," *African Repository* 42, no. 11 (November 1866); T. J. Bowen to James Taylor, May 12, 1867, BP 5: 551; T. J. Bowen to Lurana Bowen, October 31, 1870, BP 3: 173.

27 Preaching at associational meeting in Texas: D. T. Everett to Lurana Bowen, August 24, 1871, BP 4: 252.

28 Preaching around Texas: T. J. Bowen to Lurana Bowen, January 17, 1873, BP 3: 176; A. E. Vandivere to Lurana Bowen, January 20, 1873, BP 4: 254; D. T. Everett to Lurana Bowen, April 8, 1873, BP 4: 255; Fish, *When Heaven Touched Earth,* 260-1.

29 Preaching in Georgia: T. J. Bowen to Lurana Bowen, April 3, 1874, BP 3: 195; T. J. Bowen to Lurana Bowen, Undated, BP 3: 209. The references indicate this letter was probably written in 1873 from Georgia.

30 God used his preaching: T. J. Bowen to Lurana Bowen, June 20, 1874, BP 3: 202; T. J. Bowen to Bro. Gaulden, June 22, 1874, BP 3: 204.

31 T. J.'s death: T. J. Bowen to Lurana Bowen, October 18, 1875, BP 3: 207; Copied presumed original report, BP 1: 57; Orville W. Taylor, "Thomas J. Bowen: A Man for all Seasons," *Viewpoints: Georgia Baptist History* 8 (1982): 60. The author visited the Central State Hospital in Milledgeville and tried to locate T. J.'s grave. The records identifying its location do not exist.

32 Lurana grieved: T. J. Bowen to Lurana Bowen, June 21, 1867 BP 3: 162; The Bowen Papers; H. A. Tupper, *The Foreign Missions of the Southern Baptist Convention,* 261; Lurana died August 22, 1907, at the age of 75. See Family Record of Rev. and Mrs. T. J. Bowen, BP 1: 1. Her son-in-law T. B. Rice recalled, "I lived in the house with her from the time I married her daughter up to the day of her death; and I can truthfully say that no finer character than Mrs. Bowen ever lived. She lived a model Christian life and was greatly beloved by all who knew her. Her missionary zeal was greater than that of any person I ever knew." See T. B. Rice to Dr. Charles E. Maddry, March 30, 1943, BP 1: 66.

33 Few official notices: Editorial notice of Bowen's death in *The Christian Index,* December 9, 1875, BP 1: 58; *A Brief History of the Bowen Association to Commemorate One Hundred Years of Progress 1856-1956* (Bainbridge, Ga.: 1956), 14.

34 Two lines of evidence: James Taylor to Judge Thomas Stocks, July 17, 1861, FMB Copy Books; James Taylor to Judge Thomas Stocks, August 7, 1861, FMB Copy Books; James Taylor to Lurana Bowen, September 24, 1861, FMB Copy Books; A. M. Poindexter to Lurana Bowen, December 23, 1861, FMB Copy Books; Minutes of the FMB, January 6, 1862, accession no. 848 (Bowen was in the Asylum at this time.); T. J. Bowen to J. J. Toon, November 24, 1866, BP 3: 160.

35 Reports of his drunkenness: T. J. Bowen to James Taylor, June 26, 1861, BP 5: 544 (T. J. denied this accusation); D. T. Everett to Lurana Bowen, October 29, 1873, BP 4: 257; Lurana Bowen to T. J. Bowen, November 20, 1873, BP 4: 258; T. J. Bowen to Lurana Bowen, April 22, 1874, BP 3: 197-8.

36 Cover-up: Tupper, *Foreign Missions,* 386; Hardwicke, "An Examination," 199, footnote 251; I. N. Patterson to Ione Gray, April 13, 1953, FMB Missionary Correspondence, Box 9.

## Chapter 15—Leaving a Legacy

1 Inspired colonization attempts: David Carson Davis, "Thomas Jefferson Bowen and His Plans for the Redemption of Africa" (MA thesis, Baylor University, 1978), 91-2; M. R. Delany and Robert Campbell, *Search for a Place: Black Separatism and Africa, 1860* (Ann Arbor, Mich.: University of Michigan Press, 1969), 43, 36, 105, 108-9; T. J. Bowen to A. M. Poindexter, October 11, 1859, BP 5: 493.

2 British colonized Nigeria: C. Sylvester Green, *New Nigeria: Southern Baptists at Work in Africa* (Richmond, Va.: Foreign Mission Board, Southern Baptist Convention, 1936), 23-4, 29-30; John E. Flint, *Sir George Goldie and the Making of Nigeria (West African History Series,* ed. Gerald S. Graham, London: Oxford University Press, 1960), v; "Sir George Goldie," *Britannica Online,* n.p. [cited 13 May 2009]. Online: http://britannica.Com/EBchecked/topic/237858/ Sir-George-Gold...html; Louis M. Duvall, *Yoruba Life* (Richmond, Va.: Educational Department, Foreign Mission Board, Southern Baptist Convention, 1928), 26.

3 The cities Bowen toiled to reach: *Southern Baptists in Nigeria* (Richmond, Va.: Foreign Mission Board of the Southern Baptist Convention, 1940), 5; J. E. Ade Ajayi, *Christians Missions in Nigeria 1841-1891: The Making of a New Elite (Ibadan History Series,* ed. K. O. Dike, London: Longmans, 1965), 149; Taylor, "A Man for All Seasons," 57; Annual Report of the FMB to the SBC, Memphis, Tenn., May 13, 1925, accession no. 2715; Cecil Roberson, Bowen or an Evidence of Grace, International Mission Board Archives, 1969, 42. This is an unpublished book.; Travis Collins, *The Baptist Mission of Nigeria 1850-1993: A History of the Southern Baptist Missionary Work in Nigeria* (Ibadan, Nigeria: Y-Books, 1993), 43, 81.

4 Spread of the work in Nigeria and beyond: "Welcome to the Nigerian Baptist Convention," The Nigerian

Baptist Convention. [cited 21 July 2020]. Online: http://nigerianbaptist.org. Nigerian Baptists do not baptized polygamists, although they can be involved in the life of the church in many ways. See Gene Dillard Phillips, "The Attitudes and Practices of Southern Baptist Missions in Africa to the Problems of Polygamy" (M.Th. diss. Southeastern Baptist Theological Seminary, 1965), 46-7; Isaac DurosinJesu Ayranrinola, "The Missionary Program of the Nigerian Baptist Convention: Analysis and Recommendations 1850-1997" (DMiss dis., Southern Baptist Theological Seminary, 1999), 124; Marilyn R. Bonnell, "Yesterday... Today; Then...Now: Benin Baptist Mission 1970-1995," Jenkins Research Library, Richmond, Va., 25, 85-7. In 1918 Benin was called Dahomey.; Ayranrinola claimed, "Out of about 600 African churches in London, 250 are said to be pastored by Nigerians." See Ayranrinola, "The Missionary Program," 121; Bowen, *Central Africa,* 60-1.

5 Baptist Christian Education: Collins, *The Baptist Mission of Nigeria,* 81; Peter Hall Gilliland, "Thomas Jefferson Bowen: Biography and Analysis" (MA thesis, Furman University, 1970), 68; "History of Bowen University," Bowen University [cited 18 March 2010]. Online: http://bowenuniversity-edu.org/details_pages.php?page_id=24&site_id=1&page_admin=my_admin.

6 T. J. revered in Nigeria: "History of Bowen University," bowenuniversity.edu, Plate XI; J. T. Okedara and S.

Ademola Ajayi, *Thomas Jefferson Bowen: Pioneer Missionary to Nigeria 1850-1856* (Ibadan, Nigeria: John Archers, 2004), 52. Bowen is not buried in Nigeria. Thus a Bowen Association exists both in Georgia and in Nigeria; Bowen University Teaching Hospital, buth.edu.ng [cited 22 July 2020].

7 Missionary strategy legacy: "Extracts of a Letter from Rev. A. P. Davis," *Home and Foreign Journal* 10, no. 9 (March 1861): 36, accession no. 321; David Carson Davis, "Thomas Jefferson Bowen and His Plans," 123; Gilliland, "Thomas Jefferson Bowen: Biography and Analysis," 68; *Southern Baptists in Nigeria,* 7; T. J. Bowen to James Taylor, June 11, 1859, BP 5: 486; William R. Estep, *Whole Gospel Whole World,* 122-3, 208; Ayranrinola, "The Missionary Program of the Nigerian Baptist Convention," 71; T. J. Bowen, "A Missionary Agency," *Christian Index* (June 29, 1859): 1, BP 6: 585; T. J. Bowen, "Preambles and Resolutions," *Christian Index* (July 20, 1859): 1, BP 6: 592.

8 Legacy in Brazil: Betty Antunes De Oliveira, *Centelha em Restoho Seco: Contribuicao para a Historia do Primordois do Travalho Batista no Brazil* (Rio de Janeiro: B. A. de Oliveira, 1985), 6, 8; De Sousa, "A Black Heart," section 6.1; Minutes of the FMB, June 9, 1859, accession no. 732; Minutes of the FMB, September 14, 1859, accession no. 749; Minutes of the FMB, July 10, 1860, accession no. 821.

9 Ratcliff to Brazil: Minutes of the FMB, August 5, 1861, accession no. 845; Tupper, *The Foreign Missions,*

10-13; "A Call for Help," *Foreign Mission Journal* 9, no. 4 (July 1877): 2, accession no. 204; "Mission to Brazil," *Foreign Mission Journal* 10, no. 11 (February 1879): 3, accession no. 133.

10 Ratcliff's appeal and the SBC's response: A. R. Crabtree, *Baptists in Brazil* (Rio de Janeiro: Baptist Publishing House of Brazil, 1953), 36; Daniel B. Lancaster, *The Bagbys of Brazil: The Life and Work of William Buck and Anne Luther Bagby* (Austin: Eakin, 1999), 18, 30-31, 36.

11 Brazilian Baptists Today: Paul Akin, "3 Reflections from My Trip to Brazil—A Mission Force Has Grown," February 14, 2018, [cited 24 July 2020], imb.org; "Brazilian Baptist Convention," Wikipedia [cited 24 July 2020], en.wikipedia.org; "Baptist World Alliance, Statistics," [cited 24 July 2020], bwanet.org; "For over 100 years of doing missions in the world," batistas.org n.p. [cited 22 March 2010]. Online: www.jmm.org.br/index.ph%3Foopion%30com_content%26task%...

12 Overall legacy: H. A. Tupper, *The Foreign Missions*, 474-5. A mission to Japan had been attempted, but the missionaries' ship sank in route. "Ghana Baptist Convention," Wikipedia, [cited 27 July 2020] wikipedia.com; "Baptist World Alliance Statistics", bwanet.org. [cited 27 July 2020].

# Acknowledgements

N o human being could have helped me with the research for T. J.'s life more than my amazing wife, Michelle. To my joy, she became as much intrigued by T. J. as I did. She traveled with me thousands of miles to visit about twenty-five libraries, churches, associations, and other places relevant to T. J.'s life and work. She made thousands of copies of that material and organized it into nearly thirty large binders with indexes, and a master index. Michelle spent hundreds of hours transcribing hundreds of 150-year-old letters, many in bad condition. As my research assistant, she helped me survey hundreds of letters of early Southern Baptist Convention (SBC) missionaries and many on-line pages of early Foreign Mission Board (FMB) publications. She has made sacrifices, and assisted and encourage me in many other ways. Michelle made this project fun. T. J. and Lurana often became a part of our daily conversation until the point where they almost felt like family. Our children, Connie, Scott, and Thomas, as well as my late parents, Bill and Dell Hardwicke, were also an important encouragement and support.

At Southeastern Baptist Theological Seminary, Alvin Reid and Al James helped guide me through the process of writing the dissertation from which this volume is adapted. My friend, Dr. Bill Lunders, and my cousin, Dr. Alan Hardwicke, read every primary source description of T. J.'s physical and mental illnesses and gave their educated assessment of his possible diseases. Bill's wife, Rena Lunders, did some additional research in the Southern Baptist Historical Library and Archives in Nashville. The librarians there, Bill Sumners and Taffey Hall, provided great assistance. So did Edie Jeter, Jim Berwick, and Kyndal Owens at the Archives of the International Mission Board in Richmond, Virginia. I'm especially thankful to the IMB for the use of their photographs. The president of the Florida Baptist Historical Society, Dr. Jerry Windsor, and his assistant were very helpful when Michelle and I visited them in Graceville, Florida. The Providence Baptist Church in Quincy, Florida, graciously let us see and copy the original minutes of their church. So did the First Baptist Church of Greensboro, Georgia, and the First Baptist Church of Valdosta, Georgia.

My long-time friend and seminary president, Jeff Iorg, gave me the extra encouragement I needed to complete this work and was gracious to write the foreword. His assistant, Eric Espinoza, did an excellent job of editing the manuscript. Friends Jeff Green, Keith Goeking, and Dennis Brotherton gave helpful advice and encouragement. And I deeply appreciate the encouraging endorsements of leaders and authors Jim Walters, Bruce Ashford, Jerry Rankin, David Brady, Al James, and Nathan Finn.

This work has made me deeply grateful for pioneer missionaries like T. J. and Lurana Bowen. Their willing sacrifices and suffering far exceeded the bounds of what most of us would be willing to endure. They did not see the full harvest of the seeds for which they gave up so much to plant in untilled soil. For the glory of the One for whom they sacrificed, their complete story needed to be told, and to that end this volume is in your hands.

CPSIA information can be obtained
at www.ICGtesting.com
Printed in the USA
BVHW071016150421
605029BV00004B/338

9 781662 809576